GREGORY PECK

Books by Michael Freedland

GREGORY PECK

THE TWO LIVES OF ERROL FLYNN

GREGORY PECK

a biography by

Michael Freedland

WILLIAM MORROW AND COMPANY, INC.
New York   1980

For Sara
who through this journey bit her nails
with mine, smoothed the way with encouragement, love
and understanding—and, as always, smiled.

Acknowledgements

My thanks in helping prepare this book begin and end with my subject, Gregory Peck, who over two years not only devoted a great deal of time to me but opened up his personal archives and his private photograph collection.

I must also thank for their invaluable help, his charming wife Veronique, his marvellous secretary Barbara Russel and also other members of the household in California who allowed me to become a possibly intolerable nuisance too often.

My thanks, too, to Gregory Peck's agent George Chasin; to fellow performers like Fred Astaire and Dorothy McGuire, to directors Raoul Walsh, Henry King and Frank Schaffner – the last of whom tolerated my presence on the set of *The Boys From Brazil*, tangling my feet in cables and colliding with various other bits of equipment, as well as seeing me at his home in California. Neither must I forget author Harper Lee and film producer Stanley O'Toole.

The considerable problem of transcribing tapes of hours of conversation was handled expertly by Chris Robson and the even bigger problem of discovering the meaning of my scrawled notes was dealt with by Fiona Greeve, who typed the manuscript in its various stages.

But none of this could have happened without the help and advice of my two editors: in London, Amanda Girling who suffered a great deal during the course of the book's gestation and Howard Cady in New York, rightly respected as one of the great American editors and a veritable fund of information on the film industry.

Special thanks are also due to the librarians of the Academy of Motion Picture Arts and Sciences and the Austrian Government Tourist Office and the municipality of Vienna.

MICHAEL FREEDLAND, December 1979

Filmography

1943
Days Of Glory

1944
Keys of the Kingdom
Valley of Decision

1945
Spellbound

1946
The Yearling
Duel in the Sun

1947
The Macomber Affair
Gentleman's Agreement

1948
The Paradine Case
Yellow Sky

1949
The Great Sinner
Twelve O'Clock High

1950
The Gunfighter

1951
Captain Horatio Horn-
   blower
Only the Valiant

1952
David and Bathsheba
The World in His Arms
The Snows of Kili-
   manjaro

1953
Roman Holiday
Night People

1955
The Purple Plain
The Million Pound
   Note (Man With A
   Million—U.S.A.)

1956
The Man in the Gray
   Flannel Suit
Moby Dick

1957
Designing Woman

1958
The Bravados
The Big Country

1959
Pork Chop Hill
Beloved Infidel
On the Beach

1961
The Guns of Navarone

1962
Cape Fear
To Kill a Mockingbird
How the West was Won

1963
Captain Newman, M.D.

1964
Behold a Pale Horse

1965
Mirage

1966
Arabesque

1968
The Stalking Moon

1969
Mackenna's Gold
The Most Dangerous
   Man in the World
   (The Chairman—
   U.S.A.)
Marooned

1970
I Walk the Line

1971
Shoot Out

1973
Billy Two Hats

1976
The Omen

1977
MacArthur

1978
The Boys from Brazil

1980
The Sea Wolves

As a producer
The Big Country
The Trial of the Ca-
   tonsville Nine
The Dove

One

It was in La Jolla, California, that the elder Gregory Peck opened up his drug store. Years later, his greatest pride was to be "my son the fillum star of the same name," but in 1910, it was the new store that was the cause of his joy.

La Jolla was quiet, unspoiled and nothing like the affluent commuter town to San Diego it has since become. For Peck, fresh out of the University of Michigan, it was not just a good place to open up a business where none had been before, it was also an idyllic place to live. Its cliffs and rocks were alive with the screech of gulls, and the barking of thousands of sea lions echoed through the town all day.

It was his mother who first brought Gregory's attention to La Jolla. Mrs. Catherine Ashe Peck was a travelling saleslady, one of the hardy breed of career women they used to like making films about in the 1940s. She sold corsets and other items of ladies' underwear and the corset business was plainly good. By dint of her hard work and her stamina to cope with the competitive demands of a trade such as hers, she had built up connections that were quite as good as she believed her foundations to be.

She saved enough to buy a sixteen-flat apartment house in San Diego – a place she regarded as a mere step away from paradise, since she had weathered the winters of Buffalo, New York, and knew the feel of ice and cold that seemed to cut like a knife.

Catherine also knew the feel of poverty. She was born near Dingle in County Kerry in 1864 to a family who bore the tell-tale looks of the Black Irish. In 1880, with life in Ireland appearing to offer little but poverty and starvation, Catherine joined the mounting numbers of Irish immigrants travelling to the United States. She settled in

Rochester, the New York State town now best known as the home of Eastman Kodak, and it was there that she met Samuel Peck, a young man of English descent. Before long, they married and it was there that their son Gregory was born. Neither their stay nor her happiness were to last long. Samuel caught diphtheria and died and Catherine, her 11-month-old son in her arms, sailed back to Ireland.

The first ten years of the elder Gregory's life were spent on the Ashe family's farm. His closest friends were his cousins, youngsters with whom he played his favourite game – keeping hold of the iron rim of a cartwheel as it rolled along the country lanes, and then pulling himself away at just the moment that the wheel met the road. Once, he didn't move fast enough and bore the result for the rest of his life – half a finger.

It was soon after this episode that his mother took him back to America, enrolled him in a Catholic school and went off in search of a living, armed with cases of corsets. By 1910 her son had left university, a qualified pharmacist. She had saved enough to buy the apartment house and its adjoining bungalow and even had sufficient capital to make frequent visits not only back to Ireland but also to Hawaii and Australia where she had sisters. She discovered that the tiny town of La Jolla, near San Diego, (it is Spanish for The Jewel) had no drug store. She gave her son $10,000 to set up shop.

Immediately, he became known as "Doc" Peck – a commanding presence on both sides of the counter, particularly to the young girls who fluttered eyelashes when they saw the young man with the touch of Irish brogue. They followed his activities avidly – pulses raced as he captained the local basketball team and played in the town's band on Fourth of July parades. Doubtless, the young ladies of La Jolla were less than delighted with the arrival of Bernice Ayres in town. Bernice – everyone called her Bunny – had come from St. Louis to visit her sister Myrtle who had recently married Charlie Rannells, the local Railway Express representative. Bunny was 20 when she met Gregory. He was nine years her senior and was plainly smitten with her. It wasn't long before he was telling his customers that Mr. and Mrs. Gregory Peck would soon be setting up home at the Dewdrop Inn, La Jolla, neighbours to people living in houses called "The Haven" and "The Star Pine". To please her fiance, Bunny converted to Catholicism and their wedding was in the splendid setting of St. Louis's Catholic Cathedral.

What neither of them realized when they returned to La Jolla was that it was a town not too far removed from the days of the Western frontier – when a couple's wedding night was something to be shared by the other townspeople. They had no sooner locked their doors when a gaggle of the town's young citizenry gathered around the house, firing pistols in the air, beating on tin pans, pounding on the walls until Gregory was forced to plead with them to go home. Instead, he and Bunny were kidnapped and bundled into separate cars. The chivaree was one La Jolla custom that was not welcomed by the Pecks. But to the town, it represented their initiation into local society.

Two months after their marriage, Bunny announced she was pregnant. On April 5, 1916, their son was born in a bungalow Gregory had built for himself for $4,000. They called their child Eldred Gregory Peck. Eldred was Bunny's choice after thumbing through a telephone book, searching for a name that didn't sound ordinary. As soon as he was old enough, he let his parents know he hated the name and – apart from at school – was rarely called anything but Gregory or Greg.

It was an idyllic life for the boy. He would spend a lot of time with his cousins, the Rannells' children, who lived close by. There was Warren, whom most people knew as Stretch, Catherine, Bernice and Myrtle Adele. But the biggest attraction of La Jolla was his father's drug store where he delighted in watching the "doctoring" service – which included the ability to disperse the effects of a drunk's black eye without the man's wife getting to hear about it. Greg watched with wonderment as his father opened his jar of leeches, produced a hungry specimen and placed it squarely on the black eye – where it stayed until, satiated with blood, it fell fat and contented on an enamel basin resting on the patient's knee.

The smell of the store was one that lingered into later life – the aroma of liquorice root mixed with cinnamon bark; of spices and raw chemicals, all caught and allowed to mingle as jars were opened and bottles uncorked. But the happy days in La Jolla did not last.

Business did not match up to the style and dash that "Doc" brought to his drug store, and before long it had to close. To this day, Bunny talks about the young man whom she had known as the handsomest and most eligible bachelor in town – "with his own drugstore".

The trouble was that Gregory had been enjoying life too much, not watching either his business or an accountant who found easy ways of milking his meager profits. Gregory could have gone to the bank for loans but chose, instead, to put up the shutters – he couldn't face the turmoil of a rescue operation.

Nor would he collect the money owed to him by people who regarded buying on credit a natural way of doing things.

Bunny decided to chase up the debtors herself. Her husband was furious when he found out. "How dare you go knocking on people's doors asking for money?"

"We need it," she replied. "The money's ours and without it, we're in big trouble."

Doc was never to have his own business again. He worked for a San Diego druggist on the late, late shift, making up prescriptions all night. The family moved from La Jolla and the bungalow into a dull-looking apartment near where he worked. Soon after the move, the Peck marriage went on the rocks and by the time their son was six, they had divorced.

Bunny took young Gregory back to St. Louis with her, living in the kind of boarding house which she now says was straight out of a Tennessee Williams play. Mrs. Peck worked as a telephone operator and her fellow houseguests were travelling salesmen, head waiters and clerks working in local stores.

The landlady was a busty, red-headed woman who, her then youngest guest now says, was "a Tallulah Bankhead type".

Greg remembers through the blur of 55 years that it was a place that symbolized the Roaring Twenties; the women in short skirts, jazz records on the phonograph.

Greg himself was not averse to cashing in on the tastes of the clientele. Once or twice a week there were high spirited poker games for low stakes in the smoke-laden dining room and the boy found he could earn a nickel a glass for the lemonade he made in a pitcher in the kitchen, to be spiked by the fun-loving landlady's own bathtub gin. For another ten cents he'd shine the guests' shoes while they played.

He also joined the landlady's son, who was just a little older than he, in selling newspapers on the street corner half a block away, where the trolley cars stopped.

The main recreation spot to which Bunny took her son was Creve Coeur Lake – which takes the Tennessee Williams analogy still further. In 1978, the writer's play *A Lovely Summer for Creve Coeur* opened off-Broadway.

It was around this time that Bunny introduced Greg to one of the wonders of the age – the movies. The first film he remembers seeing was *The Scarlet Letter*, starring Lillian Gish, although it was an age when no one would explain to the young, intensely curious Greg that the "A" she bore stood for adultress.

When Bunny took a new job as a telephone operator in Los Angeles, Greg went back to La Jolla to live with Bunny's mother, Kate Ayres, who had herself recently arrived from St. Louis. Grandma Ayres represented whatever security Greg had during the next three formative years.

For him, the best day of the week was Thursday – when his father spent his afternoon off with his son, making the 40-minute drive over from San Diego to stay with Greg until bedtime. Because she was 120 miles away in Los Angeles, Bunny's visits were less frequent and because of this, they became occasions to treasure. On the odd weekend or vacation, she would stay at the cottage.

Doc would always spend his holidays with Greg, taking him for a week to Santa Catalina Island, a popular vacation spot, particularly for middle-class families. There was a luxury hotel there, the St. Catharine's, a place that never seemed to be open without Douglas Fairbanks, Vilma Banky or some other screen idol staying there. It was far beyond the reach of the Peck family and young Greg knew it.

He was content enough to cross over to the island by steamship and spend the next seven days living in tents without running water but with swimming every day, fishing for hours from the beach or caddying for his father on the golf course. All these things helped to make life seem perfect.

Occasionally, for the sake of young Greg, Bunny would join them for the week end; it was a glorious time as a united family.

La Jolla itself was not short of attractions, particularly The Cove, where from spring to fall, kids would spend the whole day, taking their lunch in paper bags. It was there that Greg's eyes were opened to a totally new experience that had about it all the magic of Barnum and Bailey's Circus and of Buffalo Bill's rodeos. He saw a film being made.

Lew Cody, a suave leading man specializing in playboys and seducers, was filming at The Cove, dressed in a yachting outfit and frolicking with half a dozen bathing beauties wearing the modest attire of the day. Some 50 yards away, Greg and the other "peasants" stood behind a rope barrier, gaping at the brilliant dialogue that no one could hear.

Today, Greg recalls:

"To the small-town innocent, the strange creatures with the orange make-up and black eye-shadow seemed as if they had come from another planet. Never in my wildest dreams would I have imagined becoming one of them. I still think of it when filming in small towns like that. I'm *one* of the strange creatures with orange paint on my face."

The scene closely resembled one featuring Tony Curtis years later in *Some Like It Hot*. Lew Cody sat under an umbrella smoking a cigarette from a large holder – with which he playfully flicked up the skirt of one of the prancing beauties. It seemed like the epitome of sophistication.

Greg's constant companion when he was home at La Jolla was his black and brown mongrel Bud. Bud had a bit of both Airedale and (or so young Greg liked to think) something of greyhound in him. Bud's supposed greyhound antecedents were important to the boy because he liked nothing better than to boast "my dog can run at 30 miles an hour" – and would demonstrate it whenever he could by asking his father to take him and some of his pals out in his ancient Nash car. They'd put Bud out into a country road and would watch thrilled as he'd race the car and usually win.

After one holiday on Santa Catalina in 1924, Bud was not waiting as usual for his master's return. It was, Greg now says, his first brush with the harsh reality of life, the first disillusionment with the fondly-held belief that adults were as always perfect, honest, and trustworthy as children.

Greg now says: "1924 was a bad year for me. I discovered that there was no Santa Claus, no Easter Bunny and Bud was kidnapped."

His grandmother told him that the dog had disappeared, but the truth was that the neighbours had been complaining about the noise Bud had made barking. Greg's father, never a man for confrontation, had agreed that Bud could be allowed to disappear during the Santa Catalina holiday.

Greg himself never discovered whether he was given away or "shall we say, otherwise disposed of. For the next 40 years I always took a second look at every black and brown mongrel I saw."

Greg's Uncle Charlie, who had led the gang of buckaroos at the chivaree on his parents' wedding night, would never have allowed Bud to face such a fate. He had a more open way of dealing with such matters.

Every Sunday, Greg would join him and his family for the ritual chicken dinner which followed the services he attended with them at St. James's-by-the-Sea Episcopal Church. Immediately after the services, bluff Uncle Charlie would divest himself of his celluloid collar, his tie and jacket and proceed to the chicken coop where he would grab a bird by the neck and swing it around and around in the air until the chicken's head came off like a top from a bottle.

The headless bird would then race around the yard until it dropped dead. Uncle Charlie, would sit on the back steps, pluck its feathers and a couple of hours later, there was chicken fricassee for dinner.

Uncle Charlie was as much part of the life of the West as were the Civil War veterans who dressed up in their blue and grey uniforms on the Fourth of July.

"I was lucky to have seen and experienced just that bit of the Old West," Greg says now. "It gave me a connection with those rougher, self-reliant, hardy characters I was later to play in Western films."

It was the time that Greg developed a sense of independence he was never to lose – like when he and his friend Johnny Buchanan decided to build themselves the boat they could never afford to buy. They did it properly, bought a blueprint, selected the timber and cork and proceeded to build it in the backyard of Mrs. Ayres's bungalow.

The launching of the *Titanic* could not have been received with more excitement than the builders of the Peck-Buchanan Line felt when their boat *The Tar Baby* had its baptism. Alas, it was not to have a happy ending. After a magnificent maiden voyage, the boat was tied up on the beach – and then totally destroyed by a demon storm that erupted without warning.

When he was ten, Greg experienced another major change. His father and mother conferred and decided that their son should go away to school – to the St. John's Military Academy in Los Angeles, a place where the boys wore blue grey tunics with a center stripe, breeches and a shiny peaked cap.

St. John's was not an easy place. It wasn't supposed to be. It was created in an age when the only way to guarantee a boy's decent, wholesome future was to discipline him. Hence the military association. Although it wasn't connected with the Army in any way, life couldn't have been much easier for a rookie cadet at West Point.

It was a three-storey brick building with a gabled slate roof on Washington Boulevard. But the architecture isn't the principal memory that lingers. Much more, it is the smell of wax polish that abides – and the sight of floors being mopped and wood being shined.

Once established as part of the St. John's community, it was clear that the discipline was combined with both a spirit of competitiveness and a close attachment to Catholic dogma, not all of it distasteful to young Greg.

The surplice he wore as an altar boy seemed to have about it an appeal which, in a different way, was as attractive as the blue military clothes undoubtedly were.

A ten-year-old is one of God's most susceptible creatures and Greg accepted the dogmas and doctrines of Father Timothy Crowley, the chaplain, as easily as he did the thought that there was to be a daily drill instruction. Father Crowley and most of the priests and nuns in the convent adjoining the school were Irish immigrants – nearly all of them from the same stock as his own father – so he felt quite at home with them.

Greg's best friend at the time was Augustine Mackessy, as Irish as a shamrock and the undisputed hero of the school, who came over to America after his father, a Dublin policeman, had been blown to bits by a bomb thrown by Eamonn de Valera himself.

In later years, Greg was to regard some of the things he was taught at the Academy as "rather narrow", but they made their impression on him and his own Catholicism was established for life.

By the time he was twelve he could recite the entire Latin Mass by heart – which could take as long as two hours.

The discipline was something else. Inwardly, he questioned why he and the other cadets polished their boots for at least twenty minutes every night, "like little madmen". And not just their boots. The brass buttons had to have mirror-like surfaces, too, and their belt buckles be just as bright.

For a brief time, he toyed with the idea of becoming a priest, but the more general ambitions of growing up to be a fireman or, later on, a rancher like the uncle whom he used to visit and who gave him his first experience in the saddle, were too strong for his religious training to take that deep a root.

Living in an institution like St. John's meant devoting his entire life to it – just as surely as if he were an enlisted man drafted into a war-time army. It affected the boy's whole existence. But once a month, there came a release. On the last Friday of each month, Greg would welcome the arrival of the "month end", the time when he was allowed to leave St. John's and its environs at 2.30 on a Friday afternoon and stay away until 6.00 p.m. on Sunday.

On that Friday, Greg would take the hour-long trolley ride from the college to down-town Los Angeles and then board the Santa Fe train for San Diego, 120 miles southwards. Waiting for him at the San Diego depot always would be his father, with whom he would now spend most of those precious hours away from the military discipline which he had come to accept – but which he enjoyed being able to leave behind. He stayed in the San Diego bungalow until 12 o'clock the following Sunday, when "Doc" Peck took him back to the depot for another month of parades, inspections and reciting the Mass. The military regimen began again at 6 o'clock that night – with a counting of the heads lining up in regimental formation.

The month-ends allowed Greg to maintain close relationships with both his father and with his paternal grandmother. But as the months went by during that first year at the Academy, he watched his grandmother grow more and more sick.

Doctors diagnosed that she was suffering from stomach cancer. The strapping, big woman with the Irish accent as strong as her physique, was now wasting away, although young Greg's presence was as much a tonic for her as it was a relief for him. Every day he was there, she asked her grandson to come into the bedroom to read to her. She was wracked with pain and her face had a distinctly grey cast.

From the boy's own room, he could hear her groans. She was still only in middle age. But medical science then knew almost no means of alleviating pain and she was taking the full brunt of what was still being described as a wasting disease. There was rarely a doctor to be seen on the premises.

To add to the distress of the people who came to see her, there was an ever-present, increasingly more powerful odour emanating from her bed. She had not lost her sense of responsibility, however, and passing on too many of her troubles to her ten-year-old grandson was something that she felt she ought not to allow. When Greg entered her room, the newspaper under his arm, her moans and groans were invariably suppressed to make way for a smile. It all fitted into the image that this self-made woman had created for herself. She died while Greg was away at school.

The effect of cancer on the human frame made an impression on her grandson that he would never forget. Years later, he would have cause to remember it.

At 13, Greg became Cadet Captain, which meant that 60 of the youngest benighted souls were under his charge. More important, perhaps, he had first choice of the "grey library paste" which the stews served at St. John's resembled. He also was learning to express himself – as editor of the school's monthly newspaper, *The Bugle Call*. This led to more and more reading – the works of Zane Grey and later journeys into the different worlds of Dickens, Walter Scott, Jane Austen and the Brontes.

The biggest change that being captain meant for him was that he made himself responsible for getting his team to win the gold medal for drill – a seemingly impossible task since the youngest was eight-years-old and the oldest only ten.

He worked his young charges until they dropped. As a result, the impossible happened. After putting the fear of God, the Pope and the Chaplain of the college into his boys, they won the medal. Now, he is not quite so proud of the achievement as he was then. "I shouted at them like Erich von Stroheim. God knows what I did to the psyches of those poor little kids!"

Certainly, St. John's left its mark on him. The competitiveness, the determination to finish anything he set out to do, stayed, even if the feverish assault on polished shoes did not. "I never touch them now," he laughs.

In 1930, his military school education ended as it did for all 14-year-olds, with the inevitable traumatic adjustment from the cocoon-like existence of St. John's to the wide open space freedom of the public high school at San Diego. He began to attend Mass less frequently and for a time wrestled with feelings of guilt about it.

He lived with his father in a box-like bungalow next to the apartment block in the lower middle-class part of town for a time. His father still worked at night and he and Greg usually saw each other briefly in the morning but managed to have dinner together almost every night before the elder Peck went to work.

Young Greg and his mother saw each other rarely during this period. She had by this time married a salesman of business machinery, called Joseph Maysuch – an Americanization of the original Italian, Masucci – to whom she is still happily married today, and they were frequently travelling the country on business.

When Greg was 15, Christmas morning seemed bleaker than any other day of the year. The Doc came home from work tired out, barely able to exchange gifts before he went to bed. The youth went out for a walk into the California sunshine. It was quiet and eerie. On and on he walked until he was in the city center where the streets were as deserted as for the duel scene in *High Noon*. He walked as far as the athletic club where both he and his father were members – a place that normally smelled of sweat and echoed with the sound of balls being bounced and of voices calling to each other.

That day, it was quiet. The basket-ball court was as silent as it was clean. He turned on the light and "threw baskets" alone. He says now: "I've often thought it would make a nice little scene in a film. If I were producing it, I would want a young Tony Perkins or James Dean in the role of the small town kid with nothing else to do on Christmas Day."

He went to an afternoon movie and finally wandered home in time for his father to wake up and take him for Christmas dinner at a local cafe.

He felt awkward and shy in company, particularly that of girls, who were strange but desirable creatures, completely out of reach.

He was skinny and life seemed to consist of little more than the motions of going to and from school and reporting back to his father on the sort of day he had had.

Vacations were better. His father would take him to the Yosemite and Yellowstone National Parks and sometimes they went camping. About this time, he began rowing for the first time, and with some success. He joined the San Diego Rowing Club. His height had increased from 5ft 4 in to 6 ft 2 in at 16. For a time it seemed that all his will and strength had been sapped in the process of growing. But he was beginning to escape from the adolescent cocoon.

Girls, however, still remained elusive and more than anything, he wished that they did not. When an advertisement appeared in the local paper, proclaiming: "You can dance the foxtrot . . . for ten lessons, 12 dollars," he was convinced this would help solve his problems. It made him pluck up the courage to ask an intoxicating brunette to go to the school prom with him. But she had 12 brothers on home guard and that relationship never took off.

But now, well into his eighteenth year, he began asserting himself. He calmly told his father he was going to leave school.

Two

He had decided to have a temporary break from his education. At the back of his mind he thought he might become a doctor – the same ambition his father had had before taking the second-best choice and training instead as a pharmacist. But he wasn't ready to do it yet.

He wanted not just to make some money, but also to spread himself and to use the new sense of maturity and liberty that he now actually felt. He wanted a job that not only paid reasonable wages, but one that left him time for some honest-to-goodness fun, too.

The Union Oil Company were looking for workers and the manager who saw lanky Eldred Gregory Peck walk into his office didn't think twice about handing him a cap with its "76" badge. In truth, the uniform of olive drab trousers and work shirt satisfied Greg as much as the job itself did.

For a time, he worked as their nightwatchman – an important position of responsibility for an 18-year-old in a place where fire was always a potential hazard. Promotions followed at about the same speed with which Greg found he picked up the work he was assigned. It wasn't long before he reached what he was sure was the pinnacle of all success – he was allowed to start driving the huge trucks that carried 5,000 gallons of gasoline from one end of San Diego to the other. He was paid $125 a month for his skill. One hundred and twenty-five dollars – that sounded like big money to an 18-year-old in 1934. It was enough for Greg to buy his own car.

He was very proud of that car – a blue Model "A" Ford roadster with wire wheels, a white canvas top and its own rumble seat. But no more proud than he was to be seen in the cab of the red "Union" trucks.

Drivers like him not only had to be responsible for the inflammable material which they carried, but also to have the strength to unload barrels of oil at local gas stations. Having done that, he had to be sure to pack the remainder of the load tightly and safely – to say nothing of being able to back the monster truck into a side turning or a narrow driveway before moving off.

Above all, it was a wonderful opportunity to show off to a certain young lady. For at last, Greg had himself a girlfriend. The old inhibitions had been thrown off and now Kathie Moore was both a romantic companion and soulmate. Hers was also an Irish-American family, but unlike his own, it was one of those closely-knit groups that he had envied so much.

Her two brothers were Greg's friends and she was the first girl he had successfully "squired" to a school dance.

Kathie was to change so much for him. And so were her family. It wasn't long before he was spending so much time with them in their house that he considered he had adopted them – rather than the other way about. Every evening the Moores fed this long, lean young man who still wasn't really very sure where he was heading. What he did know was that they were showing him an ease of living that hadn't exactly been normal for him up to then.

Going out in the Ford with Kathie was fun too. They went to beach picnics, played touch football with friends, who, with the Moores, were helping to make him a happy teenager. Greg could not resist driving his monster gasoline truck up to the Moores' door. If he could make it by lunchtime, he would drive the massive red machine up to the Moores' house and have a snack there with the family, which now felt like his own.

Later, when his route was widened to include La Jolla, Greg drove proudly along the roads leading to the Rannells' home and Aunt Myrtle was as thrilled by the presence of her nephew, the hungry truck driver, as was Kathie.

He was enjoying this life so much that he momentarily thought that here could indeed be his future. Why even think about going back to the hard, conventional grind of study? Certainly his manager thought he could have a career in the gas business – and if he hadn't told Greg so, the enthusiastic new driver might today be on the way to drawing a pension from the Union Oil company.

The Manager, Mr. Tilson, knew the youth could be depended

upon for conscientious workmanship – a trait that Greg had picked up at military school and which was sticking to him. He might not now have to shine his shoes until they looked like mirrors but if ten barrels of oil had to be delivered by noon to a certain customer, that customer got his ten barrels of oil before 12 o'clock. He had been with the firm for about eight months when Tilson looked him squarely in the eyes and said: "I've been watching you, Peck, and I'm impressed. I am sure you can work your way up in this company until, in about 20 to 25 years, you could be in my job."

Peck wondered about that. Could ambition take him that far? "If you don't mind my asking, Mr. Tilson," he probed gently and very politely, "could you tell me how much money you make?" "Three hundred dollars a month," the manager replied proudly. Truly in those early post-Depression days that could be made to sound like a fortune. Even so, Greg didn't think that much of it.

Neither did he want to spend the rest of his life in a routine job in a small town. He knew that he had enough ambition to try to break out of his rut. He decided he was going back to the kind of work that would lead him somewhere of his own choosing. To do that he needed a college degree.

The Moores showed true parental concern in his progress and night after night they would encourage him to sit quietly at their dining room table and study. He now had an aim – he was going to California's prestige university at Berkeley. But for that he needed not just good marks, but top grades. He had already chosen his subjects – mathematics, history, literature and science – and Kathie, who was herself a good student, used to sit with him, helping by going through the text books and throwing test questions at him.

For a time he went back to San Diego State College and from there, got such a good set of marks that he easily passed his entrance to Berkeley.

Just as Greg was about to leave home for the university, his father remarried. His new wife, Harriet, had not found it easy to communicate with the young man who was to become her stepson and for that reason "Doc" Peck had put off any thought of marriage. Now though, with Greg on his own, there was no reason not to marry her. The relationship between stepmother and stepson was still a strained one. Nothing very hostile about it, but they didn't get to know each other well for some time and Greg, who had now completely escaped from his adolescent shell, thought his stepmother was rather too strait-laced. As for Harriet, she really didn't know how to react to the idea of suddenly finding herself with an 18-year-old who seemed as tall as a house.

Harriet was very different from Greg's own mother. The second Mrs. Peck was a very conservative Protestant from Denver, Colorado, and her even more conservative mother came to live with the couple soon after the wedding.

Doc and his new wife soon had a son of their own. They called him Donald. Although there was tension between Greg and his stepmother, the love between him and his father never faltered. The relationship between the two half-brothers was good too, although Donald was virtually a generation younger.

Going to Berkeley, however, meant that Harriet would be spared an embarrassing relationship with her stepson, and he himself would be able to take advantage of the new horizons which were dawning. Besides, Berkeley was only ten or so miles away from San Francisco where his mother was now living with her new husband, and he was grateful for the chance to be with them more.

At first, he took pre-medical courses at Berkeley with considerable enthusiasm – even though he hated the physics which inevitably formed part of the course. The atmosphere was stimulating; just to be there was to be in a world in which he wanted to find himself a place.

There were 16,000 students, with 500 or 600 in individual courses from as many countries as an atlas could show. There were girls in saris and men in turbans; young people with the steel and blond look of the Norseman and with the dark hair and flashing white teeth of the Latin.

The faculty was on a par with those in other institutions which considered themselves to be the best universities in the world. Lectures were always stimulating. Greg made new girlfriends and was now speedily engaged in the process of finally growing up. He got into the college rowing crew and found the camaraderie there matched the challenges with which he had been presented at St. John's.

The tuition at the university was free, but with only the occasional $10 bill from his mother and stepfather coming in there was never a question that he had to work to pay for the rented rooms in which he stayed, and for his food.

With his two room-mates, he shared the job of janitor in the block where he was living – this paid for the accommodation of the three of them and provided $20 a month between them, besides.

They emptied the garbage, saw to the complaints of the other tenants, swept the corridors, and kept the furnaces going.

The other tenants, including some of the professors, would pound the floor if the boys overslept and neglected to provide enough hot water.

Greg worked at the same time as a waiter and dish-washer at the student co-op cafe and the sorority houses. The rule was one hour's work and all the food you could eat.

Says Greg today: "I distinctly remember sitting in the kitchen and devouring three steaks, heavy piles of mashed potatoes and then three plates of pie and a quart of milk at a single sitting. After rowing for 18 miles each afternoon we needed lots of food. Besides, we were the favourites of the woman running the kitchen."

But if he enjoyed college life and admired his teachers, he floundered in his courses. He couldn't settle down and after a year, he came to what he by then regarded as the inevitable decision that medicine and science were not for him. His happy moments were in the literature lectures and the reading that went with them. It was in that, he decided, that he really wanted to major. And because he wrote so well about what he read, his ambitions were now crystallizing. Eldred Gregory Peck was going to be a writer.

There was, after all, a confidence about him now. He was in magnificent physical shape and looked it. He had gained his "letter" in the boat crew – which in Britain would be the equivalent of winning his "blue" – and was entitled to walk around the campus with a sweater bearing a gold "C." For 12, 14 and sometimes 16 miles a day he would row – and when he came out of the boat, the lean and hard Gregory Peck was not unnoticed by the girls on the campus.

And it wasn't just the girls who noticed him. Edwin Duerr, who was the director of the college theater, approached Greg as he strode along the campus one day, tapped him on the shoulder – no mean feat – and asked if he would consider trying out for the next drama production there.

"All my actors are short," he said quite bluntly, "and I need one who's tall."

The theater was to present scenes from *Moby Dick* and he needed a Starbuck, Captain Ahab's mate. Ahab himself was to be short and burly, so his mate had to be tall and slim to provide the necessary contrast.

Peck had never given the theater a thought until that moment. He said: "OK, I'll try it out." It was then that he had to think why he had got involved.

A lot had to do with the fact that, at 21, Peck was for the first time savouring the unusual situation of being asked to do something instead of being ordered to do it. Also, he was intrigued by a wholly different kind of challenge from any he had experienced before. Perhaps, too, it offered him a chance to express himself while shaking off the last remnants of his shy, ungainly boyhood.

He says now that he wasn't very good as Starbuck, but it was the first of five plays in which he took part during that last year in college. And there were definite moments when he felt the power that all successful actors have to develop. At those moments the audience's attention was solely on him. Until then, the only time he had had quite the same feeling had been as the altar boy at the military academy. Now he is convinced that he had so much enjoyed serving at Mass because it was his first theatrical experience.

The theater at Berkeley, Wheeler Auditorium, answered all his needs. It was really a lecture hall but it seated as many as 1,200 people. The stage itself was too narrow to be really more than just a lecture platform, but every time there was a play to be put on, it would be squared by means of moveable sections. There were no flies above, so the scenery had to be in flats, brought in from the wings at the side. The theater was about 40 or 50 years old, but if it were not the ideal place for an actor, it *was* splendid experience. It was also a popular place for the audiences. Most of the time it was full and the prospect of 1,200 people staring, waiting for a "performance" was a daunting one for a green thespian like Peck. "I thought seriously of burrowing a hole in the floor backstage and digging my way to Mexico," he now only partly jokes.

There were even audiences for the dress rehearsals – which unnerved him still more, although the very nervousness was itself stimulating. It did also have its unforeseen effects. On one rehearsal for the college production of S. N. Behrman's *Rain from Heaven*, the action was constantly being interrupted by a loud clatter. He didn't know what it was – until the director asked. Then he looked down and admitted: "I'm afraid I'm the cause of it. It's this tea cup and saucer. You see, I can't stop shaking." After that, the bottom of the cup was taped and Greg kept his nerves to himself.

After that, his roles got bigger and better. In *Lysistrata*, he was the leader of the old men's chorus. He wasn't sure, though, that, dressed in their bedsheet togas and beards fabricated from old yarn, they succeeded in explaining the action of the play to the audience – even though the ladies on stage had done their best to indicate that their beds and bodies were to remain inviolate till the end of the wars.

He wasn't certain either whether he was more of a disaster in that classic or in the drawing room comedy – like the best actors he was dissatisfied with what he was doing and the inexperience *did* show – but he kept being asked to do more.

After watching Peck in the Greek tragedy, a red-haired Irishman called Kenneth Tobey stood up and talked about the play, dissecting it cuttingly. "I don't know," he said, "why we have to watch people who don't know how to speak or act. I refer of course, to Mr. Peck."

Tobey was later to be a close friend of the subject of his criticisms. Eventually he became a Hollywood character actor. He was acting at Berkeley before Peck and he was well known on the campus as a leading member of the theater group.

All the young players took their theater very seriously. They discussed the profession and drama as though they were old pros. They criticized professional performances as if knowing they could do better. And they talked about developments that might further their own careers.

When one of their number, Crahan Denton, went to New York and found a place with the Neighborhood Playhouse drama school, it was the number-one topic of conversation. Greg decided then that that was what he would do, too. He stored the thought in his mind for when the right time came.

In Eugene O'Neill's *Anna Christie*, Greg played a rough-neck Irish sailor in the steamy waterfront drama that was to beat all other steamy waterfront dramas. He was the one who fell in love with the daughter of his Swedish captain. The role of the girl has become a classic – Garbo, Ingrid Bergman and Liv Ullmann have all played her. So, too, has the situation: both captain and seaman assume the girl to be as pure as driven snow and never realize that she has had more time off than either of them ever gave her credit for having. The lady is a whore.

Oh, the opportunities that that particular discovery give an actor! Greg Peck used it by convincing the audiences that he was going berserk from personal experience, and the drunken rage in which he did it seemed to be borne of at least a couple of whiskies. It wasn't, but Peck did all that he could do with the part. Even so, he wasn't satisfied. The stage directions plainly said: "Turning purple with rage." In the privacy of his room at college, he practiced getting into that rage until he was sure that even a portrait painter would colour his face purple. But guaranteeing that colour on stage was more of a problem.

Just before the moment for the explosion came, he turned his back on the audience, closed his mouth tight, and blew – until he felt his face had turned the required shade. The director wasn't entirely sympathetic. "What the hell do you think you're doing, Peck?" he demanded, turning in the process a fair facsimile of purple himself. "How can you turn your back on the audience in this big scene?"

Peck told him that the stage directions plainly said . . . "Forget it," said the director and in so doing encouraged the young actor to be his own man for the future. "Pay no attention," he said, "to stage directions."

One of the San Francisco critics put his own stamp on the play with a review that said: "The production is all well and good. The girl playing Anna is excellent, the barge captain is good but Eldred Peck's overacting dangerously marred the production." Peck didn't bother to commit the rest of that review to memory, although the earlier part is etched forever in his mind. It was the first time that a man who could be considered a major critic saw his work. On reflection, though, he is still rather glad that the critic did accuse him of *over*acting – because there have been the critics who have accused the mature Gregory Peck of underacting. It is not a charge he accepts.

"Underacting," he believes, "is a kind of cowardice. Overacting is a self-indulgence. It is easier to take someone who overacts and bring him down to scale. Underacting comes either through a lack of talent or a lack of courage."

He believes that the public has a taste for overacting. Perhaps he is right. Undoubtedly, the professional ham can get away with theatrical murder – if he knows where to stop; if the ham doesn't take over completely. Being flamboyant is not always the same thing. As he says himself: "I love actors like Charles Laughton and Wallace Beery. They just give it all to you with gravy on it."

Gregory Peck hadn't got to the gravy stage yet himself but he was beginning to have serious second thoughts about his future. After having totally cast off any thought of being a doctor, his notion of becoming a professional writer was changing, too. Now, he thought, he might make a professor of English.

But his experience on the stage of the Wheeler Auditorium was having another effect. The "reasonable kind of literary fellow" was discovering that there wasn't quite the same appeal about reading and writing as there was to becoming an actor. Even though every time the curtain went up, he was in a cold sweat, there *was* a thrill at being out there in front of several hundred complete strangers. He hated being clumsy, but there were also times when he felt he was doing all right.

Today, he thinks that it was as an oarsman that he developed the habit of seeing things through once he had begun them. His training in the rowing eight wasn't just sport, but sport with a bite to it. The pain at the end of a race is one that rowers will talk about for as long as they are able to hold a glass in their hands. The temptation to quit is tremendous and yet they know that if they succumb, they will let down the seven men behind. Peck himself found expression in those agonizing workouts in the boats.

They certainly helped when he was picked to represent Berkeley at the 1938 Poughkeepsie Regatta in New York. He wasn't in the first crew, but the second – the one known as "the pickle boat" because it consisted of a mixture of Californians like himself and a few naval cadets from the Annapolis Academy. They won all of their races, but it was seeing New York for the first time that made the big impression on Peck. Manhattan was the center of American life and to Greg and the other oarsmen, newly released from the disciplines of the regatta, it was a place in which to soak into their bloodstream every speck of dust that came their way.

With the proceeds of the sale of the Pullman reservations that Greg and a couple of friends had made for the trip back home, they decided to take a cheap room at the YMCA and "do" New York.

Greg may have seemed a serious young man, but when the lights flickered on the theater marquees, there was no doubt where he wanted to go – to see a shapely beauty called Vera Zorina in a show called *I Married An Angel*.

They haunted the famous Savoy Ballroom in Harlem and absorbed the sights and sounds of New York until they were totally broke. For the last night in New York, they had to move out of the YMCA and sleep on the grass of Central Park.

The bus journey back to California wasn't exactly luxury. They had a total capital of 75 cents between them and for four days they survived on a diet of bananas.

It may not have been the most inviting introduction to America's biggest city. But it was enough.

The young man who had told himself never to quit, earned his degree. But he now knew that he was not going to be satisfied with anything but the life of a professional actor. And in the only place that mattered, New York.

Three

His father thought he was out of his mind. Going to New York? Becoming an actor? After his own experiences eking out a living, "Doc" Peck wanted to feel sure that his son had a career behind him with prospects that were as clear as the Californian air.

His mother and her second husband were more encouraging. Because their San Francisco home was so near to Berkeley, they had made it a rule not to miss the college plays and were distinctly impressed with the man they saw on the stage – so much more self-assured than the boy they had once known.

That was distinctly not his father's view. When Greg called on him in San Diego, the older man did all he could to discourage him. "You'll be ridiculed," he told him. "You'll be with a group of people you know nothing about. You'll be sorry. You'll have missed your chance to learn a profession or a trade. You'll be broke at 35 and you'll end up borrowing from me. Don't do it." The way he said it made it sound more like a plea than an order.

Yet it was not the kind of appeal to which the aspiring actor was prepared to listen. If he had withstood the discipline of all those years of the military school, he was sure he could cope with the stage. He also knew exactly where he was going to begin – at the Neighborhood Playhouse.

Eldred Gregory Peck boarded the train for the journey east, determined to succeed. By the time the Twentieth Century Limited had glided into Grand Central Station, New York, Gregory Peck knew he was going to make it. The journey had not only given him time to think and to strengthen his determination, it had also decided him on jettisoning his first name. When he marched to the door of the Neighborhood Playhouse and told the people there that he was their bright new hope for the future, he didn't give it a further moment's thought. They asked his name and he told them: "Gregory Peck."

The Playhouse couldn't take him straight away. But they gave him an audition, told him he had passed, and said that he could start in September.

It was early summer, 1939, and at 22, Greg, as most of the people he now met called him, had to do more than just haunt the environs of the Neighborhood Playhouse. He wanted to go to the theater but that cost money. So did food to say nothing of the room he took on West 114th Street, which was just next to Columbia University.

Somehow he had to get money. At the right moment Gregory caught up with a friend of his stepfather's, a Mr. J. W. Shillam, an Englishman who usually made marine engines but who had come to New York with an exciting invention he was convinced would draw the biggest crowds at the World's Fair.

He had a motor coach which, attached to a steel arm, travelled at breakneck speed around a steep-sided bowl. Underneath the bonnet was a powerful racing motor that made an appropriately loud noise and gave the 14 people on the ride the feel of being on a wall-of-death as they were swung upside down. Mr. Shillam normally made engines for speed ace Sir Malcolm Campbell – but now he was in show business and needed all the appropriate fanfares. He already had one "barker" to bring in the customers but he needed another. Was Gregory interested?

Greg heard the job paid $25 a week and he was very interested indeed. It was the bottom rung of the show business ladder but show business it was. His partner was a rundown old pro who had never risen much higher. The man considered that life owed him a great deal more than it ever gave him.

Since every schoolboy on both sides of the Atlantic knew of Sir Malcolm Campbell, to say nothing of his racing car Bluebird, it was Sir Malcolm's name that the barkers were given – the fact that this machine had nothing to do with Sir Malcolm was not allowed to interfere with a good story.

For twelve hours between noon and midnight, the two barkers harangued the passers-by – half an hour on and then half an hour off. Dressed in long white cover-alls and with goggles below their white helmets, the two were expected to call out to any virile-looking man who approached (using, of course, a different technique for the girls): "Hey there, buddy. Plenty of red blood in your veins? Well, just come on in and have a real thrill – a thrill a second, I tell you, a mile a minute around the upright walls of a wooden bowl. Just half a dollar. Yes, sir, that's 50 cents. Come on in."

Gregory was at the fair for a month, by which time he had heard of a less exacting job at the Rockefeller Center, which paid $15 a week more, for taking parties of 14 or 15 people on tours of the massive center. He took so many expeditions round the place that sometimes he made as much as $54 in a week.

It took some time getting used to the Radio City routine. An experienced guide could do a tour in an hour and then be ready to start another one. It didn't happen quite like that on Greg's first day.

The nervous energy required to start a new job combined with the actual energy used up in walking group after group around the complex took its toll. When it came to showing one group of tourists into the theater for what was expected to be a ten-minute "peep" at the show, Greg settled into a comfortable tip-up seat next to his party and fell fast asleep. He didn't wake up again until the lights came on. Beside him was the equally comfortable assembly of "customers" who were delighted with the opportunity that they had just had to see an entire show. They had assumed it was merely part of the tour.

On the whole, however, it wasn't a difficult job. One day he had to take a group out on to the observation roof above the 80th floor – and promptly came unstuck.

"Where's Brooklyn?" asked one woman, anxious to know her whereabouts in the big city. "Over there, madam," said Gregory, pointing confidently to New Jersey.

Finally came the time to start working for the Neighborhood Playhouse. The tall, immensely good-looking Gregory Peck was lucky to have fallen into the web of the two women who ran the drama school – both of them daughters of well-to-do New York Jewish families who were deeply involved in the cultural life of the city. Rita Morgenthau was the sister of Henry M. Morgenthau, Roosevelt's Secretary of the Treasury, and her partner Irene Lewisohn was a member of the family that had donated the Lewisohn Stadium.

Eighteen years or so earlier, they had established the world-famous Grand Street Playhouse, downtown on the East Side of Manhattan, that became one of the showcases of the great choreographer, Martha Graham. Now Miss Graham taught at their other institution, the Neighborhood Playhouse, too.

But dancing, to which Gregory felt he was no more suited than he was to misguiding the patrons of the Rockefeller Center, was not the main attraction of the Playhouse to drama students. The actors' coach was Sanford Meisner, whose reputation as a drama teacher in the Stanislavsky tradition had traversed continents.

He had taken the method to the Group Theater and given Stanislavsky's theater an American accent. With the other students, Peck was learning not merely to act but to *become* the character he played. It was no longer good enough to pretend to be the leader of the Greek chorus. Now he would have to project all their joys and agonies.

Meisner taught actors to discover the "spine" of the role. Improvisations were in themselves art and they helped the performer to find the emotional truth of what he was trying to do.

With his scholarship, Greg didn't have to pay for his tuition. But he was still constantly broke. Finally, the two fairy godmothers who admitted him to the Playhouse dipped their wands even closer in his direction. After lending him money most weeks, they decided it would be better if they paid him a $10 a week stipend instead.

He had to pay $6 a week rent now – for a room on 54th Street between Fifth and Sixth Avenues, close to the Playhouse and the other places that seemed to matter. The rest of his $10 was supposed to go on food and everything else a man now approaching 23 would need. It quite plainly wasn't enough – but he was sufficiently attractive to take advantage of the secondary occupation to which many other budding actors turned. He became a model.

It wasn't a glamorous job but it paid all of $25 a day, and anyone could see Greg's face in print 100 times every time he picked up the Montgomery Ward mail-order catalog. Peck was the one wearing long underwear on one page and a three-piece suit on the next; the one, who, in a street scene, was in a raincoat, and on the next page, in a tennis outfit. Just a flip of the pages and you saw him wearing a whole variety of sweaters, thigh-length rubber fishing boots, and a natty line in rain hats.

It was hard work, but it certainly helped the budget. All he had to do was to be prepared to wear the items with which he was presented – but fast. Of course, nothing fitted him, but standing next to the clothes horse was a company employee armed with a collection of safety pins.

Just as Greg stepped in front of the camera, the man took a professional look, sized up the situation and went to work with his safety pins, pulling the garment taut like a male nurse locking a mental patient into a strait-jacket.

He did other advertising, too.

In one shot he wore a top hat, white tie and tails, standing behind the young lady who used Palmolive soap (she got $25 too). For another job, he became a repair man – this time for the New Jersey Lighting Corporation. They used him for a public relations hand-out. He was the one smiling at the top of a telephone pole, happy in his work.

It was, in its way, still part of a show, and life really did seem as though it were all theater. Sometimes funny, sometimes sad, but, to the newcomer, usually thrilling. When he had to move rooms to East 38th Street, that, too, was part of life – still at $6 a week without bath.

Occasionally, between apartments, Greg used railroad stations for purposes other than the ones for which they were intended. When he didn't have $6 for the week's board and lodgings, he placed his belongings in a left-luggage locker at Grand Central Station and simply slept under the stars in Central Park. Mugging – in name and deed – was virtually unknown.

But he was not alone in being without money and it never really seemed to matter that much. Learning the business was much more important. Once, Greg and his old Berkeley pal, Kenneth Tobey, who had followed him to the Neighborhood Playhouse, worked out that they had the grand sum of 11 cents between them. The figure was easy enough to ascertain since their pooled wealth lay before them on the table in Greg's room. Tobey and a friend shared the room adjoining it.

The three decided also to combine their other resources – which amounted to a box of flapjack powder in Tobey's cupboard. The 11 cents went on a quart of milk and, with the two sets of ingredients, the three made an enormous pile of pancakes – dozens of them, without butter or syrup, but enough to keep starvation away for a day or two.

It was at this time that Peck's political instincts first stirred. The direction in which they pointed was left. He would describe himself as a liberal Democrat but when friends went to the Communist Party rallies at Madison Square Gardens, he went too. He moved at this time fairly far out on to the Left – without actually joining the Communist Party. But he read *New Masses* magazine which some people considered to be as good as having a party card. He was engrossed in what he read and what the articles preached.

"I was on the edge of it and in sympathy with a lot that they had to say," he recalls now. But given the choice between his personal theatrical ambitions and his youthful dreams for a better society, he had to continue dancing and training his vocal abilities as well as the process of learning how to be an actor.

During one of Martha Graham's stage movement classes – when the students were expected to sit up straight, pushing legs out and then bending heads between knees – the effect was startling. The lanky Peck body could only get halfway down. This was not nearly far enough for Martha. "Come along, Gregory," she said, "you can do better than that." And to demonstrate the fact she put one knee into his back and pushed.

His back popped like a firecracker – everyone else nearby could hear it and he knew that something inside had snapped. But it didn't hurt very much and apart from feeling slightly strained, he was able to continue with most of the day's work. The following morning, however, he woke to discover that he could move no more than half an inch in any one direction. A doctor was called and finally the diagnosis was clear. He had slipped a disc. But worse. The vertebra was displaced and the disc ruptured.

Eventually osteopathy was able to cure most of the trouble. But he had to endure years of pain, wearing the same kind of canvas brace that John F. Kennedy was to wear.

He was not so much worried about his health as about the effect it might have on his career. Even while he was studying at the Neighborhood Playhouse, he had opportunities for professional acting experience too. One of the first of these was in a one-act play which was held at the New York School for Social Research. There was just one performance and he rehearsed his role for three weeks. The experience was considered invaluable.

At the end of his first academic year, the name Gregory Peck was featured in the programs for one of the strangest outfits in the American theater – the Barter Theater at Abingdon, Virginia. Nobody expected to make a fortune from that theater, but a really successful performer could go home laden with geese and cabbages.

Customers who "bought" seats at the theatre paid for their tickets at the box office with a live duck or a piglet. There was a chart hanging by the box office which indicated what sort of seat could be purchased in exchange for each item of merchandize. A piglet could be worth six seats. A duck might merit four tickets. A quart of cottage cheese would just about be considered fair exchange for a single seat. Two pounds of spinach was likely to be worth a seat too. Various permutations were also worked out as suitable exchanges for jars of jam and marmalade or for preserved fruit and cans of vegetables. The proceeds of the local farmers' harvest were gladly demolished by the actors and others in the company.

It was the idea of a fellow called Bob Porterfield who had been fired by moderate success in New York to become a man of the theater. He thought that a bunch of unemployed New York actors could be better off plying their profession to the highly cultured people of Virginia; simple, solid folk who enjoyed good literature and fine music. Given the chance to enjoy theater, they'd flock to that too, he considered. He was not far wrong. He also had the right idea about the number of performers who would be willing to perform one play while, in the best repertory and summer stock tradition, they were learning another.

Every summer the Barter Theater took about 40 young actors and actresses to join their company. Two of them were given scholarships.

In 1940, the Barter Theater Awards were won by Evelyn Fargo and Gregory Peck. They were considered the year's best, which meant that they were also given the best parts.

Greg and Evelyn were chosen by Dorothy Stickney, the star of the long-running Broadway comedy *Life With Father*.

Abingdon had had something of a sacred theatrical tradition in days past. Sarah Bernhardt and Lincoln's assassin John Wilkes Booth had played in the old-fashioned theater there – a building which was also used for the town meetings. It was so small that it was almost possible to touch the players from a seat in the front row of the balcony.

Porterfield came on the scene intent on reviving the old tradition in his own novel way. His place is assured in American theatrical history by being the only man on record to have bought the performing rights of George Bernard Shaw's *Arms and the Man* – for a Virginia ham.

The idea for the theater had blossomed during the Depression, as both a way of feeding actors and of giving poor people a chance to unload a little of their produce in exchange for an evening's entertainment. The year that Gregory Peck joined the company seems to have been a particularly good one for the local spinach crop – and for the makers of cottage cheese. Peck ate cottage cheese and spinach for breakfast and spinach and cottage cheese for lunch. For dinner, there was usually a soufflé of cottage cheese and spinach. When a customer came in with a few chickens or a piglet, the company heaved a collective sigh of gratitude and relief.

Greg only had 102 pages to learn, he was told, and – oh, yes – he had 24 hours in which to learn them.

The play was a comedy called *Button, Button*. He will not easily forget it. Not only had he to step in for the leading actor who was ill, he also had to drive the company truck 80 miles for the performance at Big Stone Gap, Virginia. When he arrived, it was up to him to unload and set up the scenery in a school hall. Wiring the footlights and spotlights was another of his responsibilities.

He recited his lines as best he could to himself on the drive up from Abingdon. But this baptism-by-audience was tough. By the time the curtain was ready to go up, he had committed to memory only a fraction of the script. He was also riddled with stage fright.

Hard-bitten professionals will regale other performers for hours on end about the night they wished had never happened. This was to be Gregory Peck's night of disaster. Only two hours after unloading the scenery and fixing the lights, he was ready to go on stage and try to remember what lines he had learned. Even they had now vanished. All he could remember was the first line.

His mood, as he made up for his role as an old man, in *Button, Button* wasn't easily hidden. Another actor, his old pal Ken Tobey, sat on another orange box nearby and said: "Never mind, Greg. I'll be over in the wings with the book and I'll feed you every line."

There was not enough time after that to contemplate the next move – which was fortunate. The curtain went up and Greg was first on – not knowing what would happen after he recited the one line he knew.

He got that out – a word of cheer to a housemaid: "Hello, Mollie, I hope your hot biscuits are as good as they used to be."

It was then that the god of actors in trouble looked down kindly at a young player called Gregory Peck. He had a moment of inspiration. After reciting the line with all the feeling he would have given to Hamlet's soliloquy, he moved towards the maid, took one of her biscuits and began chewing it slowly. There had been no rehearsals, but he thought it was a legitimate move.

As he pensively munched the cake, he meandered to the wings and received his second line – and his confidence. He confused the second and third acts, fed the wrong cues to the other actors, but the play did go on and nobody in the audience seemed any the wiser.

No stage fright on later occasions ever equalled the experience of that night.

In eight weeks, Greg also starred in an original play, which he still remembers with a feeling of unmitigated horror – called *On Earth As It Is*. Another for which he has more affection was called *Family Portrait* – about Mary and Jesus, performed in the contemporary rural costumes of a Virginia farming family. But the really big opportunity was the title role in Christopher Marlowe's *Edward II*. The effects of that were every bit as exhausting for him as *Button, Button* – but for altogether different reasons. It was now the end of the season and the lack of energizing food had begun to take its toll. He was very thin and his long hair (for 1940) grown with the part in mind, helped complete the picture of the emaciated artist. Hardest of all was the complicated verse he had to learn and understand. But he coped well enough and afterwards he was able to accompany Ken Tobey, another male member of the cast and a girl, on the trip back to New York in a battered old truck, at the close of the season.

They decided to stop off in Washington D.C. on the way. For a politically-minded young man like Peck, it seemed a wonderful opportunity to study the workings of Government. Inevitably, he was drawn to the Capitol.

It was the time when Congress was bitterly divided over President Franklin D. Roosevelt's plans for helping Britain with Lend-Lease. The debates in the House and in the Senate were each day taking up much of the space in America's newspapers. There were endless queues outside the chamber of the Senate but that, even so, was where the actors wanted to go. They waited their turn in line for four hours – four seedy-looking, down-at-heel, long-haired young people who would have looked more at home on a park bench or in a Bowery doorway.

At last they approached the end of the line. Not quite the end – there was still plenty of time for Greg to decide to go to the men's room. There was also time to land in jail.

Before he left, he took the reasonable precaution of asking his friends: "Will you hold my place for me? I'll be right back." He was away for ten minutes, returned to his now comfortable place in the line. That was the moment when an officious looking blue-uniformed policeman tapped him on the shoulder with his night stick. "End of the line, young man," he ordered. It had been a day of disturbances in the gallery. Angry young anti-war people were shouting and yelling their views about getting involved in a second world conflict and the pressures were telling on the guards and attendants.

This one didn't like the look of the long-haired Gregory Peck at all. It was clearly no use trying to convince the official that 18 hours earlier he had been acclaimed as King Edward II.

Greg protested: "But I've been here in the line for four hours. I just went to the restroom." All the policeman would reply was: "Get to the back of the line."

The democrat as well as the actor was now riled: "That's not fair you know. My friends here held my place." The guard continued to be unimpressed. He poked Greg with his stick. "Get out of here," he demanded with a snarl – to which Peck responded by looking as purple as he had only wanted to be at Berkeley and by pushing the blue-coated man away. That did it. The policeman blew his whistle and was quickly rescued by six other officers – who wasted no time at all in grabbing Greg by the scruff of the neck and frogmarching him away from both the queue and his friends. They pulled him by the seat of his pants while the other three actors now joined in the slanging match. All four of them were eventually incarcerated in the slammer – the cells beneath the Capitol which were originally installed as a means of dealing with sudden cases of insurgency.

For two hours the four sat on a bench behind bars. Finally the chief of police came to visit them. He was a wily old bird who had spent the best part of his life dealing with disturbers of the peace.

"Were you planning to agitate in the gallery?" he asked, knowing the answer perfectly well. "We just wanted to see what was going on," Greg answered. "We've never been here before."

"Well," he replied. "You'd better get out quick if you don't want a whole lot of trouble. That guard of mine is really down on you."

With that, the party left for New York and their second year at drama school, still unacquainted with the workings of democracy at first hand.

From the Neighborhood Playhouse, Greg continued to get more part-time jobs and to borrow from his benefactresses, the Misses Morgenthau and Lewisohn. Occasionally there would be a $20 bill in the mail from his mother and stepfather.

The year ended with the school's big production at the Heckscher Theater on Upper Fifth Avenue. It was a performance of *The Chief Thing*, a Russian play. It had been selected, like most drama school productions, because of the wide variety of roles it offered – something for everyone in the Playhouse. Greg played a slick, moustachioed con-man, and had his hair dyed grey for the part.

The school had a tradition that on the morning after the play, students about to go out and look for professional work would line up at the reception desk and just hope that the phone would ring for them. All the big agents, producers and theatrical managers had been invited to the play and the great hope was that one of them might "bite."

The morning after *The Chief Thing*, nobody was more nervously chewing his fingernails than Gregory Peck. The phone rang soon after he got there. As she picked it up, the receptionist cupped her hand over the receiver. She looked at Greg and said: "It's for you." Then she spoke to the caller: "Yes, Mr. McClintic, he's here . . ."

Guthrie McClintic was one of the top Broadway producer/directors and the fact that he had been in the front of the theater the night before had been the subject of buzzes backstage from the moment he took his seat. He was constantly being examined for reaction through the spy holes in the curtain.

The receptionist seemed to be listening to McClintic for hours. Then, finally, Greg heard her say: "You'd like to see him . . . when, Mr. McClintic? This morning?"

Greg waited to hear nothing more. He tore out of the building while the startled receptionist continued the telephone conversation.

Her voice drifted out of range as Greg scrambled down four flights of stairs, sprinted half a block across 46th Street and along four blocks up Sixth Avenue, until he arrived panting at 50th Street and the lobby of the R.K.O. Building.

Peck knew exactly where the office was. He had been there many times hunting for jobs, but before, he had never got further than just leaving a secretary his name, telephone number, photograph and the important detail that he was available. Now, though, the bell had rung for Gregory Peck.

It was Saturday morning so there was no receptionist when he plunged into the office, after the elevator, taking an agonizingly long time, had dropped him on the eighth floor. The door of the inner office was open. McClintic was talking on the phone: ". . . well, yes," Greg heard him say as he stood breathless at the end of the Olympic-style run, "I have something in mind for him in *The Doctor's Dilemma* . . ." At that point, he saw the thin, lanky Peck frame, began to laugh, and literally slid off his revolving chair. "He's here . . ." he gasped into the phone. He was still talking to the receptionist at the Neighborhood Playhouse.

The phone was put down and, still laughing, McClintic beckoned Peck to sit down. That was when he told him: "You've got the job!"

It wasn't to come up until September 1941 and this was now June, but the promise of it was enough to make any prospective actor start working out the number of light bulbs that would be required to spell out his name. It was a job, and it was with a major touring company – though the part of Mr. Danby was small and *The Doctor's Dilemma* by Shaw had been played many times before.

Peck himself would only have a very few lines to say but that didn't matter.

Even more tempting, it was acting with the producer's wife, the great Katherine Cornell.

With that in prospect, he could view the summer ahead as a mere gap which he needed to fill in order to live. The experience at the

Playhouse and the mere fact that McClintic had offered him a job was enough to get him into the Cape Playhouse at Cape Cod, Massachusetts – a first-rate company in which Greg got to play opposite Ruth Chatterton in *Rebound*. She played the older woman he wooed, but who later rejected him. It had both comedy and tragedy.

Cape Cod was sufficiently near to Boston to have the attention of the city's leading critics and one of them noted in his review: "There is a young actor called Gregory Peck playing with Miss Chatterton who strikes us as the complete actor. Inside and out he gives an electrifying performance."

That, coupled with the hope of what was to come, left no doubt in Peck's mind that he had taken the right steps from Grand Central Station.

Cape Cod may have been what the profession deprecatingly called "Barnyard Theater" but the day that Greg read his first role he felt like a dog who not only had two tails but who was so excited that he didn't know which one to wag first.

Rebound was followed by several other roles, all of which were more exciting than the one that went before it. With the Viennese light opera star Fritzi Scheff – who was known as "The Kiss Me Again Girl" – he played in Somerset Maugham's *The Circle*. The only trouble was that Miss Scheff was not quite as conscientious about her role as he was. Nor did she have quite so much work to do. Greg was not only a small-part actor. He was also the company's call boy. It was his job to knock on all the dressing room doors and shout: "Half an hour please."

There were rarely any difficulties with this – apart from the sheer monotony of the chore itself. Usually the English members of the cast would react with a kind: "Righto! Thanks, old chap." The Americans would content themselves with: "Got ya. OK." On the first night of *The Circle*, Miss Scheff said nothing. At first, Greg left it at that – but since he had seen both the actress and her hairdresser enter the room earlier, he began to wonder whether they had been struck down by a double heart attack.

After talking to the stage manager, he tried again. This time he rapped hard and shouted: "Curtain going up, Miss Scheff." Finally, she responded. The mere fact that she wasn't dead was a relief in itself. But what she said was: "Young man – I'll tell *you* when the curtain's going up."

In the fall of 1941, Gregory was ready to face *The Doctor's Dilemma* and Katherine Cornell.

McClintic appreciated Peck's potential as an actor. He understood him – but he also understood the audience. During rehearsals, he always sat in the back row of the balcony – so that he could be sure that every word coming over from the stage was crystal clear.

When Greg didn't seem to be projecting sufficiently well, he shouted out from his perch: "Can't understand you! They pay to get in up here, too, you know. They pay to *hear you.*" As Greg now says: "He would stop you cold just like that. So pretty quickly you learned how to project. You didn't want him yelling at you all the time."

The play opened at the Walnut Street Theater in Philadelphia with the few lines he was due to play floating around his brain cells. Nothing would make him spoil his big opportunity by forgetting his lines. He wore a morning coat and striped trousers – the young curator of a private art gallery in London. Peck's main speech – there were only seven altogether – amounted to: "If anyone should come before the time, don't take any notice. The commissionnaire won't let anyone through unless he knows them. We have a few people who like to come before the crowd – people who really buy; and of course we're glad to see them. Have you seen the notices in *Brush and Crayon* and in *The Easel?*"

What Greg had not bargained for was the fact that the night was not merely opening night, but also the 25th anniversary of Miss Cornell's wedding to Guthrie McClintic. To help them celebrate, some of the brightest stars on Broadway had come to the opening – the Lunts among them – and the leading lady was desperately nervous. She had earlier taken advantage of the champagne being poured backstage and had revelled in the congratulations of the Lunts, trying not to show them how she felt.

It was the beginning of the fifth act when things got really embarrassing. Miss Cornell came on stage, a vision bathed in pink light, wearing an exquisite figure-flattering Edwardian dress and a huge gorgeous hat. Her large olive eyes stared directly into Greg's face as he was due to begin his first important appearance on a totally professional stage. That beautiful, exquisite mouth of hers opened – but there was nothing to say. She had totally dried.

Peck turned and, in an aside, whispered her cue line – he knew them all so well. From that moment on, she – and the play – were perfect.

After the final curtain call, she rustled her petticoats in the young actor's direction. "Gregory," she said, quite overcome with the experience, "you've saved my life. I completely dried. I didn't have a clue about what I was going to say."

She didn't keep the experience to herself. She told the Lunts about this remarkable young actor. She whispered it to Helen Hayes. Peck may have been dark but from that moment on he was her blue-eyed, fair-haired boy.

As a result, for the next two years, Gregory Peck had a job with Guthrie McClintic and Katherine Cornell.

In the spring of 1941, Greg had a screen test – and failed.

The only reason Greg made the test, he now admits, was "because I was a young fool. I really had no interest in a screen career."

An agent called Mildred Webber, who worked for the William Morris Agency, had been searching for possible talent and Gregory Peck's good looks made an impression on most women who came across him. She thought he was ideal material for the movies. Miss Webber told Katherine Brown, East Coast representative for David O. Selznick, who in turn wanted new people with whom she could impress the Hollywood office.

Remembering the day of that test – a memory he tried to drive away for a generation – he recalls feeling rather like a moth that had been impaled with a pin. The director told him not to budge from a set position – "Stand there. Don't move from your marks," he said. Greg imagined thereafter that a film actor was never supposed to move – which presented one or two problems when he eventually reached Hollywood.

The test was made at the Fox Studios on 10th Ave and 57th Street. The first words that Gregory Peck ever addressed to a movie camera were: "How should I know what a drunk has in mind . . ?"

In a somewhat stilted scene from *This Above All* (filmed the next year with Tyrone Power in the male lead), Peck played an R.A.F. officer in London during the Blitz, who had to tell his girl (Augusta Dabney, who later figured extensively in the life of Montgomery Clift), that he couldn't go back to war. He did another short scene from *The Young in Heart*, which had already been made with Douglas Fairbanks, Jr.

Peck saw this screen test for the first time – and in my company –

some 37 years later. He said then he couldn't have been sure that the young man on the screen had a future.

When the tests were completed (four scenes in which both performers are seen in long shot and then in close up), the director's comments of "Gee, that's great" were recorded for posterity. Mr. Selznick, however, thought otherwise. In one of his classic memos (and no doubt one he had reason to regret soon afterwards) he wrote to Miss Brown: "Commenting on the last group of tests: I am sorry to say that I don't see what we could do with Gregory Peck. Maybe a big studio could use him, but we would have great difficulty in either using him ourselves or in getting other studios to use him that didn't have him under contract. He photographs like Abe Lincoln, but if he has a great personality, I don't think it comes through in these tests.

"He must be a fine legitimate actor, judging by your great interest in him, and while his performance in the scene from *This Above All* is satisfactory, considering how much work was done in the day and considering the circumstances under which it was made, it is nothing to get excited about. As for his performance in *The Young in Heart*, my respect for Doug Fairbanks Jr. goes up after seeing Peck play this scene."

Greg was not totally disenchanted by this reaction. The future looked rosy enough in the McClintic Company, although he was feeling the financial pinch quite considerably. He still had no real ambitions to go to Hollywood.

After *The Doctor's Dilemma* Philadelphia opening the company toured the country for six months.

At San Francisco, Greg's mother and stepfather proudly told their friends about their boy and his international company of stars – and the theater was full every night. The local papers carefully noted that Greg was the same home-town boy who had made good after being at Berkeley.

The play closed in San Francisco, but the company stayed there – because Miss Cornell wanted to rehearse her next vehicle in the city. This was *Rose Burke*, a translation of a French play by Henri Bernstein which had been playing with success on the Champs-Elysées before the Nazis moved in. There was no part in it for Greg, but as long as Miss Cornell was running the company, there would always be work to follow it. He was assistant stage manager. He also understudied two roles.

It was a peculiar sensation being an understudy for two distinctly different parts. Actors like Peck want to get under the skin of the characters they arc playing. But without the benefit of ever doing a role before a live audience, it is really difficult to feel a part which another man portrays night after night.

In *Rose Burke*, there was the added complication that one of the men he was understudying was Philip Merivale, a leading actor of the day who was then quite 50. The other man was Jean Pierre Aumont who was merely 29. Strangely, it was the older man with whom the 25-year-old Peck felt the closer rapport, even though the actor in him believed that the younger part was the one that presented the greater challenge.

To go on in Merivale's role, Peck had perfected his own make-up devices – no make-up artist travelled with the company as it made its way from San Francisco, through Portland and Seattle and on to Toronto and Detroit. He had his own way of greying his hair, and he knew how many lines to paint under his eyes. At the same time, he had a superb silver-grey moustache ready for the day when he would go on. The day, though, never came. It is probably fortunate that it did not. As Greg himself recalls, the play, like some good wines, just didn't travel well. The frothy, light Parisian nonsense wasn't suited for an America which many believed was on the precipice of a world war.

But the young understudy did have the advantage of taking part in rehearsals – the ones in which his mentor, the beautiful Katherine Cornell, took her full share.

What worried Greg about the juvenile lead was that he had to master a French accent – while all that came out when he tried was the voice of a young actor from California trying to sound French. He looked, sounded and – worst of all – felt a phoney. It was one night in Detroit that the moment to take over that ill-prepared role looked as if it had come.

Once more he had to knock on the actors' doors and make sure they were ready to appear on stage. It was 8.15 and encouraging responses came from the dressing rooms of everyone except Aumont. At first Greg didn't worry too much but as the minutes ticked by, he got desperate.

"What'll I do?" he asked the stage manager in what closely resembled a panic. "Call the hotel, for God's sake," he was told.

47

Greg phoned the Brook Cadillac Hotel in downtown Detroit but there was no reply from Aumont's room.

He raced the two blocks from the theater to the hotel and there called the actor on the house phone. Still no reply. There was less than ten minutes to curtain time, so Peck dashed up the hotel stairs and pounded on his door. It was then that a sleepy Jean Pierre Aumont came to the door, totally bewildered by the whole exercise. Suddenly, it all dawned on him. He had been asleep and had neglected to ask for a call.

Peck got the semi-comatose actor into as decent a set of clothes as he could find, pulled him out into the corridor, through the open door to a waiting elevator, along through the lobby and out into the cold, very icy street.

A blizzard was blowing and the now very shocked Aumont hit a patch of ice and landed with a thud. It dawned on Peck that this was the opportunity that understudies are supposed to crave – his star had knocked himself out. Except that in this split second he realized that there was nothing he fancied doing less than going on in Aumont's place. It was not a role that he ever wanted to be seen playing. Peck was desperate and determined enough to drag Aumont to his feet, slap his face and haul him towards the theater like an Eskimo dragging a sledge.

They got to the theater dead on 8.30 – which was just enough time to wrap a series of cold, wet towels around Aumont's face, smear him with make-up and give him a cup of coffee to steady his bewildered nerves. Aumont went on stage and nobody was more grateful than Peck.

The play was followed by another production which was no better than its predecessor, but this time Greg did play the juvenile lead. *Punch and Julia* was about as exciting as its title, but Peck is today sure that one of the reasons McClintic chose it was because it did have a role for his former assistant stage manager. Greg had the distinct advantage of playing opposite another extremely beautiful and talented actress – Jane Cowl, who had been not only one of Broadway's most acclaimed Juliets, but who had a style that showed itself in everything she did. The ingenue was Fran Heflin, sister of Van Heflin.

Punch and Julia was a comedy. Like actors who deliberately try to be funny, *Punch and Julia* died after stumbling through Wilmington,

Washington D.C. and Baltimore – each time the notices it received were more and more ghastly.

On the Wednesday afternoon of the week in Baltimore, no more than 22 lonely souls sat among the 1,600 seats in the theater. Arthur Margetson, the male lead in the play, looked through the curtain and said to the assembled company: "I'm not going on. This is ridiculous. Call the whole thing off."

Jane Cowl, on the other hand, thought that was the wrong attitude: "Arthur," she told him, "we're going to give them the show of their lives. Take the curtain up. Everyone give of their best." And they tried – except that the 22 people out there in the shadows didn't stir. There wasn't a clap of applause or a titter of laughter.

America was now at war, and like all men of his age, Greg was medically examined for war service. The doctors took one look at the x-rays of his back and told him to return to the stage. "You're one of the people we definitely don't want," said one of the medical men. "If your trouble gets any worse, it could cost us $10,000 in surgeon's fees, and a permanent disability pension."

It left Greg free for another summer in Cape Cod – once more playing opposite the delectable Ruth Chatterton.

It was while playing the lead in *You Can't Take It With You* by Kaufman and Hart that Greg convinced himself for the first time that his future really lay in comedy. He played a ballet master of the third water – a role later beautifully played on screen by Mischa Auer – owner of a seedy, run-down dancing school. Early on in the play, he is asked by the grandfather of one of his pupils: "Can she dance?" "Confidentially," he replies, "she stinks." Now that line could be received in stoical silence – on the surface, there is no reason why it should be treated in any other way – or, if uttered properly, it could have the audience in hysterics. When Greg said it, the customers out front were howling. He had to say it four times in the play, and four times the audience was rolling in the aisles. When he had to wrestle with another of the play's characters – a banker whose son was marrying into his family – there was more than mere hilarity from the other side of the footlights.

Gregory Peck knew then he was going to be a comedy actor – perhaps with the occasional dose of high drama to spice his career. But comedy – he was sure – was the way he was going to make his life on the boards. And perhaps occasionally, a musical – like the restoration comedy *The Duenna*, in which the music was contemporary Broadway. The piece was intended as a vehicle for the pantomimist, Jimmy Savo, who now wanted to become a speaking actor. Greg did five or six numbers and danced, too. Martha Graham would have been proud of him, but it didn't seem to lead to anything.

And yet the summer of 1942 was not wasted.

At the famous Cape Playhouse in Dennis, Massachusetts, McClintic sent Greg a wire suggesting a visit to his Martha's Vineyard home. There, the producer handed him a script, entitled *The Morning Star*.

"It's been a hit in London," said McClintic. "I want you to take the lead – the one that the author Emlyn Williams has in the West End."

And, yes, there was one other point, too: he would be playing it in New York. *The Morning Star* was going to be his debut on Broadway.

Playing opposite him was Jill Esmond, the first wife of Laurence Olivier and mother of his son Tarquin. The reviews of the play were fair, but the public wasn't. They couldn't accept a story of the London Blitz – it didn't stir them or even make them laugh when a bombed-out charlady sleeps under a grand piano because it was the only kind of air-raid shelter she could find. The spirit of the Blitz was totally alien to the hard-bitten New Yorkers for whom war was still just something they read about in the newspapers or in letters home from the boys in uniform.

The play was an "honourable failure" as Greg recalls it. He himself was desperately frightened about accepting a Broadway lead, particularly one in which he had to broaden his "a's" to try to assume something of a British accent. He was well rehearsed and tried not to think of the critics out front, men like George Jean Nathan, Alexander Woollcott, Brooks Atkinson and Richard Watts, sitting in what the trade called Murderers' Row. The Butchers of Broadway had become even more deadly in recent months and actors just had to pretend that they weren't there.

After the first couple of minutes, Greg tried to rely on both the rehearsals and on his determination to justify his name writ large on the marquee outside the theatre. Before that, some of the old misgivings had entered his mind. Once more, he contemplated the notion of digging a hole in the floor of his dressing room and burrowing his way through the sewers of New York to go off to Mexico and obscurity.

It was fortunate that he did no such thing. Brooks Atkinson liked his performance: "Peck," he declared, "is an uncommon type."

It was during the run of *The Morning Star* that Greg met a man who is now one of his dearest friends – Frank Sinatra. Sinatra was playing nearby at the Riobamba night club. The club employed a press agent named Matt Miller who thought it would be a good publicity idea to photograph the new singing sensation with the new leading man on Broadway.

Peck went with Miller to the Riobamba and heard the wafer-thin Sinatra in his then high baritone, warbling "That Old Black Magic." In the last ten to fifteen years they have become very close.

Another relationship was cemented at this time. Greg took a personal step even more important than his lead debut on Broadway. He was married.

For months he had been getting increasingly friendly with a vivacious girl called Greta Konen. She had been Katherine Cornell's hairdresser and all through the period with the McClintic Company, they had been spending an increasing amount of time together – particularly since they were the youngest people in the "team."

There was no mistaking the fact that Greta was Scandinavian, although her parents brought her to America from their native Finland when she was a little girl. Her hair was blonde, her cheekbones wide and her complexion had the fresh look of one born close to the Arctic Circle.

Greta – her real name was Kukkonen, but her parents had simplified it to Konen – had already been married once to an American called Charles Rice. That marriage ended in divorce.

Greg now says that they were "thrown together" but there was no doubt that her gaiety was infectious. She loved going to parties.

On a Saturday morning in October 1942, Greg rang a few of his friends and told them: "I have some tickets for the Yankees' World Series game this afternoon. Would you like to come?" He then added that he had also bought a marriage licence.

With his friends, Greg and Greta went to the game at the Yankee Stadium – and then, almost as a casual afterthought, they all popped into the small Lutheran church on Fifth Avenue for a wedding ceremony. The marriage was not to be recognized by Greg's own Catholic church, but for the time being he was satisfied that his life, so abnormal for most of the time up till then, was now about to reach a plateau of normality.

At 26, Gregory Peck still yearned for the concrete family ties he had missed in his early youth. Greta was the one who seemed best able to give them to him. In those early Broadway days she was also willing to give him the encouragement that a young star-in-the-making needs.

The flop of *The Morning Star* was followed almost immediately with another Broadway lead role – in John Patrick's *The Willow and I*.

It was about two sisters at the turn of the century who are both in love with the same man. Peck played a double role, as the doctor they loved and as his son.

"The play," said the *New York World Telegram*'s Burton Rascoe, "is beautifully done. The casting is faultless. The settings are perfect. I especially mention Martha Scott, Barbara O'Neill (who played the sisters) and Gregory Peck only because they carried the burden of the play and did it faultlessly."

At last, Greg's name was in lights and he was paid $250 a week for the privilege. He was being talked of as the new matinee idol. Greta had moved into his apartment on East 39th Street and although he was now a star and earning good money by most people's definition of the term, he was glad not to have to pay more than $14 a week in rent.

Later, he and Greta found it difficult to pay the $200 a month rent that they committed themselves to for a charming one-bedroom, one-sitting room apartment in a place called The Townhouse on Lexington Avenue. He was also heavily in debt. Among his debtors was the famous "actors' dentist" Mr. J. Y. Pokress who was stage struck. An inveterate first-nighter, he loved being surrounded by actors and never sent them any bills. Most of the unemployed thespians of New York knew he was a good touch and he seemed to revel in that reputation. When actors made good, he expected them to pay him, but he never mentioned the matter of cash himself. He is said to have inspired Clifford Odets's play *Rocket on the Moon*.

Peck himself also seemed to be on a rocket to somewhere. When *The Willow and I* closed, he took a trip to California – at the request of his new agent, Leland Hayward. In actual fact, the request came from Samuel Goldwyn who had heard about Peck's Broadway reputation.

"How much do you want for Peck?" Goldwyn asked. "I'm willing to go to $1,000 a week."

"Make it $3,000," said Hayward who realized that the mogul had the advantage of him. He himself had never heard of the new stage star and had to check his books to make sure that he was one of the company's New York players. "Who," he asked, "is Gregory Peck?"

Greg took the three-day journey back to his home state no more concerned about a future in films than he had been when he made the Selznick test. When he met Goldwyn, he was formally offered a seven-year contract. He politely said "No thanks." There was no way Goldwyn was going to allow talent like Peck's to escape once he had him in his grasp and he only had one way of employing people – on the longest contract that Californian law allowed. No one was allowed to be tied to an employer for more than seven years. As far as Goldwyn was concerned, he either had actors under his thumb or he didn't have them at all.

Louis B. Mayer, the M.G.M. boss, also got to hear that Greg was in town. When Peck was shown into the panelled office the mogul did his best to make him feel important and wanted. And then came the offer – a seven-year contract.

"No thank you," said Greg.

Mayer came round from his desk and looked earnestly into the eyes of the young actor. "I want you, Gregory, to join my family – my family of M.G.M. stars. I have made great careers for Judy Garland, Robert Taylor, Greta Garbo ..." He was going through the entire cast list of M.G.M. standard bearers. It indeed was a compliment for any young man to be considered worthy of being included in that catalog.

"Robert Montgomery, Clark Gable ..." The list went on and on.

There was no getting away from the paternalistic stance that Mayer was taking. It was as though he were trying to persuade a green high school kid to join a particular college – which was exactly the way he liked to think of his studio.

"Mickey Rooney, Spencer Tracy ..."

"You must let me decide on your pictures for you and you must become one of us. I will make you the greatest star of them all."

He detailed all he had done for Judy Garland, how he had made Robert Taylor an actor who had been dragged away from the part of his kingdom where the shorts and documentaries were made, to become Garbo's co-star in *Camille*.

Finally he asked: "Well, Gregory ... ?" and the way he said it spoke whole movies. He was confident that his was an invitation no one in his right mind could possibly refuse.

But then came the words that he had rarely heard before: "Sorry, Mr. Mayer." Greg went on to explain, "I'm a stage actor. I want to continue to be one. I'm determined not to sign an exclusive contract for anyone. If I were to do it, I'd be very happy to do it with you because I know your reputation, of course. But I cannot do so. It's against my nature."

Mayer was certain it was just a ploy by the young man for a better deal, a man who probably knew his worth in the middle of a war when even Taylor and Gable had had to put on uniform.

Greg was astounded as the flattery and the complimentary offers multiplied – and were followed up by genuine pleas. Then, he experienced, on his first visit to the all-powerful Hollywood studio chief, the famous Louis B. Mayer crying scene, the one that had greeted Judy Garland's warbling of "You Made Me Love You" to Gable.

"Please, Gregory, understand what I'm offering you," Louis B. Mayer continued. As he strode the length and breadth of his king-size office, king-size tears dripped down his cheeks and off his cheekbones. They were dribbling down his nose. Twice he had to take off his spectacles to demist the lenses.

"*Now*," he asked, confident that his exhibition of humility had achieved its purpose, "will you sign?"

"Mr. Mayer," answered Peck. "I'm flattered. I cannot tell you how much I appreciate your offer, but I cannot consider it."

Mayer looked at him dumbfounded. But, as Leland Hayward, who had been watching from the sidelines, tapped Greg on the shoulder to suggest that it might be more sensible if they left the room, Mayer was already comfortably ensconced behind his desk rustling through some papers and pretending to be completely oblivious to the presence of such a presumptuous young man.

Outside Mayer's door, Greg shook off his amazement. "My God," he said to the agent under his breath, so that the secretary outside could not hear, "what a performance!"

"Oh," said Hayward. "He does that every day and loves it. I've seen that show a dozen times."

Greg went back to New York and accepted another starring role on Broadway – in Irwin Shaw's *Sons and Soldiers*. His agent tried to dissuade him from taking the part. He said it wasn't strong enough and Greg was entitled to more than the $400 he was now to get. But Greg wanted it.

The big temptation was the fact that it was being directed by one of the legendary names of the theater, Max Reinhardt, a man who had never really recovered from losing everything after the Nazis had come to power. He not only had had no work, but had left behind him his home, his art treasures, virtually everything but his self-respect and protean talent.

He had made his controversial screen version of *A Midsummer Night's Dream* seven years earlier with unlikely Shakespeareans like James Cagney and Mickey Rooney and had not really been able to repeat his glorious German past since transplanting himself in America. He also had lost most of his once considerable physical strength. And yet the name Max Reinhardt was still held sacred in dramatic circles and an offer to star in one of his stage productions was more than Greg, for one, could turn down.

Greg played a small-town American boy, who, against the wishes of his parents, goes off to join the R.A.F. In one scene, he had to argue with his mother and father – laugh, cry, and jump out of a window. It was highly-charged emotionally and Greg wasn't sure he was getting through in it. He was self-conscious and every time he attempted what was clearly an emotional tour-de-force, all the doubts would well inside him. Whenever he came to the difficult part, he would feel his chest muscles tightening. Worse still, his tension was having an effect on the other actors.

Reinhardt usually sat during rehearsals at the back of what in the American theater is called the orchestra – the stalls. When he had directions to give to his players, he would send his assistant, Lili Darvas, to discuss the matter. The journey from one end of the theater to the other was too much for his constitution. But now he realized that he had to make a personal appeal to his star.

He took Greg off into a corner. It wasn't a comfortable moment – Greg, 6ft 3in tall, and thin, with the slightly portly, 5ft 4in-high director, gently chastizing his performer.

He put his head close to Greg's chest as he almost whispered, his cultured German accent still very evident: "Gregory – see the great advantage of being a play actor. We do not stop being children when we grow up. Play act, play act – it's all performance and imagination. You must put part of yourself into the corner just off-stage and then you must send the player – or the child, if you will – out on to the stage to play act. Nothing to be afraid of. It's only playing."

It was difficult not to be impressed by words like that and Greg was duly affected. "It was," he recalls, "a great breakthrough. It helped me throw off my self-consciousness. You have to be willing to make a damn fool of yourself and be horrible and embarrassing before you get it right. I think fear is what keeps a lot of people from ever attempting it. I think there must be a lot of people around who could be actors if they had ever been able to overcome that fear – or even the fear of fear. They never even got around to the point of trying it."

After that salutory lesson, Greg played the hard scenes in *Sons and Soldiers* as though he enjoyed them. Before long, he actually did enjoy them.

Reinhardt died a few months after the Broadway opening of the play, but that quiet head-to-shoulder chat was a superbly valuable legacy.

The play had an impressive cast. Besides Peck, there was a young man with a powerful nose who looked promising. His name was Karl Malden. Also on stage with Greg was Millard Mitchell and Stella Adler, daughter of the famous Yiddish actor Jacob Adler, and sister of Luther. But *Sons and Soldiers* was not a success. Irwin Shaw had gone off to North Africa to drive an ambulance – à la Hemingway – and had left his wife with strict instructions that not a word of dialogue was to be cut in his absence. Since there was no way of contacting an ambulance driver 5,000 miles away, the play stayed uncut and suffered the consequences.

It ran for just six weeks. Peck believes to this day that it could still be running somewhere, had the cuts been made. But had it succeeded, Greg might never have accepted a new invitation to go to Hollywood.

Four

The offer had come from the respected screen-writer Casey Robinson, who now had plans to set up his own independent production company – an animal which, like independent actors, was a rare species in 1942.

Robinson had called round to Greg's dressing room after a performance of *Sons and Soldiers*. Accompanying him was Hal Wallis, with whom Robinson had been working at Warner Brothers. Wallis had previously offered Greg a deal too – but like the others it had been an exclusive contract for seven years labour for Warners, and Greg had rejected it just as firmly as the earlier ones. Robinson's offer was different – four pictures in four years; and since he reckoned it would only take ten weeks to make a picture, Greg could do what he liked in the other forty-two weeks of the year. He could go to Broadway, or, if the Hollywood madness took root (which he just knew it would not) he could make pictures for other people. That offer seemed not just tempting, but realistic. It was also a fairly reliable way of paying off the rent he still owed on his apartment.

In the summer of 1942, Greg and Greta took the train to Los Angeles where they were met by Robinson. He also introduced them to their West Coast home, a rented pink and white stucco house on the side of one of the Hollywood Hills. They looked round the house, summed up their new status in life – for ten weeks Greg would be drawing no less than $1,000 each Saturday – and did a little dance. "It's a honeymoon," Greg cried, and they both did a jig round the room, certain that life couldn't possibly be much better.

The film he was to make was *Days of Glory* with Tamara Toumanova – Casey Robinson's fiancee. Peck's name was to go above the title – and it has never gone anywhere else since.

Days of Glory was made for R.K.O. Pictures – then at the crest of its success as a Hollywood studio. Although it never achieved the peaks of M.G.M., Paramount or Warner Brothers, the Astaire-Rodgers pictures had lifted it from obscurity and there were a number of other features which continued to raise its status. In those days, Columbia was a fairly long way down the ladder behind it. Republic barely figured at all.

Greg's contract, however, was with Casey Robinson, personally; R.K.O. couldn't hold him to anything, but Robinson certainly could – he was able, in fact, to demand, if he chose, that Greg make one picture for him every year for the following three years.

The director was Jacques Tourneur, whose first task was to explain to the young newcomer the intimate differences between being a stage actor and a performer on the screen. Not just the fact that, on the stage, an actor goes from the beginning of the story to the end in one fell swoop, while in a film studio he is expected to do a hunk of one scene one day and then follow it a day later with a sequence that comes 35 minutes earlier in the finished picture.

Greg found his big problem was simply one of over-projecting. Having been told by Guthrie McClintic to remember the balcony customers, he was used to making the rafters ring with a whisper. Now he had to rethink everything.

Tourneur told him to think of the microphone on the boom above as the friend next to whom he was standing. He didn't tell him to attempt a Russian accent – although in the picture he played a character called Vladimir, one of a group of Soviet guerrillas who were harassing the Nazi invaders of their country. Tamara Toumanova played a ballet dancer who finds her way to the partisan lines and it is there that she entertains the guerrillas (it was an opportunity for Tamara, who trained as a ballet dancer, to practise her art before a new audience).

The first day of shooting, Tourneur told Peck that he was too precise with his diction. "Common it up," he ordered. "You pronounce too many consonants and you're too conscious of your vowel sounds. And just project your voice three feet, not three hundred. You sound like a stage actor." To Peck that was a compliment.

The film was finished and Greg and Greta planned to go back to New York. Greg seemed to be more pleased about the thought than

Greta was. She enjoyed the parties and the fun of the two of them being treated as important people. For his part, all Greg was bothered about was keeping his career moving at the sort of pace that he had got used to. It was beginning to emerge that perhaps their marriage was not quite as obviously made in heaven as the minister had said. Greta loved the whole idea of being in Hollywood, revelled in the thought that she was the wife of a film star.

Greg had no doubts that he was going to make it to the top – but as a successful actor, not just as a mysterious presence who would stare down at people from giant billboards or from the covers of fan magazines. And yet he did feel a sense of privilege at attending the same parties to which Spencer Tracy and Bogart and Cagney were invited.

"I met everybody," he recalls today. "But I can't remember being bowled over by them. I did, however, admire the big stars of the day. I did then, and I do now – simply because of their ability and because they're interesting chaps. They're not stars for no reason, you know. They're stars because they are interesting people.

"I had much earlier gained a respect for acting as a craft. It loomed larger in my mind than film stardom or glitter or tinsel."

It was a thought worth remembering when *Days of Glory* came out of the can, because it didn't make him a film star. The picture showed its lack of budget and flopped – but casting directors were taking big-time producers to theaters where the movie was playing, and they were saying: "Take a look at that guy Peck. He's a powerful young fellow."

After that first not-so-lucky experience, Greg was anxious to get back to the Broadway stage – after all, that's where it all happened for actors like him. Greta protested, but Greg didn't want to stay in California. Only one thing nagged at him, the thought that he would have to go out on a flop. No newcomer in show business likes to be anything but a brilliant hit and Gregory Peck was willing to be persuaded to stay if the right offer came along quickly.

It did; from Darryl Zanuck who, like the others, had seen Peck's performance in *Days of Glory* and was sure he had a project which not only could give the young actor a chance to shine but also his studio a sure-fire box office winner.

There were no contractual difficulties in the way. An informed look at the Broadway season also told Greg that he might have to hang around a little before another attractive stage role came his way.

When Zanuck, then production head at Twentieth Century Fox, showed him his new script, all Greg could do was accept – and do so with enthusiasm. For what the producer was offering Greg was the starring role in the film version of an A. J. Cronin best seller. Peck was to play a missionary in China. The story was *The Keys of the Kingdom*.

Today, Greg says he "fell in love" with *The Keys of the Kingdom*. He said the same thing in 1944 when he went on to the Fox soundstage for the first time. Within days, the word was buzzing round Hollywood that other people were falling in love with it – and with him, too.

Hollywood is a small, close community where people cheer the success of others openly and – sometimes after a few drinks – privately smile at their failures. When the gossips among the carpenters, cameramen and sound engineers met in the bars after a day's shooting, the cheers were heard loudly enough to be reported in the trade papers. It was apparent that Gregory Peck was already a starring, very marketable commodity.

The young Father Chisholm, the priest who asked nothing more of his life or of his God than the chance to go to China as a missionary – and was not interested in promotion within the church – was close to Peck's own idea of sanctity. He hadn't met people like this priest in his own Catholic institution days. The father and the nuns at St. John's had been simple country folk for whom the convent and seminary was a way of escaping from the drudgery and poverty of rural Ireland. Father Chisholm represented a totally different sort of man.

"He was a real priest," he told me. "Instead of being cynical and climbing the clerical ladder to success and becoming a bishop, he wanted to serve the poor and the needy."

Zanuck had been looking for a Father Chisholm for nine months. Almost all the top masculine stars in Hollywood had been tested for the role – which the mogul decided was very much the part for a strong man rather than the anaemic clergyman seen all too often. None of the men tested was considered right for the role.

Zanuck also ordered screen tests of likely unknowns. Forty went through the process and forty were rejected. When the producer heard about *Days of Glory*, he saw it with an air of detachment. It helped. As soon as he saw that movie, Zanuck called in John M. Stahl, who was to direct the new picture. Both agreed they had found their Chisholm.

What they did not know was the perfectionism with which Greg would invest the part. As soon as he had studied the script in sufficient detail to know that he could play the role, he set about deciding *how* he would play it.

He came to the set the first day knowing the script from the opening scene to the final fade out. With a few acting friends, he had already played out the role – so that he not only had perfected the lines and memorized the cues, but he had the whole personality of Father Chisholm deeply engraved in his psyche.

And yet there were problems that he didn't think he would be able to solve. Knowing the man was one thing, portraying him so that he felt he *was* that man was something else again. That he overcame that difficulty was due to a certain Father Albert O'Hara who had been retained as technical adviser.

Father O'Hara had been a missionary in China, and, like the fictional Father Chisholm, spoke fluent Chinese. Watching the priest talking to a group of Chinese extras helped Greg gain the necessary humility. The actor and the priest became firm friends and they still correspond today – Father O'Hara lectures at the University of Taiwan.

Perhaps even more encouraging for him was the fact that A. J. Cronin himself couldn't have been more happy with his Chisholm portrayal had he selected the actor personally. Soon after the film's completion, he took Greg for lunch at a New York restaurant. "Your work," he told him, "has been wonderful, really wonderful. I just can't understand how any actor could so well catch the clumsiness and the beauty of Father Chisholm's character."

Cronin later promised to write a play for Greg but unfortunately it never happened. Peck, meanwhile, continued to promise himself that he would return to Broadway soon – although he was finding the idea of making films more attractive.

A movie public suddenly anxious for a change of the usual fare in the dying days of World War Two could see in *The Keys of the Kingdom* some good pro-Chinese, anti-Japanese propaganda, but also a warm, human story that had none of the empty escapism that Hollywood was fond of turning out at that time.

Now the people who had not bothered to see *Days of Glory* waited in line for hours for the price of a ticket to *The Keys of the Kingdom*. Both Darryl Zanuck and Nunnally Johnson knew they had backed the right hunch.

"A personal triumph indeed for Gregory Peck," trumpeted the *New York Post*, who described Greg as a "dark-eyed, sensitive newcomer to pictures, whose ingratiating performance expresses dignity, warmth and on occasion, a wryly humorous controversial streak."

The *New York Mirror* also enthused about the new talent before them: "The fine direction of John M. Stahl is recognized," its critic reported in the stilted style of the day. "The star maker has treated the lead role of Father Chisholm with such delicacy that we hereby bestow upon Gregory Peck the star, the title of Most Outstanding Newcomer to the Screen."

As always, the *New York Times* was more restrained: "Gregory Peck, a tall and spare newcomer, gives a quiet and forceful performance in the role of the priest and conveys a fine impression of godly devotion and dignity."

Ironically, (as things were to turn out before long) the *New York Herald Tribune* compared Greg's Father Chisholm with Bing Crosby's recent Father O'Malley in *Going My Way*.

"Unlike Crosby, who turned in a portrayal of the lighter side of secular life, Peck typifies the earnest, hard-working and kindly type of religious man," said the paper, which chose, also, to remark on his "tall, lean" looks, "possessing all the requisites of a matinee idol . . . he discovered that his role required a certain naivety necessary to give it a more individualistic story and at the same time invoke sympathetic audience reaction. Upon his ability to do this rests much of the actor's future success."

All at once, papers and radio reporters were hailing Greg as the "most interesting new actor in Hollywood."

Darryl Zanuck was so pleased that he immediately doubled Greg's personal take from the picture with a $25,000 bonus.

There were just occasional sour notes. The newspaper *PM* remarked: "Gregory Peck is best when there is work to do; least convincing when talking religion."

The *Hollywood Reporter* – whose importance in the film town should not be underestimated – contented itself by saying: "Gregory

Peck reaches the heights in the second assignment of his movie career."

Others in the industry obviously agreed. Greg was nominated for an Oscar – for the best male actor of the year. He was pipped at the post by Bing Crosby, who told everyone how glad he had been to win the Award for a dramatic role like that of Father O'Malley – "I didn't even have to wear a necktie." Greg couldn't really have been happy to lose out. On the other hand, he had achieved in his second film what hundreds of actors never even approach in the course of long and otherwise distinguished careers.

Greg had only done the two pictures when he met Gary Cooper, by then already a veteran of no less than sixty-two.

"How many have you made?" Cooper asked him.

"Two," he replied.

"How were they?" Cooper probed.

"One good, one bad."

"You're ahead of the game right now," said the famous "yup" and "nope" actor. "Don't be worried if you get a few flops. An actor is lucky if he has two good movies out of every five he makes."

Things were beginning to get a little complicated for Greg. His new contract promised four more movies for Twentieth Century Fox. He had also signed to do four pictures with Casey Robinson – who could still claim another three from him.

David O. Selznick expressed an obvious interest in the man whom he had rejected so perfunctorily a couple of years earlier and offered Greg the standard seven-year contract, which was also rejected in his now standard way. Selznick, however, had a way of getting his man – even Greg. He bought half of Robinson's contract, which meant that Greg now had an obligation to make two pictures with Selznick.

M.G.M., too, wanted their piece of the action. They now swallowed Louis B. Mayer's pride and signed Greg to make three pictures for them in five years. The Hayward agency were making sure that their client had plenty of work in a maze of contracts that they just hoped would interlock satisfactorily. The headache, they told Greg, was not his.

Hayward was at that time married to Margaret Sullavan. He was a fast-talking, bright-eyed agent who wowed the Hollywood ladies as successfully as he was able to persuade moguls to do things for him – and both these classes of people later marvelled at the situations in which they landed themselves.

Margaret Sullavan, who had been married to William Wyler and Henry Fonda, had a personal hatred for agents and now convinced her husband that being one was demeaning for both a man's talents and his personality. Hayward agreed with his wife that it was time to try to untangle himself from some, at least, of his involvements. He gave up the agency business and left Greg with sixteen commitments that somehow had to be made good in the next four to five years. The Hayward agency was taken over by M.C.A. who decided that in Gregory Peck they had an actor who deserved to be well looked after. It was an attitude shared by the film makers who were constantly worried about the drain on their actors caused by the war.

The Hollywood studios, of course, were particularly sensitive to any suggestion that their stars were having an easy ride at this time. Darryl Zanuck had issued an earlier statement saying that Greg had been excluded from the draft because of a back injury caused during his days in the boat crew at Berkeley. Somehow it sounded better – and created a much more masculine image – than telling the truth about his back problems developing during a dancing lesson. Really, though, it was satisfaction enough for them to be able to boast an actor whose performances had already been so widely acclaimed.

As for Peck himself, he figured he had good cause to be content. Even though things were not perfect between himself and Greta, there was still reason to believe that they might improve. And in late 1943, Greta was pregnant.

To a man who had not had a normal upbringing of his own, the promise of a child did seem to offer not just happiness but a chance to establish the kind of family stability which he missed. When Greta went into labour the following July, Greg was at the hospital with her. As he waited for the birth in an outer room, he felt no different from any other expectant father: *his* baby was the important one.

"Mr. Peck," came a hidden voice suddenly, and Greg jumped up, calling out, "I'm coming, I'm coming." He might have been answering an assistant director's request to go on the set. This time the sound came through the antiseptically-protected speakers built into the waiting room wall. Before he reached the door, the mystery voice added: "Mr. Peck, your son wants to speak to you."

Greg's response to that additional piece of information was to shout: "Yippee." Then he told the nurse who came to collect him: "The Yankees have found themselves another pitcher." His son was named Jonathan.

People expected Greg to develop a somewhat swollen head about his new-found success. There was no doubt that he liked the adoration of the young women who asked him for autographed photographs and who mobbed him at the film premieres. But he did try to play it cool most of the time and most of the time he succeeded. He was always much more keen on the work that went into making a film than the ballyhoo that followed it.

Not only did his face appear on billboards all over the American continent – and in England, Australia and Africa, too – but in New York he was given THE treatment. His young features were too attractive for Twentieth Century Fox not to exploit them to the full.

Never will he forget the impact of staring across Broadway at the 50-foot-high billboard outside the Rialto. It stretched for the best part of half a block – a huge portrait of Greg in priest's attire with a group of scurrying Chinese peasants escaping from a fire in the background.

The Pecks were beginning to evolve a new life-style. They bought a comfortable but fairly small house from Boris Karloff on Mulholland Drive – the street from which Errol Flynn shot imaginary bullets into the studios of Warner Brothers and where Al Jolson lived after the immense success of the world's first talking picture, *The Jazz Singer*.

It wasn't a totally new life, divorced from everything they had known before. Sometimes there was the company of people Greg and Greta had known before – in what in many ways now seemed a previous life. Ken Tobey came out to California to try his luck and for a time lived in a room above the garage on Mulholland Drive.

Greg took up M.G.M.'s option soon after enjoying the immediate success of *Keys of the Kingdom*. They signed him to co-star opposite Greer Garson in *The Valley of Decision*, to be based on the bestseller by Marcia Davenport.

The studio manufactured stars the way Palmolive made soap – and boosted them to the same degree – so that audiences just knew that no performers were bigger or more romantic, more handsome or more beautiful than these idols from M.G.M. Gregory Peck was welcomed as the latest to join the family whose names could and still can fill a book. But because the names were so big and the legends so immense, Greg felt an outsider from the moment that he was saluted in through the studio gates at Culver City to the time he joined L. B. Mayer in the commissary and watched him enjoy his daily bowl of chicken soup (just like his mother made).

On top of everything else, he had to appear opposite the woman who at that time was undoubtedly Queen of the Lot – lot being used in both senses of the word. Greer Garson had not long before been awarded her Oscar for *Mrs. Miniver* and was treated by Mayer as though she were made of bone china. Greg understood that she had to have her own favourite cameraman, Joe Ruttenberg, working on *The Valley of Decision*. To quote Peck: "When it came to viewing the rushes, I saw that every time I was in a scene with her, her face was a lovely luminous moon floating in the centre of the screen and I was the rather dim figure beside her in semi-shadow. Not that I really minded, Greer was beautiful and all woman. Also very funny. I called her Big Red."

Soon after that experience, Greg talked about the matter with Adolphe Menjou, a man with whom he had really very little else in common: "Oh, my God," said Menjou, "I know exactly what you mean; I made a picture with her and every time we were in a two-shot, I thought I'd freeze to death."

When the film was completed, a shiny black Cadillac drew up to the Pecks' Mulholland Drive home to take them to Pasadena where a local cinema had on its marquee the time-honoured words: "Major Studio Feature Sneak Preview Tonite."

After the showing, during which most of the participants had been quite pleased with the results of their work, came the moment to go out into the lobby and read the cards filled in by the Pasadena critics – the ordinary paying customers in the theater who were asked to make their comments on a picture, about which two hours earlier they had known absolutely nothing; in fact they didn't even know the title of the film they were about to see until the credits came on the screen.

Standing with the director and the producer and with Greer looking beautiful and majestic, they waited for the cards to be brought out by the manager of the theater. A studio executive picked the first card, a smile on his face. As he read it, the smile vanished and the face turned white. Virtually motionless, he passed it to Greg. The immortal message read: "Junk it."

The studio decided not to take this anonymous critic's advice and the picture recouped its expenses – plus a respectable profit.

Soon after the take-over of the Hayward agency by M.C.A., Lew Wasserman called in one of his executives, George Chasin, a personable, friendly man, whose character and appearance totally contradicted the conventional image of the hard-bitten, cigar-smoking agent.

For some time Chasin had had a room opposite Roy Myers, a Hayward official who had personal responsibility for Greg's career. Frequently, when Greg visited Myers, Chasin would see him come and go and exchange a few pleasantries. When Myers had a stroke, Wasserman thought that Chasin could take his place.

"I understand you know Gregory Peck?" he asked. Chasin said he did. "Well," said Wasserman, "if you do nothing else for the next six months, make yourself Gregory Peck's agent because he's going to be a very, very big, important star. Just devote yourself to that."

The problem Chasin had to face was that every one of the big studios to which Greg was contracted had pre-emptory rights – each one of them could demand at any time that their contract took preference over any of the others.

It was the kind of situation guaranteed to make hard-bitten lawyers throw up their hands in desperation. The solution as Chasin saw it was simply to come clear and admit the problem to all the people concerned.

To each one, George said: "We are just going to stop everything. We are not going to do anything at all. You fellows have to get together among yourselves and figure out the priorities and the order of picture making." Studios in Hollywood were not the easiest people to get to come to any kind of gentlemen's agreement – to coin a phrase – but Chasin had a way of turning sour milk into butter. He saw, too, one distinct advantage in all this confusion. All the studios were now competing with each other for Greg's services and his prices for each picture went up as the demand grew.

David O. Selznick pulled out all the stops to make up for having rejected Greg in his New York screen test. He gave him Alfred Hitchcock as a director and Ingrid Bergman as his co-star. The film itself was to become a classic that cinema enthusiasts include in festivals whenever the opportunity arises. It was called *Spellbound*.

Selznick decided to do the picture after his own sessions on a psychiatrist's couch. He had found himself there after his whirlwind romance with Jennifer Jones and the accompanying break-up of his previous marriage. In the course of the treatment, he read the book *The House of Dr. Edwardes* about a woman psychiatrist who falls in love with her patient. Now Bergman was the doctor and Peck her patient and Ben Hecht was contracted as screenwriter.

The film was a huge success, and Greg, then 28, was himself quite spellbound by Miss Bergman, a year his senior. "I fell a little bit in love with her," he admits.

The relationship with Hitchcock was a little more sticky. Legends about the director were by then beginning to take root and all of them seemed to be true. Early in the shooting Greg went up to the fabled Hitch, and – memories of the Neighborhood Playhouse still fresh in his mind – said: "At that point I'll be thinking . . ."

"My dear boy," replied Hitchcock, making the most of his still slightly Cockney English twang, "I couldn't care less what you're thinking. Just let your face drain of all expression."

Greg couldn't take that notion – mechanical acting was contrary to all his training. Greg had to *know* why his face was drained of all expression and since Hitchcock had no interest in telling him, he made up reasons for himself. Making a face was cheap, he thought. It had to come from within. Anything else was faking.

Yet there never was a cross word between director and male star. Directors can crush their performers with a stare, Hitchcock didn't attempt to do that. But the chemistry was not there.

"I regarded him as the Master," says Greg today. "To my regret, I don't think I was his kind of actor – certainly at that time. I would like to have worked with him ten years later. I'd like to work with him *now* – because I think I could produce any kind of effect he would want."

Even then, he could appreciate why Hitchcock was the Master. He admired his construction of a picture, his careful planning which visualized the final movie in his viewfinder and which was never found to be wrong. Above all, there was Hitch's sense of humour.

He used to say: "Let's have some fun with this murder. Let's look at the dark side of life. Let's look at the violence and the corruption and the greed and rapacity that we know exists on all sides – but let's do it in terms of entertainment and let's have fun."

The director brought in Salvador Dali to design the movie's dream sequence – a collection of beautiful images that just couldn't be made to work on celluloid. In the end, the studio set designers made it all come together – the endlessly long corridors with the closing doors, the cliff-hanging.

There were other problems – and most of them were connected with getting Greg and Ingrid onto skis. Greg had never been on skis in his life, and even Ingrid, who was born in Sweden, hadn't exactly had a pair in her cradle. Alternative ways of filming the stars on skis had to be found.

Doubles were used for the long shots – filmed in winter in the Californian mountains. But most of the ski run was in medium shot or close-up – with no real mountains or real snow to be seen. All the stars were required to do was to push off from the top of a 25-foot-high slope made of gypsum and cornflakes (sprayed white of course) and stay upright all the time the camera focussed on them. They landed in a pile of mattresses.

The public had no idea that the snow came out of a Kellogg's packet. The close-ups were shot in front of a screen on which were projected the real mountain and the real snow. Greg simply had to make the right faces (he had to tell himself what he was supposed to feel) while yelling sufficiently strongly both to scare the pants off the audience and to convince his psychiatrist that he really was sliding down to madness and about to kill her.

The problems with a ski slope hardly compared with those of controlling a fawn in *The Yearling* – a home-spun story about a farmer, his eleven-year-old son (played by Claude Jarman Junior) and the conflict between the love of an animal and the necessities of life. Jane Wyman played Greg's wife.

One scene, involving the boy's pet fawn, was completed only after 72 takes. It was hot under the arc lights and the fawn – no fool, he – refused to tolerate it. Just when the actors had got through almost all their speeches and the very crucial last minute had been reached, they would hear the clump-clump-clump of little hooves running off to cooler climes. It went on for two days – in which time the director, Clarence Brown, listened for the sound of the scampering hooves almost more closely than he watched the action.

Greg got his second Academy Award nomination for *The Yearling* and M.G.M. made another handsome profit. Every couple of years, American T.V. chooses it as part of the grand fare for the holiday season. For his own tastes, despite the Oscar nomination, Peck regards it as too "saccharin". Clarence Brown discovered that Claude Jarman cried well. The tears were constantly streaming down his chin. "Too much," said Greg. "Too much."

Jane Wyman's puckish good humour helped a lot to ease away the tensions and Greg needed it. At home, Greta had given him another son, Stephen. In spite of Greg's pride in his children, he and his wife were drifting further apart, it seemed. Their life-styles were totally different and while Greg was absorbed in not just one film but two being made simultaneously, at home these differences were mounting.

While he was tidying up the last days of shooting *The Yearling*, he was also starting the shooting of his second Selznick picture – nothing George Chasin could do could completely sort out that tangle. It was worth it. In 1946 Peck co-starred with Jennifer Jones, now Mrs. Selznick, in a torrid romance set in Texas – *Duel in the Sun*.

Not only was he working for two different studios but playing two totally different roles – a kind, indulgent father in one, a he-man cowboy in the other. The studios were only a mile apart from each other and as he told me: "I'd go down the street, get out of my Southern cracker overalls and my Southern accent and then put on a cowboy suit and climb into my Texas drawl." This sort of cinematic schizophrenia lasted for several weeks and Greg loved it.

Duel in the Sun was not without its problems. The principal one was a show horse, a magnificent animal that Greg was to ride in the picture. But it was totally unused to the sort of rough terrain found in Arizona – the setting of *Duel in the Sun*.

The men working on the picture could smell trouble. The cowpokes and wranglers who made up a considerable part of the film crew warned that the horse could be a liability. Had anyone shown it a camera car before? Had it ever galloped up and down mountains?

The risk was that the horse would panic. Selznick himself had chosen the stallion because his visual sense told him it would look superb against the orange-red Technicolor sky. Greg still believed that as a horseman he could control the animal as it galloped past boulders through the scrub.

But panic it did. It began frothing and tossing its head from side to side. Directly ahead of them, as Greg rode on, loomed a saguaro

Above left: Greg, the military cadet. He loved that uniform as cadet captain
Above right: With his mother and grandmother – about 1924
Below: At 14 with his father – a treasured moment on vacation

Above: The house that Greg Senior built – and where his son "the fillum star of the same name" was born

Below: Class 5B at La Jolla school. Greg is at the extreme right of the top row

Above left: Stardom on Broadway – thanks to Guthrie McClintic. On stage in
The Morning Star with Gladys Cooper
Above right: The first film – *Days of Glory*
Below left: Greg fell "a little bit in love" with Ingrid Bergman in *Spellbound*
Below right: With the beautiful Dorothy McGuire in *Gentleman's Agreement*

The picture that really launched his movie career – as Father Chisholm in
The Keys of the Kingdom

HANDLEY PHOTO

Above left: With Martha Scott in a La Jolla Players production of Thurber's
The Male Animal
Above right: The Gunfighter with the moustache that caused all the trouble
Below left: As the General in *Twelve o'Clock High*. Dean Jagger is on
the extreme left
Below right: The Great Sinner with Walter Huston and Ava Gardner

Greg off duty in the '40s

Above: On the set of *The Paradine Case* – with Greg (extreme right) made to look distinguished and grey as the British barrister in a murder trial. Also pictured, l to r, Director Alfred Hitchcock, Louis Jourdan, David O. Selznick, Charles Laughton, Charles Coburn. Seated, Joan Tetzell, Ann Todd, Ethel Barrymore
Below: Star-studded cast of *What Price Glory,* a stage production for charity at Grauman's Chinese Theatre, Hollywood, in March 1949. Greg is in the second row from the top next to John Wayne. Among others in the picture: Pat O'Brien, Maureen O'Hara, Ward Bond, and director John Ford (in sunglasses and war veteran's cap, r foreground)

Above left: Peck's boys – the eldest Jonathan on the left, and Steve
Above right: An early picture of Greg and the beautiful Veronique
Below: "Doc" and his two sons – Greg on the right, Donald on the left

cactus. The horse looked as though it were heading smack into the bush, although Greg managed to steer it away. But that was all. From that moment on, the horse was master of its own destiny; and, it seemed, Greg's, too. It galloped as though carrying one of the Four Horsemen of the Apocalypse, see-sawing and pulling as it went with no thought of what was ahead.

Greg, however, knew. He knew a barbed wire fence when he saw one and when the thing loomed ahead, he didn't fancy the consequences of a headlong collision with it. The horse was totally oblivious – all it wanted was to get rid of its passenger and escape.

At 40 miles an hour, the horse charged into the fence – with Greg sailing some 20 feet through the air, as the animal crashed to the ground, tangled in the biting mesh of the barbed wire. Greg landed on the dusty desert soil, apparently shaken, but, amazingly, otherwise unhurt. Nearby, he could see the still thrashing and kicking horse being lacerated by the wire. As hard as it tried to free itself from its bonds, the more mercilessly entangled it grew. The horse was a mass of lacerations.

Greg knew that the only thing to do was to try to keep its head under control. If he managed that, the thrashing might stop. Gently but powerfully, he brought his foot down on the animal's head. The thrashing and the kicking ceased.

Finally, the camera crew caught up with them and freed the horse with their wire cutters and sent for veterinary help. The cuts were sutured but the horse was to be forever scarred. The beautiful animal was not going to be a film star again – nor was it ever going to take part in any more horse shows.

With a film budget that gallops as fast as any horse, there were financial repercussions to this accident as well. If the mount couldn't be used again, neither could one be found that looked remotely like it. Selznick had learnt his lesson and wasn't about to start risking another show horse. All the considerable footage already photographed featuring the original horse, now had to be re-shot.

This time, the company brought in a black and white pinto – a good "cow horse", a breed used to adapting itself to changing situations. It can move, when required, to a right angle. It knows what to do when a steer is roped, the lariat is thrown and the cord around the pommel goes taught. It can dig in its heels and lean against the roped steer.

Occasionally during the filming of *Duel in the Sun*, Selznick himself would appear on set – to see how his wife was making out as much as anything. Occasionally, too, he would make his own little directional contribution – although the director proper, King Vidor, tried to limit these interventions as much as he could.

At first there were no problems, but as the days wore on and David Selznick got more involved, the film became an obsession with him. It was *his* baby; the results his worry. He wouldn't let it alone.

Finally the crisis came – out in the Arizona desert, when Charles Bickford was proposing marriage to Jennifer Jones. It was up to Bickford to convince Jennifer that he was the one whom she should marry, not his undisciplined brother (Peck). She was trying to tell him that she was no good. "You know how people talk about me," she said. "No," he replied, "that's in the past."

They were out there alone – with just a couple of horses, a tree and the hot Western sun for company. The rest of the crew were watching the scene, and, like Vidor, they were enjoying what they saw. "Print it," said Vidor, plainly satisfied with what had been achieved. "Now we'll move in for the close up."

Selznick had other ideas. "No, let's do it over again," he said, and nobody could be sure whether he was being over-protective principally to his wife or his "baby".

All eyes were now on King Vidor, a director of experience and reputation, whose integrity was plainly being compromised. And yet as he sat on his canvas chair next to the camera, he seemed to be taking it very coolly.

Without a preliminary word, he looked at his script, shuffled his papers and reached for the jacket slung carelessly at the back of his seat. Standing up calmly, he looked at Selznick and uttered the immortal words: "David – you can take this picture – and shove it up your ass."

The rest of the company stood and watched – and continued to watch as King Vidor, now seeming to justify his majestic name, took long purposeful strides to the point where, 100 yards away, his limousine waited. He got into the car and ordered his chauffeur to drive away. The actors, the technicians and David Selznick simply stared as the car glided along the dusty road over the prairie and towards Tucson.

There, the director collected his bags from his hotel, ordered his wife to get her things too, and caught the next plane to Los Angeles.

Finally, David Selznick realized what had happened. He called out to the crew: "OK. I guess I must have said something wrong. That'll be all for today. Everybody back to Tucson."

And back at Tucson, Selznick had to decide how to solve his problem. After wrestling with it – and doubtless with Jennifer, who was none too happy about the affair, too – he decided to call off all Arizona shooting and bring everybody back to Los Angeles. Four or five days later, a new director was called in – William Dieterle, a German who was virtually the prototype of the von Stroheim character, complete with monocle and white cotton gloves.

About half the picture – all the interior shots at the Selznick Culver City studios, the barbecue dancing and the final death scene – were his. But the credits remained Vidor's. His contract had insisted on his sole directing credit and now the Director's Guild supported his case. They said he was perfectly justified in walking out.

Some of the other scenes were shot in the San Fernando Valley at a place called Lasky Masa – named after the Hollywood pioneer, Jesse Lasky – a scrub oak paradise that had once echoed to the hoofbeats of the mounts of Tom Mix and Hoot Gibson.

Duel in the Sun was a brave film – and a brazen one. Before long, it would be nicknamed *Lust in the Dust* and most people considered it went as far as the Hollywood puritans in what used to be called the Hays office (it was now the Johnston office), would ever allow. And because breasts were covered and the sex act was only suspected, the suggestiveness of the movie was more effective than many X-rated features today. Even so, Selznick did win a personal battle with the office – he said he had to show Jennifer's wiggling bottom in close up. Eric Johnston, the censor, agreed.

Peck himself describes the picture as more Oriental than Western – "a bizarre picture. I don't think the old West was ever like that." Certainly the women's lib movement of today wouldn't too much like the idea of the leading man crooking his little finger to the sensuous Jennifer Jones – who, at the signal and with fire in her eyes, crawled over to him, only to have Peck kick her in the face just before he disappeared for six months.

And the language: "I'm just trash. Trash. Trash," she spits to the good Joseph Cotten, the brother who deserved better.

Since Greg always liked to think he had "felt" his way into a character, he took as his model in *Duel*, his cousin Warren – one of Myrtle Rannells' sons. Warren was still known to his many female admirers as Stretch. He wasn't exactly a black sheep of the family, but his prowess with the young ladies of La Jolla was well known. Greg says of him now: "He was very handy with the girls. He took great pride in being a small-town Lothario, who went from job to job; was married about four times."

He had never had a serious occupation; he'd been a truck driver, delivered parcels and worked in a curio shop, but the women liked him as much as he liked them.

"I borrowed that small-town arrogance in his way with women," he told me. "He could always kid them, play tricks on them, seduce them and then leave them flat. All with a clear conscience. He was a likeable small-town rogue."

In one scene Greg had to wreck a train – just because it seemed like fun. "I was a very bad boy in that scene," he recalls years later. "I was supposed to blow up the train, watch it from a distance and then ride off singing 'I've been working on the railroad'. It got the biggest laugh in the picture."

There are middle-aged people today who became devoted Peck fans as a result of seeing *Duel in the Sun*. Yet he has always tried to play down the significance of a movie which he regards as a spoof. "I didn't do much acting in it," he said. "I just rode horses, necked with Jennifer and shot poor old Charlie Bickford."

The film was every bit the smash that *Keys of the Kingdom* had been. Once more the giant posters appeared in glorious colour – Jennifer and Gregory embracing with the golden sun in the background. It was a huge success in France, Italy and Spain. "They liked the way I used her and then tossed her away," Peck now chuckles at the thought. "That appealed to the Latin temperament."

Also it is a picture that has quite effortlessly stood the test of time. Selznick imbued it with his own sense of impish devilment and created out of his wife the sex symbol of the age. Greg comments about this: "He took the saint from *The Song of Bernadette* and the noble priest from *The Keys of the Kingdom* and turned us loose in a wild untrammelled sex story – I think he got a kind of perverse kick out of seeing St. Bernadette and Father Chisholm going at each other like that. He was chuckling all the time in the background!"

Greg was now big box office by anyone's definition. But he was still working out his commitments to studio heads as though he were a bit player picking up whatever work he could.

There was still one more picture to do for Casey Robinson. He asked Greg what he fancied doing and the new star suggested a Hemingway story that seemed to him to have most of the ingredients of a happy picture – the title alone promised to guarantee that.

It was *The Short, Happy Life of Francis Macomber*, an African jungle story with plenty of action, magnificent scenic opportunities and as much dignified love-making as an audience could take. By now, Greg was not only in a position to suggest stories but also to pick his directors.

"Who do you want?" Robinson asked and Greg struck out with a suggestion that was not altogether expected. "How about," he suggested, "Zoltan Korda?" Korda, brother of the more famous Alex, had a reputation of dealing with African films in a particularly individualistic way.

By the time the movie was ready to come before the cameras, it had a new title, *The Macomber Affair*, although the search for that name was itself worthy of a screenplay.

It was during rehearsals that the producer, Benedict Bogeaus, a man Greg recalls as "handsome, expensively tailored and always moving in a cloud of cologne", approached Korda with his solution to the problem of finding a name for their picture, one that would be brief enough to fit on to the theater marquees.

"Zolly," he said, bursting into the sound stage. "Zolly, I've found it. Get this – 'Congo'!"

Korda was a man with his own way of expressing his displeasure with ideas that he did not consider worthy of any association with his name. A deathly silence descended on the company, as the director reached into his back pocket, pulled out a switch knife, clicked a button and jabbed the blade against Bogeaus's rib cage. As he began twisting it, he sneared at his producer: "Stupid son of a bitch. You come on my sound stage again and I'll cut out your liver!"

The producer made no other suggestions, although he received a number of them himself. As for the title search, it was the subject of conversations everywhere on the lot, particularly over lunches at the elegant dining room which Bogeaus had provided for the studio elite – his stars, his director and the important visitors who always seemed to be hanging around.

The producer talked on about the title search and the difficulty of getting a buffalo to charge the camera and fall down to order; to say nothing of allowing the cameraman to survive to tell the tale.

Instead of having a real buffalo they made one that ran on tracks. For a mere $30,000, a taxidermist's delight was created out of rubber, hair and a genuine horned buffalo's head.

To please the Johnston office, still the guardian of the cinema-going public's morals, the final moments of the movie had to be changed. For five-sixths of the action, the story and dialogue was pure Hemingway. But the tale of the sexually-frustrated wife (Joan Bennett) who shoots her husband (Robert Preston) and gets clear away with it, had to be altered to make it seem that she got her just desserts.

All that would have been easy enough, if only Hemingway could have been found. The writer, however, was content to make off with the $80,000 he had accepted for his story and let the studio do the worrying.

At his Cuban hideout, he refused to answer the telephone or to reply to telegrams. Finally, the studio produced its own ending – the woman went to jail but the audience just knew that somewhere in a Nairobi white hunter's bar, Greg, would be waiting for her.

The Macomber Affair will not be remembered as a great film, and Greg knew it, but there was now another picture on the horizon that involved a different kind of Gregory Peck; the Peck who had a social conscience.

Five

1947 was a difficult year in Hollywood for people who recognized that there were injustices in this world and that the film industry should be honest enough to come out and say so. Distinct sniffs were being made around the town for people whose favourite colour was suspected to be red. It was, in fact, the colour assigned to anyone who adopted any attitude which could conceivably be regarded as liberal – even when it had no connection with communism. One of the issues was anti-Semitism.

When Laura K. Hobson wrote *Gentleman's Agreement* — a novel about a magazine writer who thought the best possible way to research anti-Semitism was by living as a Jew – the book apparently stood about as much chance of getting filmed as Hitler's *Mein Kampf*.

Darryl Zanuck, however, had his own ideas on the matter. The book dealt with a fascinating subject and it was beautifully written. It had all the hallmarks of being a success in an age when returning servicemen fully believed that the war they had fought was for a noble purpose. The studio asked Greg what he felt about playing the writer. He was enthusiastic and said so.

But from the moment word got out that he was to do the picture, the telephone wires buzzed between Darryl Zanuck's office and all the "Jewish" studios. One studio head followed the other, each of them stressing that they represented the feelings of the industry, for the good of them all. Louis B. Mayer called; the Brothers Warner managed to find excuses to ring; Sam Goldwyn added his ten cents' worth:

"Why do you want to rock the boat? Why bring this up on screen? Just to anatagonize people? Because so many of us are Jews, they'll think it's some kind of self-preserving propaganda."

Zanuck, born in Wahoo, Nebraska, of Swiss parentage, was not Jewish. He also had the rights to the book and they didn't.

"You make your pictures and I'll make mine," he told them.

But Greg himself was not left out of the controversy. The letters and the calls started coming to him, too. "Why do you want to play a Jew on the screen?" they all asked. Some came from Jews who were genuinely puzzled that a man born free of their problems could even consider taking the risk of sharing them (on the assumption that "mud" can be made to stick if it's thrown hard enough). Some letters came from anti-Semites who said they genuinely wanted to protect him from their future tirades. Gregory Peck was too nice a guy, too good-looking for comfort to fit in with the propaganda image of Jew. Yet people would say: "He's very dark, isn't he?"

Greg brushed it all off without any soul-searching and went ahead with the production, keener than ever. He researched his role just as the writer he played had done his. It all seemed not just controversial but, for 1947, brave, daring, pioneering and exciting.

Elia Kazan – of Turkish descent, also not Jewish – was brought in to direct and Dorothy McGuire, as attractive as she was considered WASPish, was signed to play Greg's girlfriend. The writer Greg played was a widower. Dean Stockwell played his young son. The Jewish connection was there, however, via Moss Hart who wrote the screenplay and John Garfield, who was featured as the star's Jewish friend who, newly out of the forces, faces him with the facts of life and tells him from personal experience of the problems of being a Jew.

Roy Myers, who was still Greg's agent at the time the film was first talked about, tried at the last minute to dissuade him from taking the part. "Don't do it," he said. "You've got other commitments to Fox." He admitted that there would be no problems with his salary, simply it was a matter of what was going to happen to the Peck career afterwards.

"Please, Greg," he said. "Think again. People are going to think that you're a Jew."

"Well, that's all right," said Peck. "If they do, they do. If they don't, they don't. It's a good story. I've been given a good character to play and it's a subject on which I'd like to have my say. Maybe we can have some effect on public opinion by bringing anti-Semitism out of the closet. Maybe we'll help to change people's attitudes."

One thing was proved by making the movie: anti-Semitism was not a subject some Americans liked talking about. Certain scenes were filmed in Darien, Connecticut. Greg told a newspaper there about the film's theme and how he hoped that it might have some effect in countering anti-Semitism. On publication, the piece turned out to deal only with real estate.

It is doubtful if attitudes were changed in any mass way – although it's possible that someone sitting in a theater somewhere had second thoughts about a business deal or about excluding some neighbours' children from their kids' birthday parties. And it did bring anti-Semitism out of the closet – the country did start talking about it and other films followed, to deal with the subject, as well as with racism in general. Most notably, there were *Crossfire* and *Pinky*.

John Garfield and Greg struck up an immediate friendship. "Oh," Peck recalls, "he was a sweetheart." He was also a different kind of movie star in the days when Peck, Gable and Gary Cooper were the heroes of the girls in typing pools and riding on suburban buses. He was short, Jewish and from the hothouse of the New York ghetto.

He and Greg toyed with the idea for a time of setting up a repertory theater in Los Angeles which they were going to call The Actors' Company, but it never materialized.

Garfield had a coronary attack playing tennis soon after making *Gentleman's Agreement*. His left arm went numb and there were pains in his chest. He went to hospital for tests where, with a lot of colourful language, he told the doctors what they could do with their EKG. He simply didn't believe that a man of 38 could get a heart attack. "You don't know what you're talking about," he said. With no nurses or doctors around, he gathered up his clothes and walked out of the hospital.

There was no more pain, so he was certain he was all right – and went about his hard-working, hard-playing business. A year later, at the age of 39, he was dead. Just before that, he told Greg: "Dammit, if I'm going to die, I'm going to die with my boots on. I'm not going to be a frigging invalid."

Gentleman's Agreement was a good picture to work on. A bond between the company seemed to link all of them outside the studio as well as inside it. Greg and Dorothy McGuire, peculiarly beautiful in a fragile, vulnerable way, were good friends – each with a genuine respect for the other's ability, since both were trained in the hard school of the live theater. Dorothy remembers Elia Kazan as being the catalyst that made it all work.

Kazan and Peck were, nevertheless, not the ideal combination. The director saw the character of the magazine writer as that of a man who gave vent to his emotions more openly than Greg thought natural. When Peck was supposed to seethe with anger at examples of anti-Semitism, Kazan wanted him to pound the wall in frustration. But that is not the Gregory Peck way. Kazan probably would have been happier with an early Brando–James Dean type of performance. Nevertheless, *Gentleman's Agreement* did win Greg another Oscar nomination – and the film got the Award for the best movie of the year.

The abiding memory Dorothy McGuire has of working with Greg at this time was that the man whom she had heard had no sense of humour was constantly outrageously funny – "without ever trying". They became very close friends and remain so to this day.

If espousing causes like fighting anti-Semitism meant Greg was taking a political stance, then a few black marks were already being chalked up against him. He had long since given up his association with Communists and he himself clearly saw the danger that Russia was presenting to the world at that time, swallowing up Eastern and Central Europe. But there were murmurs about his political views which would be expressed more loudly before long.

Meanwhile, he and Greta were still outwardly living a harmonious marriage but their paths were beginning to diverge like the roads at a freeway junction. Their tastes changed as Greg's financial state improved. He had taken out an endowment policy for his future for the then colossal sum of $150,000.

With that new-found security and with the assured knowledge that the studios were anxious to get Greg to do everything he possibly could for them, it was hard for Greta to understand why he wasn't able to socialize and enjoy the same friends. Greg liked the company of the sort of talented accomplished people with whom he worked. Greta, meanwhile, had developed her own set of friends.

Yet he was working six days a week – with dialogue to learn each night, and on Sundays too. His only night off was on Saturday, which was a good time for dinner parties and for fairly raucous drinking sessions with pals.

In some ways, play-acting in the studio each day was better than what other people might call "real life." It was stimulating and he had the satisfaction of seeing his career advancing all the time. The best producers working for the best studios were sending him scripts every day and he liked a lot of what he read. All he had to do was to continue giving his all. The marriage, however, suffered as his career prospered.

He brought to the studio the concentration and discipline of the military school and of the boat crew. When he had worn the blue uniform or the white singlet he had had to do his best – or face consequences that he did not dare to think about. It was the same with Hollywood.

He had never knowingly quit anything that he had started before and that went for his career as well. "Anyone who's rowed in a four mile race knows what's expected of him. He understands the joy of total team work and rhythm – with everyone giving equally – and then the agony of the last mile or half mile and the knowledge that you can't quit even if you die. That has to have some effect on his character."

For a time he felt exactly the same way about his marriage. He had to see it through – for the sake of the boys if not for himself.

There were, however, things about being a big star that did not jell quite as easily in his mind as the need to rehearse, to be word-perfect with his dialogue and then to give only his very best performance. By 1947, he was the recipient of one of the biggest mail bags in Hollywood. Fans daily wrote to him by the bundle for autographs and pictures. Not one was ever turned away – although he found that task a chore. "I didn't feel like a little tin god because people wrote and asked me for my autograph," he told me. "It was just part of the business." He has never believed that fan mail and talent necessarily have anything to do with each other.

Sometimes the requests were for more than just autographs or stills. There were persistent demands for money from people who believed Gregory Peck was obviously a soft touch. And there were women who asked for more – and were prepared to pay for it. There were always appeals from over-wrought girls who wrote saying: "Please let me spend a night with you. You can do what you will with me. It would make my dreams come true."

His reaction was to tell his secretary: "Tell 'em I'm all booked up."

Six

There was still one nagging thought in Greg's mind: in Hollywood he was now what a later generation would call a superstar, but he still missed the special excitement that came only from playing before a live audience. He was still enmeshed in his Hollywood contracts, like a fly in a silken spider's web. There was plainly no easy way back to Broadway, but he asked himself: "Is Broadway the only stage that counts?"

Then, in 1947, Greg, with other Hollywood stars – including Jack Benny, Rosalind Russell, Mel Ferrer, Dorothy McGuire, Gene Kelly and Joseph Cotten – decided that the answer was "No".

They set themselves up in a group they now call The Actors' Company, pooling the money they earned from a radio version of *The Man Who Came to Dinner*, starring Jack Benny, to open a theater on Wilshire Boulevard in Beverly Hills.

For various reasons, that theater never happened.

The notion of a live theater, though, did take root the following year, and in territory that was once much more familiar to Greg than Hollywood – his birthplace of La Jolla. He, Mel Ferrer and Dorothy McGuire decided that this now select seaside resort might be the ideal center for a summer theater. David O. Selznick agreed and put up the money to launch the venture. The auditorium at La Jolla High School was available, although the seats were anything but comfortable and the sight lines of people in the rear seats were constantly blocked by the ones in front.

However, the La Jolla Playhouse, as they called it – operating during the school's summer vacations – was a start. La Jolla was undoubtedly a good town for a theater. It was convenient for most film actors in between film commitments to get to and from. There was a ready-made, local, culture-hungry audience – to say nothing of star-struck youngsters from all over California – ready to buy all the tickets that they could get hold of.

The La Jolla audience hoped that they would get Gregory Peck, too – especially the ladies of the area. But at the last minute film work prevented his appearing in a planned production of *Rope* and the veteran Dame May Whitty opened instead in *Night Must Fall*.

There was great excitement about the theater's first season. *Time* magazine described it as "America's most exciting star-studded summer theater".

The comment was well-justified. The theater went on to produce plays like *The Glass Menagerie* with Richard Baseheart, Ann Harding and Betsy Blaire; *Serena Blandish* starring Jennifer Jones, Constance Collier and Louis Jourdan; *Summer and Smoke* with Dorothy McGuire; and *The Silver Whistle* with José Ferrer.

Greg himself closed the first season, starring in Patrick Hamilton's *Angel Street*, which was twice filmed under its original title of *Gaslight*.

The following summer Groucho Marx starred in *Time for Elizabeth* by Norman Krasna. Neither star nor author was considered quite right by some of the snobbier residents of La Jolla.

The town had never seen anything like either of them. To the conservative, WASPish residents, these were two exotic birds indeed. The quick-fire wisecracks they spewed out in all directions were not the sort of thing the locals were used to hearing at all.

Groucho and Norman sensed that the townspeople were not exactly overjoyed by their presence and reacted accordingly. Dressed in the most outlandish Bermuda shorts, they trooped down to the beach and stepped over the tanned bodies lying on the sands, flicking cigar ash over the Southern Californian business executives and lawyers and their chic, fashionable families.

The message got across. The act first stunned vacationers and residents caught on and began to enjoy the best vaudeville show La Jolla had ever seen.

Greg's faith in the La Jolla venture was justified. People came to see their movie heroes and for the most part the stars came, too. Some were, however, less enthusiastic than others. Joan Crawford flatly refused to appear.

"You couldn't get me on that stage for a million dollars," she said when asked to star in a play there. "It's one thing to act before a camera, but if I had to get before all those people, I'd be scared stiff."

Greg still nurtured the idea that one day he would go back to Broadway, but his current love affair was with motion pictures and for the present he was not going to forsake that love for an old flame. He had gone back to the Cape Cod summer stock theater for a short run in *The Playboy of the Western World* and that, and La Jolla, were the sum of his stage activities now.

The second summer, Greg played the lead in James Thurber's *The Male Animal* with Martha Scott in 1948. In this he was declared "sensational" by the local critics, who didn't realize they were seeing the real Gregory Peck who still longed to play comedy.

For much of the time Peck acted as producer, ringing, flattering, and cajoling other film personalities to appear, arranging play availabilities, contracts, sets, everything.

For many of the stars, La Jolla presented a challenge and one that they were delighted to see they could meet. Many of them had not had to learn a whole play-load of lines in one go for years, nor had they experienced the terrors of a first-night audience. "We were scared lots of times," even the experienced stage actress Dorothy McGuire remembers. "And then there were the dress rehearsals, which were always before an audience, and that really was a full opening too. You just took it for granted that you damned well got that show on and got it opened."

No-one expected to make money out of La Jolla and they were not disappointed – although costs were usually covered. The company operated on the basis that they would sell two-thirds of the 500 seats at each performance and that a week of them would gross between $5,333 and $9,000. The cost to them of the auditorium was $120 a week – plus the janitor's salary.

Being a producer was a challenge to Peck. And sometimes he was extremely glad that it was the other people who were doing the work before live audiences.

One night, Greg and Robert Ryan became deeply enmeshed in a convivial conversation which neither of them saw any good reason to end. Ryan was the star of the current production *Born Yesterday* and Peck the producer.

They began talking about the play over a glass of Scotch. Before very long, the conversation had switched to a hundred other topics and the Scotch was disappearing as fast as the talk changed direction. A bottle and a half later, to quote Peck, "We had gotten completely pissed" and because they both decided that some fresh air might do them good, they went out swimming in the surf.

It was a senseless diversion and could have been exceedingly dangerous. Two very sozzled men swimming in the fast current at that point – and in the dark – was a sure recipe for a drowning accident. But they were lucky and survived without, at that time, giving the matter much thought. The next night, Ryan gave a performance that didn't betray too much evidence of their spree. "As I sat in the theater," recalls Peck today, "as I watched him, all I could think of was that I was so glad it wasn't me up there."

Ryan, who was constantly being retained to play a reactionary blue-collar worker living on a diet of racial prejudice, had an important characteristic in common with Greg. Both were political liberals. This fact was to cause Greg especial difficulties as the House Un-American Activities Committee got into gear and started turning its attention to Hollywood.

Senator McCarthy had not yet come to the fore, but the shadow of the hearings that were to put a blot on the reputations of so many stars, writers and producers was already beginning to lengthen.

Seven

Greg's social conscience, which first bloomed in his college days, had not faded. Then, as now, he saw no reason why just because he had considerable personal success, he should change his liberal politics.

In 1948, that attitude was enough to make him fair game for red-baiters like Myron C. Fagin, who claimed to have "unmasked Hollywood". In a book called *Treason in Hollywood*, he included Greg in a list that also featured Fredric March, and his wife Florence Eldridge, Eddie Cantor and Edward G. Robinson (who was soon to be demoted by Warner Brothers to "B" pictures because they were worried about the effect of his left-wing politics on the box office).

Fagin alleged that Greg had been "barred from a personal appearance in Dublin because of his red activities". It was not true and a few days after the book was published, Greg said, "There is more than one way to lose your liberty. It can be torn out of your hands by a tyrant – but it can also slip away day by day while you're too busy to notice and too confused or too scared."

It was to prove a prophetic statement. Before long, stars, writers and directors were to be black-listed, some of them not to work again for years because they had belonged to the Communist Party, to organizations said to be red fronts or simply because they wouldn't name the names of other people who had once belonged to them.

Now Greg was being put into an impossible situation. He didn't want to have to justify what he believed were simple democratic principles and statements of the obvious. Yet people were saying ridiculous things about him. The mere fact that he had made *Gentleman's Agreement* was surely proof enough of the way his mind worked, the red-baiters pointed out.

At about the same time, the 1948 report of the Joint Fact-Finding

Committee to the California Legislature recorded his association with six groups they claimed to be Communist front organizations. This was enough for a lady from La Jolla anxious to protect the fabric of her idea of America to write Greg a concerned letter.

Mrs. C. P. Lineweaver, Chairman of the local chapter of an organization calling itself Pro-America, said her members were concerned about the La Jolla Playhouse.

"We have been most happy and enthusiastic about the project," she wrote to Greg, "and are great admirers of your histrionic ability and charm," but, she added, her members were "anxious not to support any person or project through which encouragement and help might be given to radical groups who are seeking to undermine our Government."

Greg replied that her fears were unfounded. The Playhouse had "absolutely no political motive," he said. "As for myself, I am a liberal Democrat or could be so labelled on the basis of my voting record. The domestic policies and the international views of President Roosevelt met, for the most part, with my humble approval. However, I would not hesitate to vote for a Republican candidate for President this year or for any office at any time should that candidate offer the kind of leadership I, as an individual citizen, think is needed."

His letter continued in the form of a challenge: "I hold no brief for Communists or communistic doctrines, but I believe – and will defend – their right to think and act independently within the law. Therefore, I question whether the members of the fact-finding committee are interested in enforcing the laws designed by our finest legal minds to defend our form of constitutional government or whether they are attempting to suppress political opinion at odds with their own. If laws are being violated, let them instigate prosecution. If they disagree with the ideas and principles of certain groups, or feel that violation of law is imminent let them defend their principles on proper grounds, not by labelling people or issues 'Communist'."

He then proceeded to deal with the organizations mentioned: The Actor's Laboratory. His function as "audience sponsor", he said, was to contribute $20. It was an organization which "trains young actors and technicians in their crafts and produces plays on a modest scale. They needed money. I gave a little. All I know is that the

Actor's Laboratory puts on first-rate non-political plays, one of which I happened to see."

The China Conference Arrangements Committee was another organization named. China was a continuing problem in America. The U.S. Government was committed to maintaining General Chiang Kai-Shek in power and would stay supporters of his for another generation, although Mao Tse-tung was about to oust him from the mainland. "But," said Greg, "every good American must oppose the feudal system which still exists in China and at least hope that an extension of democracy in China will help China's 400 million to catch up with the modern world in education, industry and in their living standards".

That was also why he supported the Committee for a Democratic Eastern Policy. "My interest in these two organizations was in issues – one of which was India's independence which can certainly no longer be considered a subversive idea since it is an established fact. If there are Communists among those members of these organizations, I never heard them voice their subversive ideas."

The Committee for the First Amendment was fourth on the California legislature list. It was set up to "combat what we in Hollywood knew as a direct and vicious attack on our civil rights". Its members at one time included names like Humphrey Bogart, Danny Kaye and Fredric March.

"The list of names," he declared, "speaks for itself. What subversive propaganda has been discovered in my pictures or Fredric March's or Myrna Loy's, William Wyler's, Groucho Marx's or Danny Kaye's? We resent, and most of Hollywood resents, the tactics of the Thomas Congressional Committee. They have uncovered no subversive propaganda in pictures; they have succeeded in smearing the picture industry; they have made headlines and blatantly publicized their own members in a manner no Hollywood press agent could stomach. Which pictures have been subversive? Which scenes? Which lines? They have not named them. In the case of John Lawson . . . whose personal reputation has been destroyed, who is now considered unemployable by producers because his reputation has been ruined with the American public, the members of the Thomas Committee admitted that they had not even seen any of his pictures. The ten 'unfriendly witnesses' are now being prosecuted for contempt of Congress, because they refused to answer questions about their political affiliations. Why are they not being prosecuted for treason or for being unregistered agents of a foreign power?"

But after this campaign on the offensive, Greg muted his anger for the last two listed organizations – the Hollywood Independent Citizens' Committee of the Arts, Sciences and Professions, and the Progressive Citizens of America.

Yes, he had belonged to them, but had resigned some time before. "My reason for doing so was that I did feel that the stand these organizations were taking on several issues was too far to the left for my taste," he explained.

Greg was not to be subjected to the haranguing and cross-examination of right-wing senators who were quickly making careers for themselves at the expense of artists who refused to name names. But the Chairman of the Californian State Committee for Un-American Activities did ask him to come to see him.

After about 45 minutes – in which Greg repeated what he had said in the Lineweaver letter – the conversation ended. "I admire you," said State Senator Hugh Burns, "for coming in and stating the truth. I believe you when you say that you were not a Communist and I'm going to report this to my committee."

Others were not so lucky, and Senator McCarthy (aided by the less than courageous moguls, to say nothing of top film names like John Wayne, John Ford, Robert Taylor, Ward Bond and Adolphe Menjou) became the hero of the American newsreels which gleefully pictured him booting out the Reds whom he alleged were Techni-coloring the movie industry.

It was not a happy time for America.

With the lifting of the cloud over his own career, Greg was in a position to think of his next film commitment. As his fans testified, Greg was increasingly seen to represent the virile epitome of American manhood. At 32, he was in great demand in the industry, still young, still with an always well-groomed head of black hair, still, for the man in the street, inhibitingly handsome. When he opened his mouth, he was speaking for America at her best.

But David O. Selznick had a cunning scheme that would change that image, in a film called *The Paradine Case*. He had a part for Greg in which not only would his hair turn grey – very distinguished it would look too – but his nationality would become British.

That presented a challenge. "I shall have to study the accent and spend time with a dialectician," he told Alfred Hitchcock who was once again to be his director – and who once again didn't want him to go too deep below the surface of the character he was playing. "Don't bother," said Hitch.

And so audiences were treated to the spectacle of a bewigged barrister who – for no apparent reason – spoke, apart from a conscious broadening of the "a"s, with an American accent.

He played counsel for a woman (Alida Valli, who played Mrs. Paradine in the script) on trial for her life at the Old Bailey on a charge of murdering her blind husband. His work as defense lawyer turns into an infatuation for his client – until he not only cannot believe her to be guilty, but tries to find ways of incriminating other people, including the dead man's valet (Louis Jourdan, who was making his American debut).

The picture cost $4 million, a vast sum for 1948, and was made with the David Selznick stamp – a determination that nothing was ever going to be allowed to get in the producer's way.

Earlier, Selznick had tried to interest Greta Garbo in the Valli role. When she said no, he was still certain that it was a film that should be made. Selznick chose Hitchcock because the director had a contract for a film for him and had to be given something. Theirs was not a happy relationship.

First, Hitchcock wanted Laurence Olivier to play the barrister. Selznick insisted on Peck – who was big enough box office to take any part and get away with it, and who still had one of his many contracts with the studio.

There were more problems over the script – which Hitchcock had got his wife Alma Reville to write, in tandem with James Bridie. Selznick didn't like their work and notified Hitch that he would be rewriting it himself. This he proceeded to do – a couple of pages at a time, after filming had begun. Neither Hitchcock nor his actors ever knew what they would be saying the following day for the simple reason that it hadn't been written yet.

Selznick, who wasn't worried about having an American barrister, was insistent on the most meticulous detail being observed in the court scenes. He sent artists to see London's Central Criminal Court in session and then rebuilt the Old Bailey's No 1 Court in its entirety in Culver City. The set was so heavy that, once built, it couldn't be moved. So Hitchcock's love of unusual camera angles had to be buried along with the cast he had planned and his original screenplay. Selznick later accused the director of getting his revenge by taking twice as long as he needed to make the picture.

The film flopped, but it wasn't a total disaster – at least as far as Greg was concerned. It introduced him to Charles Laughton with his menacing eyes and sagging jowels, who represented the case for the prosecution in the picture.

Laughton was impressed with Peck's performance. After two days of experiencing his "advocacy", the English-born actor button-holed Greg. "You know, you should be doing Shakespeare," he told him. "You've got the voice. You've got the breath control and you've got the energy." It was a tempting prospect and for days they talked of little else, although it never happened.

Peck regarded him as a "pussy cat – but a dangerous one. He could be a threat. Laughton was the kind of actor who always projected a sense of danger. That's why I say he was a threat. He was a ham – but a great one. I love characters like that. Too bad it's gone out of style in a way."

Eight

Greg's first film of 1949, *Yellow Sky*, was a post-Civil War western that was to turn out more interesting in the making than the script could possibly have indicated. It was intended as a quality western – and looking at it today, it bears out that description.

Peck played the leader of a group of bank robbers – but he was a robber with a heart, especially for Anne Baxter who played the daughter of the house where the robbers hid after the heist. When the gang realize that there is hidden gold in that house, Greg falls for Anne and fights Richard Widmark in his attempt to wrest the loot from the household.

William Wellman directed and brought out every ounce of the talent that his gifted company possessed. But it was a dose of morphine that brought out a different kind of behaviour from Greg.

Peck has always believed in sizing up a part; making sure that no aspect of a film or a role he has to play escapes him. So when it came to working out the western scenes in the picture, it was the most natural thing in the world for him to map out the locations and survey the horses from which he would make his choice of mount. After what happened with the horse in *Duel in the Sun*, he felt he couldn't afford to take chances.

He went to a ranch in the San Fernando Valley to make his choice. He tried three horses and thought it was wise to look over a fourth. This last one seemed fine – with him up in the saddle, it trotted to a gallop beautifully. But as it galloped into a turn, the horse lost its footing and went down. It fell so fast that Greg didn't have a moment in which to pull his left foot from the stirrup. As the horse thudded to the ground, it took Greg with him – crunching his leg on the wrong side as it did so.

Fifteen hundred pounds of horse snapped Peck's left leg like a piece of firewood. He could hear the limb crack. The horse was totally unhurt. Having unceremoniously unloaded itself of its burden, it bounced up, galloping off in the wrong direction.

Meanwhile, Greg was lying sprawled in the dirt. At first he was numb with shock, but as he looked at his twisted ankle, there was no doubt it was completely smashed. He felt the pain at about the same time as the realization. Had the situations been reversed, the horse would have had to be shot.

Some of the film crew who had come out with Greg for the reconnaisance visit had by now rushed to his side. They, too, saw the damage and immediately one of them ran to the ranch house and phoned for an ambulance. It arrived within minutes and, after some careful handling by the ambulancemen, Greg was carried to the hospital in great pain. As he waited for the surgery that would reset the leg, the doctor in charge ordered his nurse to inject morphine.

The effect that the drug had was to give his patient an incredible sense of well-being. Suddenly, the pain and the hard world outside had been transformed. The universe looked good. The middle-aged nurse who had given him the injection looked down at her patient and as she did so, she became the most beautiful woman in the world.

Her figure suddenly took on the dimensions of a Jane Russell in starched white. As he looked, Greg's eyes focused on the nurse's breasts – exquisitely beautiful, they seemed at that moment. And from his prone position on the hospital trolley, Peck stretched out his hands and placed them reverently but firmly over the breasts.

A big smile was on Greg's face. "You have," he said, "the most beautiful breasts in the world. You are a lovely, *lovely* woman."

"Morphine addicts," said the nurse, now quite composed, "say that to all the girls."

"No," he replied, "you are an angel. I love you."

At which point, two burly porters came to take him away and into surgery.

The leg was reset – but not properly. Studio officials had told the surgeons that *Yellow Sky* was an expensive project and Gregory Peck an expensive movie star. Could they please get him back to work soon?

When he finally persuaded the doctors to let him go back to

work – which in turn signalled the start of production – none of them insisted that he needed still more rest. If he didn't get it, the leg could be damaged for life. After four weeks, they gave him a walking cast – with the result that the leg *was* damaged for life.

When today he plays tennis or has to appear to run in a film, he wears a support which immobilizes it – and hopes that heavy-soled rubber shoes give him the movement and flexibility he needs. "When I play tennis I do some fast walking around the tennis courts."

On the whole, despite the injuries, Greg enjoyed *Yellow Sky*. Anne Baxter, never more beautiful, was a delightful companion and his fellow actors, Richard Widmark and James Barton – an old vaude-villian turned legit – shared his own sense of professionalism.

On top of that, the director, William Wellman, figures with Harry King and Raoul Walsh on the list of Peck's favourites. Wellman was one of that rough-hewn band of directors who made the transition from silent movies to sound and never allowed anyone to forget it. He was boss – a sarcastic, profane, leathery-skinned man who gave the impression of being a martinet.

He never spoke when he could shout and never used conventional language when he could swear. His sarcasm was rarely matched by any other man in the movies and as he yelled and barked, there wasn't a man or a woman in his company who could shelter in the comfort of a canvas chair. He kept everyone moving – stars, extras, technicians and secretaries alike. Yet most of them loved him for it.

His work for *Yellow Sky* seemed to show. It was a film that earned respect. A western that became a prestige movie *after* it was shot – which is not always the usual way round.

In July 1949 Greg went home to Greta and the two boys and talked about the month's delay in schedules that the accident had caused the studio. Greg and Greta were trying hard to keep their marriage going and another child was now on the way.

In July 1949 Greta had her third baby, another son. They called him Carey, after Greg's friend, the old-time western star, Harry Carey. Their marriage proceeded much as before and to accommodate their expanding family they moved to a bigger house.

Whenever Greg told himself that his marriage was a mistake, he had to jolt his thoughts into remembering that it had given him three fine sons, none of whom showed any signs of suffering from the strains under which his relationship with Greta was operating.

But it was clear that he and Greta were not meant for each other. They had vastly different interests and it was hard for them to communicate. It wasn't possible for him to come home from the studio and discuss the everyday problems of his work or differences with people with whom he was working. Everything about the couple's relationship spelled that one word: differences.

Greg was now spending half the year at La Jolla with the Players and this was taking more out of his home life. There was rarely time for a holiday and in the year that Carey was born, Greg expanded his stage activities still further. He still had at the back of his mind the hope of going back to Broadway, but there was no more time for that now than there had been in earlier years.

He did, however, find an opportunity to join a company set up by veteran Western director John Ford to give five performances of the World War One classic, *What Price Glory*. Wearing an old-style tin hat, Greg joined a whole cast list of other Hollywood celebrities in the play held at Grauman's Chinese Theater in aid of the Purple Heart Recreation Center for Veterans in the San Fernando Valley. Greg didn't have a star role. Ward Bond and Pat O'Brien had the lead parts. John Wayne also played a supporting role.

The next picture he made was for MGM. He played a Russian novelist who turns compulsive gambler in *The Great Sinner* – an adaptation of Dostoevsky's *The Gambler*. Greg at the time registered a complaint about the change of title. "I thought it was pompous," he said. The film had a marvellously strong cast, Ava Gardner playing opposite Greg for the first time and with those fine veteran performers, Ethel Barrymore, Walter Huston and Melvyn Douglas in important roles.

The film was set in Wiesbaden, Germany, and the cast was supplemented by an assembly of fine actors who had been refugees from Hitler's Germany. The producer was Gottfried Reinhardt, son of Max, who even had his mother playing a cameo role.

Most of all, though, Greg enjoyed working with Walter Huston, a man it was difficult for any professional player like Peck not to admire.

One day, he asked him the secret of being a great actor. It was the sort of question fans ask their heroes all the time, but Greg could ask it with professional concern. "I really like what you do," he said. "I admired *Dodsworth*. It was my favourite picture. Have you any advice for a young fellow that's just getting started?"

"Yes," said Huston. "Give 'em a good show and always travel first class."

Peck chuckled and decided to bear it in mind. "It was good advice. That's one of my favourite one-line summations of what it's all about. Among others is James Cagney's advice to 'plant your feet square on the ground, look 'em in the eye, say what you mean and mean what you say'. Spencer Tracy's was the simplest of all: 'Learn your lines'."

He liked Huston: "So warm. So loveable. So believable. A rich personality."

All that is not to say that Greg didn't have his problems with Huston. It was taken for granted that when the two of them were on camera, they would share the scene, 50–50. There would be a chalk line on the floor, imaginary or not, over which it would be agreed the other would not step. Yet Huston had a habit of upstaging Peck in a way that might have taken violence to stop.

Just as they were going through their dialogue and with the cameras purring, Greg would feel a pressure on his arm and notice that Huston had taken hold of him and was gently but firmly pushing him. "With the result that I'd have the back of my ear to camera. At first I thought it was his enthusiasm. Then I realized what it was, he was hogging the camera."

As Huston did so, there was a twinkle in his eye, as if to say: "What are you going to do about it, young fellow? How are you going to handle this situation?"

The final upstaging, in reality, was done by the cutter – who would decide how much of this he was going to allow. If an actor really was being badly treated, there would be compensation in the close-ups that finally appeared on screen.

Greg was now due to make another film for Twentieth Century Fox. Zanuck – a very insular man in some ways who had few personal friends and who generally didn't like meeting agents – called George Chasin with an idea for Greg's next Fox commitment.

"It's called," he said, "*Twelve O'Clock High*."

Greg read the script and rejected it. It seemed too much like MGM's big flop *Command Decision*, which although it starred Clark Gable and a galaxy of top flight personalities like Van Johnson, Walter Pidgeon, and others, couldn't be translated into good box office.

But Zanuck possessed all the characteristics of the business mogul – including the one that said "Once you have an idea, don't give it up." A year went by. But Zanuck was still determined not to lose this one. Once more, he said to Chasin, "You've got to bring Greg in."

Once more Chasin said, "What about?"

And once more Zanuck repeated, "About *Twelve O'Clock High*. I've got a new approach," he said, "You've got to bring him in." Greg and his agent agreed to talk to Zanuck.

"I've been running *Command Decision* over and over again," said the studio boss once the pleasantries of small talk had been gone through, and Peck and his agent were seated in front of Zanuck's regulation-size desk. "I realize now what went wrong. I've got it. I've got it. The picture was three-quarters over before you lost sight of the fact that these were stars you were looking at, not characters. You were overwhelmed, overpowered by the stars. But it's not going to happen with *Twelve O'Clock High*. I want to make it with unknowns. You'll be the only star and there'll be just one other actor who's known to the public and he's promised to play it without his toupee on – that's Dean Jagger." Greg was persuaded to do the picture.

Twelve O'Clock High came in the midst of a burst of popular enthusiasm for World War Two films. More than four years after the end of that war, audiences had now come to appreciate pictures about it that didn't have to be flag-wavingly patriotic. You could be cynical. You could see that heroes weren't always men who shot down ten Germans or Japanese planes in every fight. Sometimes they had problems.

The film was about those problems – seen from two different directions: popular squadron commander in a U.S. Air Force base in England (Gary Merrill), is relieved when he becomes too tired to carry on. A young, ambitious, serious General (Peck) is deputed to take over from him. He bears all the stamps of a martinet – humourless, pedantic about detail – who puts the guard on a charge for allowing him through without showing a pass. "But you're the General," protests the guard. In the end, the General, too, becomes over-protective of his men and has a nervous breakdown.

It was great stuff – and it remains so today – especially as it is seen through the eyes of Dean Jagger, playing the adjutant who goes back to see the site of his wartime experiences. As he looks at the former airfield with its long, long grass where aircraft once stood on what were virtually manicured lawns, he remembers the scene five years before – when the squadron was planning the first daylight bomber raids on Germany.

The idea for the film, in fact, came about before Greg was brought into it. Zanuck asked veteran film maker Henry King to direct. He had been making pictures since 1916, with classics to his credit like *Stanley and Livingstone, Wilson* and the first *State Fair.*

Two or three other players were in mind for the hard-nosed General and one by one they were rejected. Finally, Zanuck called King and said, "I want you to meet Greg Peck. I believe that Greg would be ideal for this – better than anyone we have negotiated for up till now. I wish you'd see him and talk with him."

By this time, Zanuck himself had talked Greg into it. But there was a remaining probem. "I've never had any real military experience in my life," Greg told the director.

King understood his diffidence and explained ways round the problem. "You'll be so surrounded by military people who'll be giving us advice," he said, "that you'll find yourself thinking like a military man."

Peck shook hands with the silver-haired, wiry director with the crisp Southern voice, and said; "Yes, I'll do it."

He then proceeded to give a demonstration of Gregory Peck toning up for a new role. He studied Generals at close range – asked them the sort of questions that didn't appear to have any bearing at all on the script in front of him, but which would shape the man he was playing. Once more, the experiences of the Neighborhood Playhouse and even of St. John's Military Academy were playing their part in his creation of the character. He had disciplined himself to do his job properly and there was no other way he wanted to play the part.

He insisted on always having a script properly prepared and he did this by bringing in one or two young actors to go through the motions with him – to prepare him for all the cues. It let him feel his way into the role in a manner which the more conventional film rehearsals never could.

"It's a lot more stimulating," says Greg, "than locking myself in my study and pacing back and forth on my own."

But even when starting new films today the main stimulation in creating a role comes from Elsa Schreiber, the Viennese-born lady who has established an international reputation for helping stars dig down into the depths of their roles.

Mrs. Schreiber, who at 18 played Juliet in a Max Reinhardt production of the Shakespeare play, acts as rehearsal director, continually offering advice and insights into a role that even experienced actors like Greg might have missed.

"She is," he says, "a dramatic coach – but a super one. She could have been a great director but there was even less opportunity for women directors in 1949 than there is today."

But in America, not just Greg but Lilli Palmer, Rex Harrison and the late Tyrone Power could testify to her skills. In England, Valerie Hobson and Kay Walsh both came under her watchful eye.

Mrs. Schreiber provided a proper working atmosphere as well as good rehearsing for the finished product. They worked in a fairly small room and in addition to providing a suitable disipline, she also acted as a story analyst with an exciting insight into a script's possibilities – a number of which were carried over to the film itself.

The preparations worked so well that Greg has invariably repeated it for most of his films, and gives great credit to his old friend, Elsa Schreiber, for his success.

Henry King now says, "When you start rehearsing with Greg, he's in the part there and then and stops being himself. He's the hardest worker I've ever seen."

In one scene, Peck the General takes away the stripes of his office clerk sergeant – because he had hitched a lift on a bomber and taken part in the raid. A brave thing to do – but against orders.

Peck bawls the hell out of his underling. There was something about that which looked wrong to King but he couldn't decide what. When the film was shown to Darryl Zanuck, he, too, felt all was not right.

"I'm sending back the rushes you made for you to review," said Zanuck's note to the director. "I wish that you would look at it and see what you think. It seems to me that a boy who was trying to win the war wouldn't deserve the bawling out which the General of the base gave."

Greg was brought in to see the rushes with the director. He looked at his own performance. "My heavens," he said. "That's an awful lot of acting."

King said: "Yes, I think so, too. We'll do it over again."

The scene was shot again – with a totally different feel to it. This time, an audience was left with the understanding that what the General was saying was, "You can't break regulations and disobey orders – but I'm proud of you for doing it."

The picture was a huge success. Not only did people line up for blocks for tickets, but the critics loved what they saw, too.

Greg won the New York Critics' Award, the Paris Film Festival Award for the best foreign actor, and another Oscar nomination. So far the Academy Award itself was still eluding him. But there were compensations. *Life* magazine featured Greg on their cover in his flyer's kit.

"Gregory Peck," said the magazine, "give a forthright performance at the head of a strong cast of male actors (a single woman makes a brief appearance) who recreate all the urgency and the strain of men face-to-face with the grim business of air warfare."

Even more important was the reaction of other people in show business. For most actors, the judgement of their peers is even more vital than that of the paying customers or critics. Greg was particularly cheered when he received letters from people like Fred Zinnemann and William Wyler commending his performance.

He says that he was just playing it the way he saw it had to be played. A martinet having a nervous breakdown had for Gregory Peck to be played by a man who really felt that he *was* a martinet having a nervous breakdown – at least while he was making the film.

From the moment that the critics began saying nice things about it and the box office started pouring out the stream of tickets, the offers came flooding in for more of the same. He was offered military martinets and business martinets, martinets on the sea and martinets on dry land. Once more, Greg dug in his heels. He had no intention of being type-cast.

Yes, he admits, he did know a few martinets among the directors for whom he worked – although he was not consciously modelling his General on any of these. "Some of them are martinets, I think," he says. "It's the only way they can function. I suppose it's tough on their families."

He is able to empathize for, like them, Gregory Peck making a film has never been the Gregory Peck who eases his way enjoying life when there are no film commitments. When he makes a picture, he *becomes* the character he is playing, almost totally oblivious to the real world outside. He scans the newspapers over his morning coffee, but doesn't really know what is going on outside of the film set. He is, he says, "a total fanatic but harmless".

Nine

The Western is a genre often disparaged by the so-called art lovers of the cinema, but every now and then one comes along that has about it the feel of folk history, and is not merely a good yarn.

The Gunfighter – in which Peck played the classic character Jimmy Ringo with a sympathetic intelligence rarely seen in that kind of movie – was one of those. It wasn't an easy role; had he not been careful, Ringo could have developed into just another "bad guy".

Instead, Greg created a man with whom the audience could sympathize – a one-time villain who desperately wanted to go straight, but who wasn't allowed to; every time he entered a town, he'd be challenged to a gunfight by the local bravados and would eventually die at the hands of one.

It was a story with its roots deep in Western folk culture, the tale of an uneducated man, who, Greg says, "had an innate intelligence and who, I think, in other circumstances could have gone on to become a Senator."

The story appealed to him from the moment he was first shown the script. "I remember reading it and feeling certain this was going to work into a fine picture."

It remains today one of the best Westerns ever made.

Right from the time that Darryl Zanuck showed Greg the script, he wanted to make it. But he wanted to be sure that all the other factors in the movie would jell exactly the way that he saw them. Zanuck went off to Europe convinced that Peck would do it well, and leaving all the remaining details to the studio and its Senior President, Spyros Skouras.

Nunnally Johnson had been deputed to produce it. Johnson knew that Greg had a director in mind – Henry King again. The two had got on so well in *Twelve O'Clock High* that there was not another one who could handle him quite so sympathetically. In a way, the parts of the General and the Gunfighter were not unalike: both men had to try to overcome their reputations.

It was Greg who cemented the deal. "Have you read a script called *The Gunfighter?*" he asked. "No," said King, "but I know about it. Nunnally Johnson told me."

"Please read it," said Peck, "because if you do it, I'll make the picture."

King decided he liked it, too, and the film went into production. Once more, star and director sat down and worked out what sort of man Ringo was – how he would feel and how he would dress.

"Greg," said King. "In the days of this man, they put a pot over the head and cut their hair right round it. And every man had to have a moustache or he wasn't a man at all. I think you'd better grow a moustache."

"If you say so," said Greg, and prepared himself to grow a fuzz on his top lip. Two days later, Peck walked into King's Hollywood office with a basin hair cut and a growth of unshaved moustache.

Daily, King surveyed the Peck upper lip like a horticulturist watching the growth of a plant. Finally, he announced, "Enough. Keep it right there. Don't let it grow any more." The make-up men were given their instructions to keep the growth in check, and filming began.

The day after the first rushes were processed and shown, Nunnally Johnson phoned King. "Henry," he said. "Do you like that moustache on Greg?"

King repeated his belief that it was the declaration of Ringo's manhood. Johnson was decidedly unhappy. "I don't think Zanuck's going to like it at all," he declared.

"What are you going to do?" King asked. "Just take him out of uniform and turn him from a general to a gunman? He has to have the right clothes, too."

"I don't like the clothes either," said Johnson.

Indeed the trousers were baggy and the shirt unkempt. The Peck sex symbol had gone through a transformation. It seemed likely to send all his admirers rushing to the nearest Post Office to mail back their fan club membership cards.

That was another thing that worried Johnson. What would it do to the box office? Peck had the largest teenage following in Hollywood. Could they afford to slight this?

The film was allowed to proceed. But the question of the moustache came up again when Spyros Skouras saw the rushes for himself several days later. He saw Peck lumber into the saloon wearing a dusty swallow-tail coat and what had now become known on the Twentieth Century Fox lot as "That Moustache". Skouras positively bounced up in his seat in the plush darkened projection room and screamed. It was as though one of the guns used in the film had been directed at his own brain. He shouted. He ranted. He demanded. "Take off that . . . that . . . "

Two weeks of filming had gone by. With King, Peck went to see the production manager of the film. "How much," they asked, "would it cost to refilm those two weeks?"

They knew the answer would send Skouras into another fit of apoplexy, but neither wanted to change what they thought had been done well. The Wild West characters were America's peasants. They were immigrants or the sons of immigrants from Ireland, Scotland, Scandinavia and Germany, and they wore whatever assortment of clothes they had brought with them on the cattle boats or had "borrowed" from the bodies that were taken into the neighbourhood undertakers' parlours. There were no rules – except the ones laid down by Hollywood over the past fifty years.

The studio man totted up the expense account of the previous fortnight and announced it would cost a frightening $150,000 to reshoot the film that had already run through the cameras and been processed.

"Tell Mr. Skouras that it's going to cost $300,000," suggested Peck. "I can't do that," said the man. "My job depends on my being accurate."

Eventually, the man sent a written memo to Skouras, setting out the $300,000 figure. He didn't have the nerve to tell him so to his face.

Skouras was furious. He repeated his worries over the effects of the moustached Peck on the box office. "This man is a sex symbol," he said again. "Women will hate it! Women won't come to see it." But then he looked at the figures and decided that $300,000 was too much to add to the budget. "We can't do that either," he admitted.

Skouras might have been right. The film barely covered its costs.

Zanuck got back to Hollywood and proclaimed; "I'd give $25,000 of my own money if I could get rid of that moustache."

Twenty years later, Skouras, the Greek immigrant who began life in America as a dishwasher, met Peck and greeted him with; "Oh, that God-damned moustache! It ruined my picture!"

Even if it were no blockbuster, *The Gunfighter* did well enough at the box office. If proof were needed as just how successful it had been, it came in the trade talk and in the offers emanating from the Hollywood studios. The situation that had arisen after *The Keys of the Kingdom* had now happened again – except that instead of seeing Greg in a cassock, the moguls wanted him in cowboy boots and a wide-brimmed hat. Again he didn't want to be typecast just when everything was going so perfectly.

One role did tempt him, though. He was offered a chance to star opposite a young, pristine beauty called Grace Kelly in a picture with an engaging theme song. The principal focus was to be on a duel scene on a deserted Western street. But Greg thought better of it. *High Noon* seemed too much like *The Gunfighter* and he turned it down. "I thought Coop was great in it," he told me with the benefit of some 26 years of film history behind him. "I would have liked to have won that Oscar. It did occur to me that it might have been me up there getting it instead of him. But he was perfect in it. I admired him. It's not that I'm a plaster saint, without envy. I just respect good performances, that's all."

Peck is not afraid to say that turning down *High Noon* was "the greatest mistake I ever made." Although he does add, "Of the two, *High Noon* was by far the greater success, but I'm not so sure today that *The Gunfighter* doesn't wear better. I think in a way it was less compromising. It was pure. *High Noon* was a bit theatricalized. It was, though, a fine picture and there's no sense making any unfavourable comparisons."

Greg certainly has never denied the power of Westerns. Unlike some other "serious" actors, he doesn't despise and dismiss them as the kind of hokum that has brought Hollywood into disrepute. On the contrary, he has always respected the genre as a perfect synthesis of history and folklore combined with a generous amount of entertainment. Making them, however, can be another thing entirely.

"I wouldn't like to play nothing but these inarticulate cowhands and the like," he told me. "I wouldn't like to make a whole career out of that. I like people who know how to express themselves. When you make a Western, you do a lot of waiting around in the Arizona desert, and when you are called on more often than not it's for action with very little dialogue involved. It doesn't tax the intellect."

But in the late 1940s, Gregory Peck became a cowboy – for real. He began leasing grazing land on which he would place his own cattle. It was not only a fascinating business for a man who played cowpunchers on the screen and who had been brought up on the West Coast, but was also considered by his financial advisers to be a good use of tax dollars. The expenses for running the ranches were deductible, as were those for the feed and the land. The animals themselves were not. The land was in Santa Barbara County, in Mercedo County and in Modesto.

There have been few films that Gregory Peck has made simply for the money, but *Only the Valiant*, which was produced immediately after *The Gunfighter*, was one of them. Except that the money went to David O. Selznick and not to Peck.

Selznick was in desperate financial straits and sold the Peck contract to Warner Brothers. Greg got $65,000 for undertaking *Only the Valiant* – while Selznick pocketed no less than $150,000.

It was all the result of an overnight deal – which, in turn, was the effect of Selznick being in debt. It also turned out to be the worst film that Gregory Peck ever made. He didn't even have a new wardrobe for the picture and a bespoke selection of clothes is a fundamental requirement of any star. On this occasion however, he was handed some of Rod Cameron's old Cavalry boots and pants. Everything about it amounted to a quickie – something that Warner Brothers didn't do that well.

The first that Greg knew of it was when he received a call from Selznick's office, telling him to report the next day at Warner Brothers for wardrobe fittings. He hadn't even been sent a script, just an order to report. When he did get a screenplay, he felt worse than ever. In his own words; "I raised holy hell." But it was not enough. The lawyers said he had to go through with it.

Every time he tried to contact Selznick, the producer was conveniently out. Finally he was met by his deputy, Danny O'Shea.

There was a fire raging inside Greg's head. He felt as if smoke must be coming out of his ears. He fumed as he was shown into the office. He didn't even sit down. Before he could say anything, O'Shea got in first.

"Look, Greg," he told him. "He's done it. He needs the money. What are you going to do? He needs the cash. He's been selling quite a few people like you."

Greg knew that Selznick had the right to invoke his contract – and he had no right himself to choose his own subjects. Peck could have tested it in the courts but that wasn't his way. On the other hand, it also meant that he would now have one fewer commitment to worry about. His ambition to be a freelance player was getting closer.

Only the Valiant, in which he appeared opposite Barbara Peyton, was a horse opera with what has rightly been described subsequently as a *Dirty Dozen* theme. Peck played a cavalry officer in the midst of the Indian Wars, in charge of a group of tough misfits employed on escort duty for an Indian Chief. There were gunfights, fist-fights, knife-fights, horses and women, and Greg was not unhappy to get it over with.

Captain Horatio Hornblower was something else again. Once more, he was supposed to be British and once more he wore a uniform – except this time it was that of a naval officer at the time of the Napoleonic Wars.

The Pecks moved to London for the making of the film and lived in a house in Gloucester Square. The English house was staffed by a trio of Irish girls. In an off-guarded moment, Greg confided to a friend: "It's all very fine – except the cooking. But they are such nice rosy girls that I don't have the heart to let them go."

Princess Margaret came to see Greg at work in Elstree Studios and looked at him through fluttering royal eyelashes much as would any other young woman gazing face-to-face at Gregory Peck.

"I think it's wonderful to see such an exceptionally good-looking man who is also such a fine actor," she told executives. "I think he is wonderful."

The filming process proved something of an education for Greg – in more ways than one. Not only was he being educated by the technical adviser in the ways of the Royal Navy at the time of Nelson and Napoleon, but also by director Raoul Walsh – known to many of the people with whom he worked as "Uncle" – in the ways of raucous high living.

Walsh was the actor who played Lincoln's assassin, John Wilkes

Booth, in *Birth of a Nation*. He switched to directing after a jack rabbit had an argument with the windscreen of his car on his way to shooting a film. The windscreen shattered and the glass impaled itself in Walsh's left eye.

From then on, Walsh became one of the characters of Hollywood, directing movies with an eye patch that never prevented him seeing what he needed to see – but which, like Nelson's, he found very useful when there were sights that were better unseen. He was the man whom Errol Flynn used to call his "One-eyed Bandit" and who shielded Flynn from much of the wrath of the Warner Brothers when the Australian-born star's excesses got in the way of the comparatively simple business of film making. (Flynn had earlier been selected to star as Hornblower himself, but was now considered too much the worse for wine, women and drugs.)

Today, Walsh, well into his nineties, lives in the Simi Valley, totally blind but with a memory as crisp as a new dollar bill. In 1951 he knew what made a good roustabout yarn – and the sort of people who could tell it.

Naturally, there had to be a love interest in the film – the English lady to whom Captain Hornblower Peck would tie himself for the duration of the picture. Jack Warner, with Walsh's advice, had chosen Virginia Mayo – then best known as the glamorous female in the Samuel Goldwyn Danny Kaye sagas. Walsh pictured her in the comparatively (for the early '50s) daring, low-cut gowns that would set off Hornblower's uniform, and decided she was right for it.

Peck wasn't so sure. The perfect Lady Barbara, he thought, would be the genteel Margaret Leighton. Who better, he considered, than a woman who looked and sounded like an English aristocrat? The more he pondered, the more he liked the idea. He put it to Walsh as an honest suggestion for the good of the movie.

"OK, kid," said the director, peering at Greg – or so it seemed – through his good eye. "Don't know this broad. She's good, is she?"

Peck hoped he might be getting somewhere. "She's very good, Raoul. I think she's the one we need. I've seen her on the New York stage with Laurence Olivier, and with the Old Vic. She's very good. One of the great actresses of England. This is an English lady. You couldn't wish for anyone better."

Margaret was young and beautiful at the time. Very refined.

"OK.," said Walsh. "I'll tell Jack. See what he says."

A couple of days later, star and director met at the Warner Brothers lot. "How did you make out with Jack Warner over Margaret Leighton?" Greg asked him.

"It's no soap, kid," Walsh said. "It's Virginia Mayo."

"What is the matter with Margaret Leighton?" Greg demanded.

"Simple," Walsh said. "No tits."

The film marked one to the earliest appearances of James Robertson Justice – playing not a well-spoken eccentric but a rough-hewn sailor. Greg enjoyed working with him and with other stalwarts of the British screen like Robert Beatty and the late Stanley Baker.

Once more Greg steeped himself in his part. He read all the Hornblower novels, seeing himself in every one of the situations that C. S. Forrester had created for his character. But it was his education at the hands of Raoul Walsh that will stay with Peck for the rest of his life.

Walsh is one of those earthy characters who are impossible to duplicate. Little habits of his create a mood of kinship with others – like the way he would roll his own cigarettes, holding the paper and a little tobacco pouch in the same hand that he used for the rolling operation.

He was a fastidious dresser in those days – appearing on the set usually in an immaculate pair of riding jodhpurs. One day, early on in the shooting of *Hornblower*, he looked his star up and down and came to a serious conclusion. "Gregory, old boy," he said, in a booming voice that had been known to terrorize leading ladies, "you're a lousy dresser, you know that?"

Gregory, old boy, didn't know that. "I've never thought about it much," he said. "I've always let the studios worry about how I was dressed."

"That's not the idea at all," Walsh announced. "You must come along with me."

Indeed, Greg had always admired Walsh's clothes and was willing to be taken in hand. On the first day away from the shooting schedule, the director took his star to the Savile Row premises of Huntsman & Co. and proceeded to order a wardrobe suitable, or so he considered, to Mr. Gregory Peck's station in life. It plainly made an impression. Greg has been going there ever since.

Part of the shooting was in the South of France. At La Reserve Hotel in Beaulieu, one of the world's finest hotels, the top members of the crew lived the lives of kings.

On a Saturday night, with a day's filming to look forward to the following morning, Walsh conducted his band of followers – Peck and other members of the crew – to the Chateau Madrid high up on the Haute Corniche. Not many other people were around that night – except a little quartet playing a medley of sedate chamber music and the sober hits from shows 20-years-old.

Among those present was an assistant director on the picture, known – because of his former career as an all-American football player – as Racehorse Russ Saunders. As Peck put it; "He was loaded to the gills. But then none of us could feel any pain."

The quiet music was getting to the point where the film makers were wishing that the gut had been put back into the cat. They couldn't stand the calm, unhurried playing of the musicians who seemed on the point of falling asleep.

"Play 'Yes Sir, That's My Baby'," called Saunders. "Do you know that?"

"No, make it 'Home on the Range'," suggested Peck – who now decided it was his bounden duty to explain what he meant. While the quartet manfully tried to follow him, Greg zig-zagged his way to the platform where they were sitting, rendering as he weaved his way towards them, "Home, home on the range . . . where the deer and the antelope play."

The perhaps half-dozen diners who were not in the Hornblower party tried not to notice what was going on.

"We were polluting the atmosphere with our loud talk," Greg recalls. But even that failed to satisfy the roustabouts. Saunders decided to demonstrate American football prowess.

A couple of serviettes were knotted into the shape of an oval football, two teams were chosen from the members of the party and the normally sedate Chateau Madrid center dance floor became a football stadium.

In a corner of the room sat Walsh – who had thought better of joining in the more active part of the sport himself – chuckling quietly and watching the game between sips of Jack Daniels. Eventually he thought it time to sound a warning. He told the "players", "Boys, the cops will be here in a minute. Watch it. The gendarmerie is on the way. You'd better cool it, boys."

At four o'clock the following morning, a woozy party of movie folk crawled out of the Chateau Madrid and made for La Reserve and about two hours of sleep. They had to be back on location at eight.

That day, the sweat poured off the participants in the previous night's football match. Raoul Walsh for his part, was on duty. "If you want to stay up all night, you can!" he declared. "But you'll have to work all day too!"

Had there been a lot to say, they never would have made it, but since the film's characters merely had to pretend to be Dutch sailors in uniform, madly escaping, scampering and hiding behind corners, they managed.

Years later, Greg took Walsh to a session organized by the American Film Institute where students and young film makers could question him on his career. One of the youngsters was amazed to discover that Walsh had ever been on the other side of the camera. "Well, for Christ's sake, sonny," said the then 91-year-old director. "I was John Wilkes Booth, don't you know that?" None of them could believe that the blind pirate with Gregory Peck ever jumped off a balcony on to the stage and, as his ankle snapped, shouted "Sic semper tyrannis!"

Any observer who had strayed onto the set of *Hornblower* wouldn't have found that at all hard to believe. And press acclaim for the film proved that the spice that Walsh was able to add to this dish had had nothing but advantageous effects on the finished product.

Greg could be happy with his part in the film, too. The plaudits of the critics and the ever-mounting black totals in the box office ledgers told him that he was a success. But something new was happening in his life. Well into the new decade and with barely nine years in the motion picture industry behind him, Gregory Peck was having to take a fresh look at the life he had made for himself.

Ten

To a casual visitor, the Pecks' life in the early 1950s was a mixture of professional satisfaction and domestic tranquility.

Newspaper reporters interviewing Greg on a visit to London for the Royal Command Show noticed not merely that the actor "towers over his petite, slim wife" but that the blonde Greta "with an open fresh face" plainly adored her husband. Well, it *was* the thing to say and the traumas of their married life had to be kept out of the papers for both the good of their children and of the box office.

And there was still so much to do. Six months of the year were being devoted to the La Jolla Players. When the productions worked – as they did with plays like *The Hasty Heart*, starring an "outstanding" Richard Baseheart, or *Serena Blandish*, featuring Jennifer Jones – Greg felt as though he himself had been cheered by the delighted audience.

As far as films were concerned, he still had not yet won his own Oscar, but the fan mail he received justified the confidence placed in him by the studios and their bosses. Similarly, the box office takings for his films continued to expand without the assistance of inflation.

And even if he couldn't achieve the coveted prize of the Oscar, other awards did come his way. In January 1951, the *Hollywood Reporter* published an advertisement proclaiming: "Twentieth Century Fox congratulates Gregory Peck – winner of the World Film Favorite Award. This award is based on a world-wide poll of more than 1,000,000 votes gathered from picturegoers of fifty countries by 1,000 roving representatives and 900 newspapers, magazines and radio stations." The poll was conducted under the auspices of the Foreign Press Association, and the Award was known as the Henrietta.

At Reno he won the local Chamber of Commerce's Silver Spurs Award for being the outstanding Western star of 1950.

All these honours were the result of a lot of hard work.

But Greta was not happy about the boys being taken from one place to another and said it was unsettling for them. Greg, on the other hand, thought that as long as they were all together, the change of atmosphere – even sometimes having tutors for the older boys – didn't matter in the least. They tried to keep the children out of the goldfish bowl of snapping cameramen, but they didn't hide them. It was just part of the job to be photographed getting on and off aircraft and it became so usual that the kids took no notice; that, too, was all to the good.

The three boys gave Greg his greatest private joy at this time. He desperately wanted to be a family man, an instinct bred of his strong desire to recoup what he himself had lost as a child.

There were no moments happier than when he and the boys went on beach picnics of the kind he had treasured with his own father. Together, too, they went horseback riding and made trips to the mountains and to Big Bear and Arrowhead Lakes.

Often, Greg's father – their grandfather – would visit them. And Greg took them to visit their other grandparents too – sometimes to San Francisco, sometimes to La Jolla where they would joyously stay at the Beach and Tennis Club, delight in its own private beach, swim in its pool and play on its tennis courts. He took them there when he was running the Playhouse, and sometimes they would rent a beach home for the summer.

But the pressure of work combined with the difficulties of his marriage were finally taking their toll. More than once Greg packed his bags and left home, only to return to make the best of what he told himself had been a "rocky patch".

By October 1950, it had all become too much. When there were no domestic worries, there were the pressures of three films a year, producing plays at La Jolla and sometimes merging the two occupations, producing plays from his dressing room on the set where he was filming 100 miles or more away.

The mountainous work load and the unrest at home did not make for happiness. Finally, while going through the rigours of early costume fittings for his forthcoming role as King David in *David and Bathsheba*, Greg collapsed.

It was early morning – the usual time appointed for stars, known to their public as he-men and the possessors of fine physiques, to subject themselves to the sort of agonizing treatment for which perfumed women at more civilized hours pay good money in the beauty parlour.

But Greg felt something different this time from the normal inconvenience of a long spell in the make-up chair. There was a stiffness about his chest and a numbness in his left arm. The pain was excrutiating. He was convinced that, at 34, he was faced with imminent death.

He felt himself break into a sweat. As he touched his arm, he looked into the face of the make-up man poised above him and said, "I think I'm having a heart attack."

Immediately, the Fox studio doctor was called. "I'm not sure whether you're having a heart attack or not," said the medico, "but I don't think we can afford to take a chance. I think we ought to respect these symptoms and get you into hospital. I don't think you can work today – and maybe not for a while."

Studio executives joined the make-up men and the doctor hovering around Greg, who was now lying on a couch. He didn't feel frightened at that moment, although no-one yet had any idea how serious the attack – or whatever it was – had been.

But he was in a general state of terrific tension. His mind seemed to confirm at that moment what he had been feeling for months – a generalized feeling of doom; that there was no way out. At that time he had begun dosing himself with whisky during the day – totally contrary to his old habit of reserving the hard stuff for Saturday nights. Now he even added a Seconal tablet or two for good measure. This combination seemed to ease the feeling of imminent death and doom which crept over him all too often.

The tensions of his marriage and work had convinced him that without the comfort of some kind of soporific or other, it wouldn't be long before he was carted away. And now it seemed that moment had come. Strangely, he felt quite sanguine about it. He still wasn't afraid; it was almost as though he had prepared himself for the worst and if this was it, he was ready.

But in hospital, an electro-cardiogram revealed that he had not had a heart attack after all – it was merely a spasm.

He went home. But life was no better there now than it had been before the pains went cascading through his system. There was yet another stormy row between him and Greta. This time Greg packed a bag hurriedly, rushed to his car and drove out to a hide-away he had been saving for just such a moment as this. It was in Apple Valley in the Upper Mojave Desert – an isolated spot where the well-heeled had for years been taking advantage of a sparse population and an ideal climate to be able to unwind. In a bungalow there with its wood-burning open fireplace and a Navajo rug spread on the bare floor, Irwin Shaw had written *The Young Lions*. Greta Garbo, to fulfil her dream of being "alone," had taken up residence in another bungalow.

Greg rented a bungalow with its own private patio, a place where he could sunbathe and where he could read the kind of thick books that he had been wanting to get into for years but for which he had never found the time.

The resort was run by a woman who understood the temperaments of writers and artists – and entertained them accordingly. She gave them the opportunity of either eating in the big ranch house or, if they preferred, in the solitude of the patio. Greg chose to eat alone. A car would rush a hot box to his bungalow and there on a table neatly set out for him by the mobile waiter, he would eat and think.

He stayed in the desert for a month, providing for himself what he later decided was self-psychoanalysis, feeding his stomach with the extremely good food served from the hot boxes and his mind with the works of Anthony Trollope and Jane Austen.

When he began to feel a little more relaxed, he rode horseback. It felt better here than on any film set. Now there was the sheer exhiliration of knowing that as he sat in the saddle there were no camera cars trailing the scrub with him and no director watching anxiously to see that he galloped in just the right posture to fit into the frame of film – simultaneously hoping that the mount wouldn't buckle under him.

Sometimes he walked in the desert, feeling the hot sun pounding on his back and allowing his mind to switch and focus on whatever he wanted to think about – anything but his marriage and the studios.

He didn't take a drop of alcohol but when he laid himself down on the comfortable wood-framed bed inside his bungalow, he slept the deep sleep of the drunk – and woke up feeling marvellous.

It was the first time in his life that he had spent so long in total solitude. All the month that he was there, the only people he saw were the waiter who brought his food and the women who came to clean his bungalow. He didn't go into the central house once. He left, feeling as though a sense of stability had returned to his whole being. But it was also the moment he knew for sure that his marriage was not going to last – and conversely the one when he decided that for the sake of the boys, he had to try to patch it up for the time being.

He felt that he could take anything that came to him. He didn't pretend that he could be happily married to Greta – but he felt that he could cope with it.

He coped with his work, too.

Hedda Hopper, one of the *grande dames* of Hollywood gossip, spared Greg some of the sympathy and admiration that almost any other female filmgoer would have been prepared to echo. "At the beginning of his career," she wrote in a nationally-syndicated column, "the young actor is often humble and eager to please. By the time he's famous, temperament has reared its ugly head. But Gregory Peck, who stands top rung in Hollywood, is as humble and co-operative today as he was with his first picture. He has never allowed fame to lessen his natural quality of greatness."

Greg himself put it all down to how lucky he was.

"Acting," he said at the time, "it's the best profession there is. Loving the job, meeting talented people and getting well paid for it. No matter how long I work at it, there'll be things to learn, doors to open, new roads to travel. I'm glad it's a life's work and one that's never finished within a lifetime."

Greg's success was undoubtedly that he tried to keep his problems to himself. When reporters asked him about the secret of being able to stay well-adjusted and successful on the screen at the same time, he would generally reply with a pat on the back for Greta. "I'm lucky," he would tell them. "I've a very tolerant wife." There was no reason why he should allow his personal crises to infect the work of other people and spoil the investments of his backers.

Indeed, producers and directors for the most part felt that Greg was one of the most co-operative actors with whom they could work. That is not necessarily why he succeeded. "I think you can succeed as an absolute son of a bitch and have nothing to do with the publicity people, be indifferent to or intolerant with the crew – just so long as you deliver the goods and the public likes you and the pictures make money."

Peck had doubts about playing King David in *David and Bathsheba*. He certainly didn't want to be type-cast. But perhaps adding a Biblical king to a line that had already included more than a sprinkling of Western heroes, an Air Force General, a British barrister, an American writer and a white hunter may have been taking faith in providence too far.

"Are you sure I'm right for this?" he asked Darryl Zanuck when the idea was first put to him. Zanuck didn't answer straight away, but pulled his chair back slightly, opened the drawer of his desk, and from it he produced a little blue book. It contained, he said, a list of all the Gregory Peck films made for Twentieth Century Fox studios. On one side of a page was an itemized account of what each had cost. On the other, details of the films' profits. All of them were healthily in the black.

"The total profits of these films add up to something like $100 million," Zanuck told him. "Now, I think you *are* right for this picture. But it wouldn't matter what I thought if your pictures didn't come out well at the box office. You shouldn't forget that. We're not sentimental in this business. I'm not giving you good roles because I like you – although I do. The reason is you're box office."

Greg had just been taught a lesson he was not going to forget. What had just been offered to him were the ground rules of his profession. As he says now, "It's lovely to get good notices and to be well thought of by discerning critics. Most pleasing of all is to be well thought of by your fellow actors and directors – that's why the Academy means something to me – but the thing that keeps you going is the one that keeps the old bicycle wheel a-turning – it is that your pictures make money for the studios. It's a business."

David and Bathsheba was good business and good cinema – better than many of the Hollywood people had thought it could be. Greg surprised himself by enjoying it very much. The dialogue by Philip Dunne was much better than the usual phoney adaptations of the King James version to which film audiences had become accustomed. Of course, he was helped by the original King David himself.

The Psalms of David – including the majestic 23rd Psalm – were gifts to any screenplay writer and the colours those words conveyed were, in turn, brought to life by the dialogue.

The relationship between Greg and Susan Hayward was not quite as close as that between David and Bathsheba. Greg says he admired Susan as a professional actress – who gave what she was supposed to give in the love scenes. But although they kissed as enthusiastically as the Johnston Office would allow and convinced the public that they were locked in embraces that were very real, they hardly knew each other. What they did know was how the two lovers were supposed to have felt for each other. Both made love with the same sense of devotion to duty that Greg had himself used to study the behaviour of a General having a nervous breakdown. It was artificial, but it looked right.

Peck was, however, never better than in the scene where David realizes his folly in wooing the wife of one of his soldiers – sending the man to his death in battle so that Bathsheba can become his. The film not only had Biblical splendour but taste – from the way Henry King directed Bathsheba's nude bathing to the prayers of David before the Ark of the Covenant begging forgiveness for his sins.

Directors make a great deal of difference to a performer's work – just as a conductor can change the very sound of a symphony. Certainly, they make all the difference between creating a happy crew and one where all the participants are just anxious to get finished so as to move on to other things.

Henry King is not one of Gregory Peck's favourite directors without cause. Like Raoul Walsh, he is an actor's director – he understands actors because he has been a performer himself. Before he started work on a scene he always planned it out for himself, imagining as he did so that it was he and not his stars who was in front of the camera.

He always started a new scene by pacing up and down on the lot and going through the actions of the various performers. If any seemed to be studying him too closely, he would assuredly tell them, "Don't watch me. Don't see anything I do. I'm trying to design this scene to fit it to the room." Greg, of course, never wanted to be left out of anything that might concern his performance. Once, King caught him watching his movements too intently for comfort.

"Greg, please," the director said in his rich, Southern patrician drawl. "Don't do anything that I do, will you please? I am only doing this to design the scene." Greg responded: "Well, it doesn't look too bad to me."

Raoul Walsh was a different sort of director, one who appeared to operate a lot more casually – until, that is, a performer failed to deliver the goods. For the most part, however, he would limit his instructions to his actors with choice phrases like "Speed it up a little, kid. Keep it moving. Keep the screen alive." It wasn't difficult to know what he meant.

For some actors he reserved a special code. Anthony Quinn was featured in *The World in His Arms* with Greg. To Quinn, Walsh used to say, "Too much garlic, Tony. Do it again."

A Latin like Quinn didn't have any difficulty in responding to such gastronomic direction. He wasn't any less happy to be told, "Do it again, Tony, with a little more garlic."

In *The World in His Arms* both actors were rivals for the affections of Ann Blyth, a countess who got involved in the life of an adventurous seal poacher, played by Greg, who tries to buy Alaska for himself.

Of course, America bought that tract of snow-covered Mother Russia without the help of Gregory Peck or the character he played, but the story was a good enough yarn, aided considerably by the acting of both Peck and Quinn and by the beauty of Miss Blyth. Perhaps because they were so different, Greg and Tony Quinn hit it off splendidly. "Our relationship is friendly," says Greg. "Friendly rivalry – there's always room for two on the screen. He does everything he can think of to attract attention to himself. I don't mind that. He's a good, salty actor, one of the best."

Their friendship was not too obvious in *The World in His Arms*. Most of the time they were looking for ways of breaking bottles and jugs over each other's heads.

The World in His Arms was the first picture involving Greg as a partner of the studio – in this case, Universal. It was an idea that had first been tried out as early as 1927 when Al Jolson made *The Jazz Singer*. At Universal in the late 40s, when James Stewart wanted to make *Winchester 73*, the studio couldn't afford both his salary and the rights to the story. They settled on the idea of paying him a slice of the gross. When it came to *The World in His Arms*, it seemed the most sensible way of drawing up the contract to everyone's mutual benefit.

Universal Pictures gave the film a big build up as the movie that marked their 40th anniversary, but Gregory Peck and Raoul Walsh were both more interested than anything in the fact that it was their second film together. They both were quite clearly more than grateful for the opportunity to work together again.

Every lunchtime Peck and Walsh went off for the obligatory steak – washed down by two big slugs of Jack Daniels bourbon. Their steaks were the biggest that an American restaurant could provide. It was man's food in a man's world.

Back on the set, Walsh once more used his one eye to good effect. Unlike Henry King, he didn't size up every scene. He knew when the action was going right somehow without looking. But he could be guaranteed to spring to life when things got too slow or leaden.

Occasionally the effect of the steaks and bourbons would take their toll during an afternoon's filming. Gregory Peck, always the lively professional, would get just that little bit sleepy. Walsh didn't miss it. "Wake up, Greg," he called. "Wake up. Give it all your energy, kid."

The make-up man on the set always carried a portable ice box well stocked with chamois leathers to wipe away the perspiration. The hot Technicolor lights frequently took the set temperature up to 120 degrees, even when, as in the *The World in His Arms*, the movie was set in Alaska in winter. Peck made good use of the leathers. He had to. Whenever he appeared to flag, Walsh was there to provide encouragement: "Wake up! Keep going! Keeping running till you drop, like a thoroughbred."

For a time it looked as though Peck were consciously dividing his future filming schedules between his two favourite directors, Walsh and Henry King. He was lucky to be able to do so. His next film, *The Snows of Kilimanjaro* gave Peck the opportunity to translate a Hemingway character into the real-life proportions of a screen adventurer.

The picture opens on the slopes of Africa's tallest mountain with Greg lying outside his tent, wondering whether the searing pain coming from a leg wound means the end of his life. He wonders out loud – and then he begins to speculate about his first love (Ava

Gardner) who died in the Spanish Civil War. His wife – Susan Hayward again – is constantly reminded of the earlier woman in his life. "Did I ever tell you about my first love affair?" he asks her, the effects of the whisky he is downing having its effect. When she replies, "No and I don't want to hear about it either," oblivious to this reply, he proceeds to detail his previous life with the intensity of a man not totally responsible for his actions.

While struggling with the agony of a decaying leg, Greg had worried a lot about getting into the right mood. Finally he told King, "If I had a drink, I think I'd feel a lot better."

"You know, there's one thing about that man," the veteran director told me. "I actually believe that he felt that pain in his leg."

Not long afterwards, a pain in his leg was real enough. In the scene which flashed back to the Spanish Civil War and Ava Gardner's death, Peck was driving an ambulance at the front. It was being filmed on the back lot at the Fox studio. Greg was supposed to be pulling the dying Ava out of a shell hole. With her weight in his two arms, he was supposed to climb out of the depression and lift her to the flat ground above. He crouched down and lifted the supposed dead weight in his hands. As he did so, he felt an agonizing pain in his leg, all too clearly reminiscent of the one he experienced when the horse had rolled on his leg not long before. That time, he had broken his leg. Now he had torn a ligament in his knee. For two weeks, Greg wore a plaster cast and the filming had to be done around him without the benefit of any action shots.

Of course, filming in those circumstances somewhat stretched the credibility factor. When Greg appeared to be shooting a wildebeest in the African jungle, he was really standing in the midst of a few potted plants with a back-projection screen to his rear. He had to keep his eye on a tiny light that blinked at just the moment when he was supposed to fire his rifle – for that was when another screen showed a hippo charging towards him. The back-projected film had been shot by a second company.

Between pictures, Greg was still playing the part of the producer at La Jolla. Mel Ferrer and Greg were acting not only as producers but as agents and managers. Greg himself would often go over the heads of the conventional agents, cajoling stars into taking miniscule salaries for leading roles in their plays and, when they arrived at the coast town, treating them as royalty whose every wish had to be regarded as a command.

For himself he was always looking out for new acting challenges. The one he hadn't yet exploited was comedy. George Chasin promised to do what he could.

The notion that Gregory Peck wanted to do comedy struck a chord with Alan Miller, who was soon to become Vice President in charge of new productions at the M.C.A. agency. "There's a script out at Paramount that's on the shelf," he announced. "It might be very good for Peck. The title is *Roman Holiday*."

What Miller proposed, of course, led to one of the most notable movies in Peck's career. He asked Chasin, "Why don't I get a copy of it and sneak it to you? You read it and if you like it, perhaps we can do a deal."

The script was "sneaked" out and taken to Greg on one of his now frequent lonely holidays in the desert. Both Greg and Chasin agreed that they liked the story, but they also agreed that the principal part was that of the leading lady.

"There are two women who can play it," said Chasin. "Elizabeth Taylor and Jean Simmons. If we can get either of them, I'll try to acquire the rights from Paramount and get a deal set up somewhere."

Meanwhile Paramount had learned a certain big star was interested in playing in *Roman Holiday* but they didn't know who. They said, "Since we're not going to sell you the rights, at least tell us who's interested."

Chasin said, "Gregory Peck." "Right," said the Paramount bosses. "If Gregory Peck wants to make it, we'll make it."

A deal was concocted whereby Peck had approval of the choice of leading lady and all the other protection a top movie star has ever needed. He would be billed above the title alone, and no-one else would be referred to as co-star without his permission. Peck never mentioned the matter himself, but Chasin felt he ought to protect his client. As it turned out, neither Elizabeth Taylor nor Jean Simmons was available. William Wyler, however, had been selected as director and he decided he had to go to Europe to scout for a leading lady.

It wasn't long before he sent back a message to Paramount that he believed he had found the girl he was looking for, a Dutch-born, elfin-like creature who had had small parts in English pictures. Her name: Audrey Hepburn.

Wyler wasn't able to direct the test himself. The British cinema union, NATKE was very tough about importing technicians from overseas, so Paul Stein was retained to direct the test while Wyler positioned himself by the camera. The result was exciting. Since Audrey was already a client of M.C.A.'s London office, there was no difficulty in bringing her over to America, personally carrying her own reel of test film.

Greg was one of the first to see it. He decided immediately that both Wyler and M.C.A. were right. Audrey Hepburn did look sensational and she had clearly been wasting her time playing cinema usherettes in British "B" movies.

With all the details finalized, Peck and the *Roman Holiday* unit moved to the Italian capital. Two weeks after the cameras began to roll for the first time, Greg buttonholed George Chasin and asked. "What's my billing?" It was an unusual question from the one star who had the reputation for not bothering about such things.

"Greg, you've got top of the bill as usual. Nobody can be billed above you and nobody can be billed with you."

Greg replied, "You know the real star of this picture is Audrey Hepburn. It would be pretentious of me to take the billing alone. Go to the studio and tell them I want Audrey Hepburn to be billed on the same line."

Frank Freeman, who was in charge of production at Paramount, didn't see it that way at all. "Absolutely not," he said, conscious of the box office as ever. "This is an unknown girl. Our job is to sell Gregory Peck."

"Mr. Freeman," replied Chasin who knew his client well enough, "you're going to have a very unhappy actor."

Finally, Freeman agreed to discuss the subject with his publicity department.

Later that day, Freeman rang to say that the publicity people had decided to go along with the idea of projecting a new star. The next year, Audrey Hepburn won the Academy Award as the best actress of 1953.

Audrey definitely added to the spirit in the company. The story of *Roman Holiday* is of an incognito princess who takes a sleeping pill and is mistaken for a slightly tipsy commoner by the American newspaperman who finds her. It still holds up well whenever it is shown on T.V. Gregory Peck himself experienced the joy of seeing it cheered and applauded at the 1977 American Film Festival at Deauville by young people who weren't even born when it was made.

Audrey has said that her success in it was due in no small part to the way Greg put her at ease before every scene. For himself, he says he only wishes the comedy potential she showed at the time had been exploited in the years since. "She has a delicious sense of humour, always making faces like a clown, yet the producers saw her mostly as a 'classy lady' and seldom gave her zaniness full expression."

Eleven

All the time that the fun-loving reporter in *Roman Holiday* was scraping through one incident after another with Audrey Hepburn, the real Gregory Peck was going through the torment of his broken marriage splitting ever more wide open.

The more fragmented his private life became, the more determinedly and solidly he performed in front of the camera. He may have had the latest upset with Greta ringing in his ears, but on the sound stage he was putting everything at his command into getting the right touch of comedy. This had to look as light as a soufflé or was not worth the effort. The Pecks had taken a delightful villa outside Rome, but Greta did not stay for the whole period of filming. Halfway through, she took off to visit her family in Finland. At times like that, both realized they were happier apart than they were or ever could be together.

She returned just before it was time to wrap up the *Roman Holiday* filming. Greg still had more European-based films to make and they agreed that the sensible thing would be for them to rent a house in Paris.

They settled on a place in a rather dismal village just to the west of the capital called Les Temps La Ville. They had rented it through an agent and in the photographs it all looked fine. But the day they arrived it was grey, dull, and muddy – a French winter at its worst – and the sad-looking surroundings only seemed to echo the state of their relationship together. It took very little time for them both to realize that they weren't going to be able to cope and that it had to come to an end.

In a quiet moment they agreed that it would be best if Greta and the boys returned to California while Greg stayed on in Paris to work. And, yes, it was now only right that she begin divorce proceedings. The struggling was over.

The parting was amicable. Greg drove the family to Le Havre and saw them on to the ship, the *Ile de France*.

Both Greg and Greta had tried to keep the burdens of the broken marriage off the shoulders of the boys. It didn't always work. As in all similar cases, they knew they were not living in a happy household – even if they didn't actually hear their parents quarrelling.

The divorce proceedings, now that they were about to begin, came as a relief to both parents. There was no bitterness on either side, although – as Greg said – "you get divorced because you can no longer stand each other."

It was as he drove away from the quay side that the effects of the wound he had inflicted on himself struck for the first time. He felt, as he slowly put his car into gear that day, that it was the blackest moment of his life. The picture of his tearful sons was vivid in his mind. The look of farewell on Greta's was just as clear. As much as anything, it seemed a moment of intense loneliness – and of failure.

As a child, he had yearned for a stable family life and now the one that he had, he knew had sailed off with the *Ile de France*. He directed the car on the *N*13b road to Paris and all the way along the autoroute he could think only of that wrench and that failure. He had not only failed himself, but had failed his boys, too. Was he now giving his sons the same kind of family background that his parents had given him? They, too, were a couple who had unwillingly faced the same circumstances and reacted with the same fatal decision. The feeling he had that day, he now remembers, was "very Dostoevskian, practically suicidal".

When he stopped the car, it was so that he could go into a cafe and order a double cognac. The first was downed with the memory of the farewell in his thoughts and the feelings of anguish gnawing through his subconscious. As he followed it with another double, the feelings became more muted. By the time he got to his Paris hotel and unlocked the door of his room, he wasn't really aware either of his state of mind or of the reasons for it.

He didn't leave that room for two weeks. A minimum of food was supplied by room service, but mostly he drank. It was a totally unfamiliar, out of character performance by a man who had always been too solid in his devotion to responsibility to risk losing control of his senses.

Certainly, he had always enjoyed his Saturday night drinking, American-style. He and Greta moved in a hard-drinking circle and each Saturday night they had consolidated the habit of gathering at one or other of their friend's houses – sometimes the Pecks' – for dinner, pre-dinner drinks, dinner wine, after-dinner drinks and lots of conversation, story-telling, singing, playing games and more drinks.

Greg didn't consider himself a hard drinker because that would have meant breaching his own code of ethics – which said that you don't let anything interfere with your obligations to the job of work you have in hand. The only exception to his firmly-observed code had been on location shooting when at two or three o'clock on a cold morning, the actors would creep away for a warming nip of cognac between takes.

This particular drinking spree was altogether different. So was his depression. In all the "down" times before in his life, nothing had compared with this.

But at the end of a fortnight, Greg began to come out of his comatose state. Night after night, he spent hours walking the streets of Paris, meandering along the side streets, pausing momentarily to look in the windows of a tiny *boucherie* or to chat to a worker sipping a Pernod at a roadside cafe. Sometimes he would walk over to the Madeleine and on to the Left Bank or even go as far as Montmartre. Occasionally, he would stop for a brandy or a coffee in a bistro.

All the time he thought and worried, torn up over what would happen to the boys. He decided he would go back to California between pictures so that he could be with them.

Paris can be the loneliest city in the world for a man who is conscious of being alone and the ladies on the prowl couldn't offer what Gregory Peck wanted most. He was young and he knew he had a lot going for him. His resilience was going to be a stronger factor than his emotions.

Back at his hotel, he began thinking about the future and the possibilities for companionship. With whom? It would never have been difficult for Peck to find a companion but he didn't want to spend time with film people he knew well or have friends fix a blind date for him.

As he sat in the hotel room thinking, he had the idea of calling an attractive, wide-eyed girl who had interviewed him for *France Soir* six months before. A short while later, a friend had sent Greg a copy of her piece – a light-hearted account of their meeting which, even with his less than perfect command of French, struck him forcibly. Her name was Veronique Passani. The next day he rang the newspaper. They told him she had moved on to *Paris Presse*. He phoned that paper and asked to be put through. His name, he told the inquisitive operator, was Gregory Peck. She didn't appear particularly impressed. The next thing Greg heard was the sound of a loudspeaker system calling the young writer to the phone: "Mademoiselle Passani – c'est Monsieur Gregory Peck qui vous demande au téléphone."

At that point the clacking typewriters in the busy newsroom came to an immediate halt, and 20-year-old Veronique, on the threshold of what seemed a promising career, became the focus of attention. She wasn't at all happy about it. But she took up the phone.

Greg knew what had happened by the strain in Veronique's voice, although he felt he had a great opening patter for her. "Hello, I'm Gregory Peck – do you remember me?"

She replied, less than over-awed, "Yes, of course I remember you – what are you talking about?"

"Well," said Greg, conscious that something had to be done at that stage to ease the tension – even if he had felt like backing down: "I realize that you are in an embarrassing position there, but I'll make it short. Why don't we meet and go to Auteuil, the race track? There's a steeplechase there and we could have a nice afternoon."

There was no response. Greg broke in, "Are you still there?"

"Yes," she said. "I'm still here." But nothing more. No further information. No questions. And still no response to his offer. Greg understood why. The whole newsroom was gathered around Veronique Passani taking a phone call from a Hollywood film star.

"Well," he said. "Last chance. Will you go to the races with me?"

Finally she said "yes" and they made a hurried rendezvous. Veronique tried to get back to her typewriter, looking indifferent to what had just happened. She couldn't, though, keep it entirely to herself.

That afternoon she had an interview arranged with Albert Schweitzer and her news editor had to be told that she would not come straight back to the office after completing it. Meeting Gregory Peck offered possibilities every bit as intriguing as her first appointment – although the benefits to her newspaper were not uppermost in her mind.

Veronique regarded herself as a serious journalist and not just a star-struck fan – although she had seen a number of the Peck films, and thought she liked his work. But she was very professional in her attitude to interviewing and writing and earlier that year had been delighted that Greg had turned out to be such a willing subject, talking freely about his plans for *Roman Holiday* and about working with William Wyler and Audrey Hepburn. But it was just another of the interviews she had been given to do with Hollywood personalities because she spoke better English than most of her colleagues. At the time, however, it certainly hadn't seemed to be any more important than the one she was about to have with Dr. Schweitzer.

She waited with rising impatience for the great man at the flat of Jean Paul Sartre, his cousin; Dr. Schweitzer was staying there. She waited for hours at the apartment for him to arrive, sustained all the time by cups of coffee brought in immaculate china by Sartre's butler.

Finally at three o'clock, she had to make the big decision: give up the interview or forgo the chance of going to the races with Gregory Peck half an hour later. Schweitzer lost; Peck won.

Their first date turned out an idyllic afternoon, driving to Auteuil in Greg's Jaguar. That night they had dinner together and afterwards, he drove her back to the apartment where she lived with her mother and grandfather.

Veronique's mother and father were divorced, although they now lived only about two miles apart. Her mother's father was a powerful burly White Russian who had lost a fortune with the Revolution. He had been a paper manufacturer and all his factories and forests had been confiscated in 1918. The following year he had taken his family to Berlin and then, like so many other White Russians, had settled in Paris.

Every morning M. Passani, Veronique's father, would come to have coffee with his ex-wife and daughter. During the war, Mme. Passani had married an American colonel and a child was born of the marriage, a little boy who didn't speak anything of his father's language. The second marriage had lasted only two years. When it was over, Veronique's father adopted the boy and gave him his name. It was all very French.

Greg's single date with Veronique turned into another and another and . . . they saw such a great deal of each other that before long there was an understanding between them. They were very much in love.

Greg took an apartment of his own in Paris and when he went off shooting on location to make *Night People* in Germany, Veronique flew to West Berlin to join him. It was the beginning of what was quickly developing into a regular pattern.

Greta, meanwhile, said she was looking forward to Greg's finishing his film commitments and to his returning home. "I do my best," she said, "to make our home worth coming back to – warm, friendly and interesting. It was impractical to remain together and have the children travelling all over Europe."

As 1953 progressed, Greta was asked whether divorce was on the cards. "I've taken no steps along those lines," she said.

In December 1953, nine-year-old Jonathan joined Greg at St. Moritz for Christmas. Greg still wasn't a skier but Jonathan was taking lessons on the nursery slopes.

When one newspaperman caught up with Veronique on Greg's arm, his picture was captioned, "Here's the mysterious Veronique Passani, journalist and travelling companion of Gregory Peck."

Veronique's own journalistic training had taught her more than a little about the mind of journalists and she knew that it was best not to try to play cat-and-mouse with them. The less interesting she and Greg made their romance seem, the less they were troubled by newsmen – although in Rome, they suffered the fate of all people in the public eye by being hounded by the paparazzi.

By now Greg and Greta had no thoughts of patching up their broken marriage. As soon as Greg could, he was determined to set in motion the divorce process, although he had to go to America to do that and film commitments in Europe were still taking up all his time.

The first of these was *Night People* made in Cinemascope by Twentieth Century Fox. It was about the Cold War. Once more, Greg appeared in American military uniform – this time a mere lieutenant-colonel working in Intelligence, whose job was to find a young corporal kidnapped by Russians anxious to do a barter deal for two elderly Germans.

He had the good fortune of balancing his role with Broderick

Crawford, who was playing the heavy-handed father of the kidnapped corporal. But if it all looked good from a seat in the theater, that was not altogether the way it was in and around the Berlin location.

As usual, Greg learned the entire script. The picture was to be not just written by his old *Gunfighter* associate Nunnally Johnson, but directed by him too. Early on in the discussions about the film, Johnson had approached Greg and said, "What would you think if I directed it?" Usually, like most writers, Johnson would have been satisfied simply to hear his words coming out of the mouths of the actors the way that he had written them. Now, however, he was getting more ambitious. Darryl Zanuck was not totally opposed to the notion, but it was Greg who had director approval – and he agreed.

Zanuck had taken a number of precautions to protect his interests. He may have had an unknown as director, but as producer he picked a man whom he felt could keep a watchful eye on any excesses Johnson might be tempted to undertake.

He was a German called Otto Lang, who was Zanuck's own ski instructor from Sun Valley. To complete the surveillance, another German, Gerd Oswald, a man renowned for discipline in the Teutonic mould, was appointed as production manager.

Greg met Lang for the first time in London when he went there for his wardrobe fitting. "Everything's all right," said the producer. When Greg put on the Army uniform Lang had chosen for him, the shoulders seemed four-feet across and the jacket came down to what looked like a wasp waist. Peck wasn't impressed. "Otto," he remonstrated, "this is out of date. I look like an usher at Radio City Music Hall."

Otto was prepared to argue. "What do you mean 'out of date'?" he demanded. "A powerful man with big shoulders . . . a tough guy."

"Sure, he's a tough guy," said Greg. "But you don't have to prove it by stuffing his shoulders with cotton. I can't have that."

It is fairly traditional that in matters of this kind, it is the star who has his way. But Lang proceeded to make a big issue out of it. Tempers flared. However, once it became clear that Gregory Peck was determined not to be mistaken for a Radio City usher, it was inevitable that he would win. "I'm going to my own tailor," he said. He walked out and took a taxi to the unchanged splendours of

Huntsman. The uniform was ordered and later shipped to Berlin to await the arrival of the star.

Usually, actors of Peck's stature are met at the airport of a foreign location centre by one of the V.I.P.s in charge of production – the producer or the production manager. This time, neither of the two Germans was in evidence. Instead, a lowly publicity man was waiting on the tarmac at Tempelhof Airport to greet the arrival of the propeller-driven aircraft bringing the star of *Night People*. As soon as Greg checked into his hotel, the phone rang in his suite. It was George Chasin, sounding very agitated.

"Greg," he asked. "What are you doing? There's a terrible editorial on the front page of today's *Hollywood Reporter* about your holding up production and insisting on having your own way. They say you've been pushing the producer around. What's going on?"

"Nothing," said the incredulous Peck. "I'm ready to start. I know the part cold and I haven't even seen Nunnally yet."

"Boy," said Chasin. "You're in trouble." And he proceeded to read him the piece from the *Reporter*. The studio publicity department had put out the story at Lang's insistence. Both he and the editor of the newspaper had decided this was a good opportunity to put temperamental actors in their places.

When Greg heard the piece, he was – in his own words – "madder than a boiled owl". Accordingly, his meeting with Nunnally Johnson was less than cordial.

"What the hell's this about?" he demanded.

"I don't know what it's about, Greg," he said. "But put all the trouble out of your mind. Of course, you don't want a uniform with padded shoulders. It's ridiculous."

The night's rest hadn't cooled Greg's anger one bit. The first scene to be shot involved some ten pages of invective against Broderick Crawford, and everything that Greg felt against his producer and production manager he vented against the actor playing what Peck describes as "the axle-grease tycoon from Akron, Ohio".

The scene was scheduled to take two days. Greg ripped into it from the first moment he stood before the cameras. By 10.30 that morning the ten pages that represented two days' filming were completed – in one take. With interruptions, just over two hours. Since these were the early days of Cinemascope, an unwieldy medium in which it was difficult to feature close-ups, the whole of the scene was filmed virtually in a single master shot – with the camera moving in and out to emphasize certain aspects. It was mostly devoted to Greg's shouting at Crawford across a desk.

"Print," said an ecstatic Johnson, who had just discovered how easy it was to be a director. "What's next?"

The two Germans who had been so eager to bring Greg to heel, stood there slack-jawed, wondering how to cope with a totally unexpected situation. There was no set yet ready for the next scene, so the entire company was sent home until the following morning. Peck left the studio that day beaming.

When all the filming was finally completed, he returned to his rented apartment in Paris and once more spent his spare time with Veronique. For her part, she had by now given up her plans for professional journalism and was regarding herself as unofficially engaged.

Together, they left Paris late in 1954 for London. There, Greg was once more given a chance with the kind of role he enjoyed most – a comedy performance in *The Million Pound Note*.

Because it was a good comedy opportunity, Peck loved making the film, although it didn't exactly set the film world on fire. Nevertheless, no expense was spared on the best and sometimes ornate interior sets and Greg himself says he was given what was probably the most elegant wardrobe he had ever worn in a film.

Greg took a house in Victoria Square, not far from Buckingham Palace because, he said, he liked seeing "open space in front of me". Working with A. E. Matthews was one of the delights which the picture offered Greg personally. Matthews was then about 80-years-old and only a few years earlier had earned the Peck admiration for remembering a whole book of lines in his original stage role in *The Chiltern Hundreds*. For *The Million Pound Note*, he was not quite so well prepared.

He had to be fed his dialogue on the set, a line at a time. But the way he recited those lines, the timing still as perfect as that of an old-time stand-up comic, earned the affection of the people working with him.

Matthews needed a turn-of-the-century riding outfit for the film and the wardrobe department wanted to send him to Monty

Berman's costume center to be kitted out. "Never mind that," he replied. "Don't need 'em. Got me own – at home." And he came into the studio next day with a perfect pair of riding breeches, the right tweed jacket and the exact bowler the script called for. Haven't changed my weight or size in 60 years," he said proudly patting his jacket on the back. "Great bore, fittings, terrible bore."

For Gregory Peck, the chance to work with A. E. Matthews was filed under the same heading as sharing scenes with Lionel Barrymore and his sister Ethel, and with Walter Huston and Charles Laughton.

The picture was known in America as *Man with a Million* and deserved to be remembered as a better box office success than it, in fact, was.

There wasn't much humour about his next picture, *The Purple Plain*. This was set in Burma with Greg playing in Air Force uniform yet again – although this time the uniform was Royal Canadian Air Force tropical khaki.

The Canadian character is shot down in the Burmese jungle, and, heedless of all the warnings of the training manuals, leaves his aircraft to go in search of help. He is clearly disturbed – the reason is later established as the death of his wife in a London bombing raid – yet he manages not only to crawl to safety, but to rescue one of his crew members too.

Location shooting was done in Ceylon. Anyone involved in the actual making of the movie could see that it was all a lot funnier on the set than the script suggested. Certainly, the off-screen story today sounds rather more exciting than any synopsis of the actual picture could possibly be.

It was the presence of Win Min Than, a Eurasian girl, part German, part Burmese, playing the inevitable love interest, that gave *The Purple Plain* story a different perspective.

The beautiful Win Min Than had been educated by nuns in a convent in Darjeeling and had lived in both Germany and London where she studied ballet. The minute the company landed in Ceylon, she became completely Burmese in manner and bearing, which looked great on film but brought a few unforeseen difficulties off-camera. These were largely heightened by the continuing presence on the set of her fiance, a big businessman who was immediately tagged the Tycoon from Rangoon.

He was not a totally likeable character. Legend had it that he had been educated at Oxford. He was very anti-Western and was rumoured to have been a Japanese collaborator during the war. Now he was dealing in motor vehicles. He was also insanely jealous about his curvacious young lady.

He studied her every movement on the set and was constantly gesticulating to her when he considered her sari too tight or revealing too much of her breasts or showing curves of her rounded bottom that should have remained hidden. Such behaviour called for stern measures on the part of the production company. It was agreed that they had to be administered by Mr. Peck.

The young lady and Greg were called together by Bob Parrish, the director who told them that he had decided that the picture needed one additional scene, one that was not in the original script.

In this, the pilot (Peck) would put all his inhibitions aside and make passionate love to this beautiful virginal creature from the Orient. Greg, of course, was in on the whole thing from the beginning, and he helped the director explain in his best gentle manner why it was necessary for them to go at each other with such passion. "Every consideration will be paid to you, of course," they both insisted, knowing the young lady would report it to her fiance immediately.

The next day Win Min Than turned up on the set with a distinct odour of garlic emanating from her person. It was there the following day too and the next – and the next. She was also actually seen to be eating a mixture of cloves and garlic, followed by beetle nuts which made her teeth and gums blood red.

When there was no real evidence that this was having any effect on either Mr. Peck or any other member of the crew – who had all been apprised of the game afoot – she began to douse her hair in coconut oil, which is guaranteed to turn rancid after an hour or so beneath the harsh tropical sun. From most camera angles she still looked pristine and beautiful. Within twenty feet, she smelled according to Greg, "like a badger".

Peck and Parrish found it very difficult not to crack up completely at this exhibition of defiance, Burmese-style. But they knew that the Tycoon from Rangoon was never far from sight – and in this instance they had seen him standing in the bushes, just out of camera range, wearing a black homburg hat, an English-cut jacket and a Burmese skirt over black shoes. He peered through thick pebble glasses at the scene being acted in front of him. He was in a nervous sweat as he wondered what the barbarians might do to his treasure.

By now the smell was quite overpowering but giving in to Miss Than would have meant admitting defeat. Finally, the moment came for the big love scene, after the young lady had indicated that she hoped it would never be exhibited in Burma. If it were, she and her fiance would both be socially ostracized.

The tycoon had positioned himself behind a palm tree and was dashing in and out of sight like a man possessed. Meanwhile, Win Min Than was trembling and shaking, all the time making funny little noises bred from her anxiety.

Finally, came the big moment, when Greg did what he and Parrish had planned all along. He put her head on his shoulder very gently and placed an arm very firmly around her waist. In that moment of peace and tranquillity, the scene gradually faded.

When the director called "Cut," she practically fainted from the utter relief and joy of it all. When he said: "Print – that's all. Next scene," the tycoon could be seen dancing with frantic joy behind the palms. No one enjoyed it more than Messrs. Peck and Parrish.

Greg's next picture was to be his last for the time being in Europe, *Moby Dick*. Making it was a different story altogether from his previous picture.

Playing Ahab (with his real leg strapped behind him to make way for the wooden hulk that was meant to look like a whalebone), provided another example of the Peck policy of diversifying as much as possible. When he accepted John Huston's offer of the role, his theatrical background was showing itself again, in the idea that the consummate actor had to be able to put his hand and his mind to everything.

The *Moby Dick* project was fraught with problems from the time that John Huston finally convinced Warner Brothers – it is said against their better judgement – to remake the Melville classic for a third time.

First, Huston thought the part of Ahab would make a marvellous swansong to the movies for his father, Walter. That was not to be because Walter died before the film could get anywhere near the production stage. Then he wanted Orson Welles – but it appeared that nobody would put up any cash for a Welles picture.

When he accepted that Peck was the only "bankable" name that would allow the film to get started, there was confusion between Huston and his star as to which role he was expected to play. Greg was at first enthusiastic because he thought he was going to play Starbuck – the part he had already played in college and one which he felt was part of his own fabric. When Huston told Greg that he wanted him to play Ahab, the actor accepted the part as a challenge but with some misgiving about Huston's casting talents.

Looking back now on the part in the film that anticipated *Jaws* by almost a quarter of a century, he says: "I don't regret it. It's been a career of ups and downs . . . peaks and valleys. I don't think you can stay around for over 30 years in pictures without having regrettable episodes."

The early part of the picture was filmed at Youghal, on the Irish Channel coast north of Cork, which was thought to bear the strongest resemblance to the New Bedford setting of the original Melville novel. The team then moved across the Irish sea to Wales. The action seascape shots were all filmed off the Welsh coast, on an inhospitable stretch of water where nasty grey squalls can come up out of nowhere and which was unlike anything that could be captured in a studio water tank.

Unfortunately, one of these precarious nautical disturbances occurred when Greg was astride his white whale, harpoon in hand. He was clinging to the 85 foot whale, made largely of solid white rubber, attached by a towrope to the launch in front.

Unexpectedly, the heavens, cursed so colourfully by Ahab, apparently attempted to revenge themselves on the mere mortal film-makers who were trying to imitate nature. The whole area was blanketed by fog. But Gregory Peck was meanwhile still painfully stabbing the rubber whale with a prop harpoon, and being tossed about by waves that sometimes reached twelve feet high – while no one, let alone a camera, could see him doing it.

However, Greg couldn't be sure about that. But at the moment when the harpoon was striking home, he felt himself beginning to drift. The towrope looked incredibly slack – as well it might have done; it had snapped in the squall and the wind had by now turned to near gale force. Greg was totally alone with his rubber companion, which didn't offer too much in the way of comfort.

That was the moment Greg said to himself, "Good God, I'm going to die. And in this ridiculous way. This is no way to go." He kept seeing in his mind's eye the headline: "Movie Actor Lost on Rubber Whale".

He may have been frightened when he thought he was having a heart attack, but now he was scared rigid. The sea was rough and the wind was blowing at 60 miles an hour. When the rope snapped, he was, within seconds, totally out of sight of all other human life.

The rubber whale was heaving and rolling and it seemed it would be only minutes before the whole thing turned over in a violent somersault.

As the waves lapped the sides of the brute and the wind howled, not even a bo'suns cry of "Land ho!" could have been heard – let alone the stage-school trained voice of the lonely actor.

He didn't even know in which direction lay the nearest expanse of dry land – the Welsh coast eight miles away. Had he jumped off and tried swimming against all the elements, he wouldn't have been able to tell whether he was making for Wales or Ireland. And while there may have been an even chance of making Wales, there wasn't any hope that he could aim for Ireland and survive.

"I think that for the first time in my life I experienced real physical fear," he told me. It had a curious affect of hitting him in the stomach, an unusual strain of nausea coupled with a very strange lassitude. He was weak in the arms and legs and as this reluctance to help himself (borne from a certainty that there was nothing to be done to achieve it) increased, so he felt himself get smaller and the sea and even the whale grow larger.

It seemed to go on like that for an eternity. And then, quite suddenly and by that time unexpectedly, the launch broke through the fog and bumped its way by the side of the mad, white rubber creature.

It wasn't even funny for the crew of the launch. The whale had been built on the hull of an ancient derelict Irish potato schooner – with an engine inside to enable it to spout water not too convincingly and for its tail to wag – and was heavy enough to have sliced its way through another boat without anyone being the wiser.

It was easy enough for Greg to slide down the monster and jump into the launch. As he did it, so the whale sailed away into the fog, doubtless consigned to the big props room in the sky. It was never seen again. A warning was that night issued for shipping to be on the lookout for "a white rubber whale". It could still be floating today, a sea phantom, somewhere in the Atlantic!

Compared with all that, the matter of getting used to a whalebone leg made of wood was child's play. The leg was dispatched by special messenger several weeks before filming began. Every day at the Victoria Square house that Greg took again, he would practice thumping up and down the ornate staircase with his own leg strapped uncomfortably behind him. It was not enough for him to be merely *word*-perfect in the role of Ahab.

After a couple of days, he wore it around the house constantly – pretending that his real leg wasn't there; Ahab would be seen wearing it in all sorts of shots – up and down stairs as he was learning to promenade, and across decks. As far as the cinema public was concerned, they could only imagine what Peck had done with his real leg. It was fortunate that the seafaring costumes of Ahab's time meant that he would be wearing a long frock coat.

The reviews for *Moby Dick* stung – they were the first really bad ones he had had in his career and after receiving four Academy Award nominations in his first five years, he had come to accept that the critics liked what he did. Now, however, he is philosophical about it. "I'm not sure," he told me, "it can be done at all. I saw both previous versions with John Barrymore, and they were perfectly awful, too."

Greg was still keeping his relationship with Veronique a very private affair. When a newspaper discovered that the two were both in Madrid together, Greg would say no more from his sumptuous suite at the Phoenix Hotel than, "It happens that the young lady is in this city and that is all I'm going to say."

After each film they either took short vacations together or he would go back to his apartment in Paris between film engagements. He had not been to America for two and a half years.

But at the end of 1954, Greta finally initiated divorce proceedings against her husband. California law stipulated that a year was needed before a divorce could be finalized. Greta was charging, said her lawyers, that "Gregory Peck has pursued a course of conduct towards his wife of such character as to constitute in law extreme cruelty." And she added herself: "He is cruel because he stayed away from home nights."

In December 1955, the divorce became final. On New Year's Eve, not much more than 24 hours after the decree was made final, Greg and Veronique were married.

When asked today what might have happened if she had not broken that appointment with Dr. Schweitzer, Veronique laughs and says, "I might be a widow in the Congo!"

Gregory Peck, movie star. An early publicity portrait

Above left: In *Moby Dick.* It was while making this film that Greg feared he was going
to end his days tied to a mammoth rubber whale lost in a storm at sea
Above right: In fighting form as *Captain Horatio Hornblower*
Below left: Roman Holiday, the classic film, with Eddie Albert and Audrey Hepburn
Below right: Surrounded by babies and good fortune in *The Million Pound Note*

Above left: A more cheerful moment while making *Pork Chop Hill*. Also in the picture is
TV actor Norman Fell
Above right: With Deborah Kerr in *Beloved Infidel*
Below: Greg particularly enjoyed *Designing Woman* – seen here with co-star Lauren
Bacall – for its comedy opportunities

Above left: The affectionate Atticus Finch – even when the cameras are not rolling.
An off-set moment during the making of *To Kill a Mockingbird* with Mary Badham
Above right: Behold an intense moment in *Behold a Pale Horse*
Below: Royalty on the set of *The Guns of Navarone*. With the cast are ex King Michael of Roumania,
the now Queen Sophia of Spain, Queen Ingrid of Denmark and King Paul and
Queen Frederika of Greece

Above: In style at Royal Ascot – Greg and Veronique with Hjordis and David Niven
during the year they made *The Guns of Navarone*
Below: Sizing up to each other – Greg and Anthony

Veronique, 1967

Above: The sign says it all. Musing in a London mews with Cecilia
Below: With Cecilia, a festive moment on the Universal set of *To Kill A Mockingbird*

At the White House the night Greg received his Medal of Freedom from President Lyndon B. Johnson. Also in the picture with the President are First Lady Ladybird Johnson, the Vice President and Mrs Hubert Humphrey. Behind the President stands Leonard Bernstein

Twelve

Financially, Gregory Peck was almost back where he had been on his arrival in Hollywood. A property settlement had made deep inroads into his economic stability. The Los Angeles judge had awarded Greta more than $100,000 a year as well as $700 a month for their three sons.

To complicate matters, the U.S. Treasury had decided that the time had come to change American tax laws under which, hitherto, there had been advantageous deductions for stars making European films. The law was made retroactive and Greg suddenly found that 80 per cent of his income over the past two and a half years was now to be taxed. He told a reporter at that time; "One day, I was a millionaire. Then the phone rang and I was told the tax law had been changed. I don't think anyone ever said 'goodbye' to $900,000 as suddenly as that before."

There were, of course, essential differences between Greg's position and his situation 12 years earlier. He was then an unknown in Hollywood; now he was being trumpeted by the valuable trade press as one of the industry's three biggest international money spinners.

The civil marriage ceremony was in the guest house Greg often used on the Santa Barbara County ranch of his friends, the Channing Peakes at Lompoc.

Greg's parents were there – Gregory Peck Senior with Harriet, and Bernice with Joseph Maysuch, as well as the Peakes and their other friends Adolph and Helen Pedotti, writer Sy Bartlett and his wife and various locals. After a few days on the ranch, they took off for a brief honeymoon trip, before Greg's next picture, *The Man in the Grey Flannel Suit*.

It was Veronique's first visit to America and her excitement was

Greg's, too; seeing the country through her eyes. With him, she went to Texas, where she was made an honorary citizen of the state, probably the first French girl to be treated in that way.

They saw Chicago, which Veronique described as the most romantic city she had ever seen (quite a compliment from a Parisienne). In New York they covered the length and breadth of Manhattan, from its restaurants, theaters and concerts to the tourists spots like the top of the Empire State Building.

They went to museums and haunted art galleries. They saw the Yankees play baseball. "It's not exaggerating to say that we were wildly happy, as happy as two people have a right to be," says Greg now.

The relationship between Veronique and Greg's three sons was a delicate one. At first, they were painfully shy of this beautiful young Frenchwoman who had entered their lives. Greta had been granted custody of the boys, but Veronique made it clear from the earliest days that rooms would always be kept available for them at their father's house whenever they wanted to come to stay.

She also made up her mind what sort of relationship there would be between them. It would not be one of stepmother, stepchildren. They were simply going to be friends. Veronique told Greg at the beginning that that was the way she wanted it. Today she says; "I can never understand women who complain about their husband's children from a former marriage."

Things were helped rather than hindered by Veronique being so young. Certainly the fact that she had a younger brother who was in their age group only eased the difficult early days of their relationship.

Greg, for his part, made it clear that he wanted his young brother-in-law Cornelius Passani to come to America eventually to study, which he later did, graduating from Harvard University and U.C.L.A. Medical School.

It did all look very good for a happy marriage. There were not even the convential mother-in-law problems. Both of Veronique's parents adored their new son-in-law.

Veronique's father was a French-born architect, every inch the aristocrat, who did everything as though governed by a strict regimen that parcelled out not only his day but the way he lived, like the regular morning coffee visits to his ex-wife.

He always drove an Alfa Romeo car that was kept perfectly in tune. He wore well-tailored sports jackets and black shirts – but never a tie. His hair was always neatly cut and shaved very close to his head. Soon after the wedding, the Pecks invited him to Los Angeles. Greg then took him to Manhattan where the architect was beside himself studying the skyscrapers in minute detail. Together they went to the top of the Empire State Building and then spent a whole day prowling the streets of New York.

Veronique never once doubted the wisdom of giving up what was a highly enviable job as one of the very few successful young women journalists in Paris.

Like most journalists, she had made important contacts. Now many of them were also friends. Very often, French artists whom Veronique had known in Paris would call on the Pecks in Los Angeles. Frequently, Greg would take them to the ranch were he would demonstrate the roping and branding of steers and entertain them to a barbecue lunch with the real cowboys. It was very different from the Beverly Hills Hotel where they stayed on visits for the Academy Awards presentations or to promote new films. It was certainly very different from Paris.

Gerard Philipe, the leading French romantic star of his day, enjoyed it all even more than most. Completely at home in the rustic surroundings, he ate the barbecued steaks, spare ribs, and corn on the cob and drank Californian wine without a murmur.

Greg was able not merely to give a commentary on roping and branding but could demonstrate the work well enough himself.

Before long, his cattle were spread over something like 150 square miles of central California – which is an awfully big area to be able to supervise with any degree of efficiency. His cattle grazed on the land of seven different ranches.

That period of his life was to last 15 years. For many of those years, Greg dreamed of one day having a ranch of his own, treading his own soil, surveying his own acres of fertile grazing land with its air scented by salt wafted in from the nearby Pacific Ocean. But you can't run an operation like that and still be a film star, or follow any other occupation for that matter.

He had to rely on partners, which is rarely a satisfactory arrangement for any businessman. And that, like it or not, was exactly what he had become. He did not like it; a man he had met

143

only once and then briefly, could be responsible for 500 head of his cattle.

Cattle ranching is a full-time job. To be successful in business, the rancher has to be a boss, and a boss who knows everything that is going on, be able to solve problems on the spot and see at the same time that his solutions to those problems are put into action. Greg couldn't do that from afar. There was no way of producing the best herds when you were 6000 miles away on a sound stage wearing Royal Canadian Air Force uniform. The choice had to be between being a rancher and having a film career. On balance, he decided he preferred having a film career.

It was as a film actor that he shared the cover of *Look* magazine with Veronique early in 1956 – it was a demonstration of how well the new Mrs. Peck had taken to her role as a star's wife. "Veronique is very special," he said at the time and most of the people with whom she came into contact seemed to agree.

When Greg went to the Twentieth Century Fox studios to work on *The Man in the Gray Flannel Suit* it was his first American film in nearly three years.

Greg played an ex-Paratrooper captain who is personal assistant to a dynamic tycoon – played by Fredric March. He had to project all the tensions of a man in a Madison Avenue world where he had a continual tussle between ambition and integrity.

When he and Veronique turned up for the British premiere of the picture in May 1956, none of the reporters noticed an important development in the Peck story: Veronique was pregnant. Back in Los Angeles in October, Anthony, their first child, was born. Ecstatically happy, Veronique and Greg said at the time: "This is the greatest thing that could happen to us." Both parents had already decided that the new arrival would not prejudice the good relationship between Greg and his three elder sons, all of whom were pleased to welcome a new brother.

This was the time that Greg was making *Designing Woman*, another comedy spot, the kind which he has always regarded as a great test of any actor's ability.

Greg likes to tell the story of the last conscious moments in the life of the British-born actor, Edmund Gwenn. As he lay on his death bed in the actor's home of rest, a friend asked him gently; "Is it very hard for you Teddy?"

"Not nearly as hard as playing comedy," Gwenn replied.

Designing Woman, co-starring the tempting Lauren Bacall, gave him all the comedic opportunities he wanted – and a reward he never expected.

It happened as a result of a scene where Greg invites his fiancee, Dolores Gray, to lunch to tell her that he has surprised everyone, including himself, by having had a whirlwind romance with the beautiful fashion designer, Lauren Bacall. To complicate matters even more, he has just married her.

He knows she'll be a pal, that she'll understand, that she'll shower him with congratulations and lots of love. She listens patiently, as he had expected, and then empties a plate of ravioli in his lap. "I'll be seeing you," she says as she gets up to leave, while Greg sits with a lapful of ravioli.

Not long after the film was released, George Burns, who is revered in show biz as the comedian's comedian, patted Greg on the back and told him; "That was the funniest 'take 'em' I've ever seen." It was the supreme accolade. Each time Peck and Burns meet, the octogenarian comic reminds him of that moment. "That was worth more than an Oscar," Greg says now. "To be told I could make George Burns laugh!"

When he has surprised people by the breadth of his range, writers always want to know what makes for such versatility. In the 1950s, he told one journalist; "Whatever I've got, *if* I've got it, I'd better be thankful and leave it alone."

In May 1958, 18 months after Anthony's birth, Veronique gave birth to their second child, and after four sons, Greg's first daughter. They called her Cecilia.

It was the beginning of that special relationship that fathers often have with daughters – although for Greg to find himself the father of a girl was to take some getting used to.

Filming in Mexico – which Greg did in his picture, *The Bravados*, took no getting used to at all. It's a country he loves, among people whom he adores, folk who are much more energetic than the legend allows.

The film was shot in Morelia, St. Jose and Guadalajara, place names that have become immortalized in popular songs. Some of the filming was done eight thousand feet high in the mountains of

St. Jose Perua – famous for its beautiful citrus trees, tropical flowers and a spa based on a natural spring which produces an effervescent pink water said to be a powerful aphrodisiac. The film team delighted in watching a succession of aging optimists bathing in the water while their wives rocked themselves on the verandah, patiently tapping their feet.

Once more Greg was working with his favourite director, Henry King. He co-starred with the British actress, Joan Collins, then on the threshold of the career she has carved out for herself as a young beauty. Greg now recalls; "She was a sensational young girl . . . a kind of knockout. I see Joan today and, if anything, she is prettier now than she was then."

Joan played Greg's first love – and the one on whom he falls back after killing three members of the gang who he too late discovers were innocent of the deeds for which he holds them responsible.

Once during the making of the picture, a young inexperienced player went through his lines and then stood back waiting for the satisfied pay-off from the director: "Cut and print." Instead, he heard King demand that he do it again.

"Why?" asked the actor. "I know the scene perfectly."

"Well," agreed the director. "It isn't just knowing your lines. It's believing them when you say them. I don't believe a damned word you said. You were just talking because it was in the script."

Fortunately for Mr. King at that moment in another part of the vast street set, Greg was to be seen just walking up and down the street – nothing else, just walking back and forth.

"What's he doing?" asked the actor, noticing the satisfied, admiring way in which Henry King was watching the Peck walk. "He's preparing himself," said King. "It's the next scene and Greg is preparing himself physically and mentally for it – getting involved in it."

Whatever he did for *The Bravados*, the next Gregory Peck picture needed a great deal more mental preparation. It was more than just a new part. It was entirely different situation. Greg was going to be a producer and in the course of it, get involved in a huge row.

Thirteen

The Big Country was the name of the picture and big it was. Everything about it. Big screen, big budget and big fights. When it was made in 1957, it cost over $4 million and they didn't come much dearer than that in the 1950s. Had it gone out to the movie houses in its original entirety it would have lasted well over four hours. As it was, it ran for 165 minutes and any unsuspecting adventurer into the cutting room would have drowned in discarded film littering the floor.

But none of the finished product – which eventually earned a modicum of profit for United Artists – gives any indication of the problems that were hidden from the movie goer. It was a motion picture success that arose from a series of mistakes; many of them as big as the project and its title.

For Gregory Peck, it began with a cancelled film, continued with a decision to broaden his sphere of activities and become a producer – and ended up with his rowing with his director and threatening a lawsuit. In between, there were sleepless nights, a lot of bad feeling and a decision to walk off a set, never to return.

Greg had originally been going to Spain to make a picture with William Wyler called *Thieves' Market*. The project was dropped when everyone concerned decided the script was not worth the effort.

But with the investment of time that had already gone into the idea of Peck and Wyler working together, both agreed quickly to look for a substitute.

George Chasin was called to Greg's house where the star and the director were anxiously trying to get out of the problems that had beset them. Both had turned down other engagements to make the Spanish picture and it didn't make sense to let everything slide.

"Do you know of any other picture we can do?" Wyler asked the agent who had the great talent of being able to find out news about possible film properties as quickly as a fox could discover a rabbit. "Well," said Chasin, "there is a book treatment I've been sent for Marlon Brando – and I know he hasn't even looked at it."

It turned out that Chasin had been sent a 50-page treatment of a book called *The Big Country*, which had started out as a *Saturday Evening Post* story and now he was suggesting that both Wyler and Greg read it quickly.

"It's a Western", said Chasin. "I know United Artists want to get this tied up very quickly."

"I've made Westerns in six or seven days," said Wyler, only partially joking. He was a product of the old school of film making and had been introduced to the business by his uncle, Carl Laemmle, one of the industry's pioneers.

No one thought *The Big Country* could be completed in that time, but it was generally agreed that it was worth doing anyway.

Ironically, as things turned out, Greg says it was Wyler who had first put the idea of being a producer into his mind. When they were making *Roman Holiday* a chance remark by this old hand at producing had taken root. Wyler had said; "Greg, it's a hell of a thrill to make a movie. We start with just an idea, get it on paper, put it before a camera and then people pay money to look at a blank wall to see what we've put up there."

Somehow Greg thought he wanted to see for himself what he could put on that wall as a result of his own ideas, not those handed to him in a bound volume of typewritten papers. He was to have the star part in the picture, but, in addition, he was also going to be William Wyler's co-producer.

The contracts were drawn up. Greg set about being both producer and star; he helped with the adaptation of the story. Basically it was about two cattle barons at war. One of the men was, on the surface, a highly prosperous rancher. Nevertheless, he ruthlessly denied watering rights to the other, a crusty, homespun individual who had more guts in his little finger than anyone roundabout (including his own son) had in his whole body.

Charles Bickford had been selected for the successful landowner, the one who controlled what everyone in the area knew as the Big Country. Carroll Baker played his daughter who fell for a retired sea captain making a new life for himself out west, Gregory Peck. There was Jean Simmons in the role of the neighbour whom Greg takes instead of his intended bride, and Charlton Heston as Bickford's number-one whipping boy, a resentful, bitter man who wants nothing more than to see Peck out of the way.

All these roles were easily filled.

It was Greg who suggested for the rival landowner the big bulky frame of Burl Ives, a man who had endeared himself to Peck years before as one of the Saturday night drinking crowd.

In those days, Ives was best known as a wandering minstrel. He would travel from town to town, and sometimes from house to house, singing ribald ballads which were almost as old as the hills about which he used to chant in his distinctive velvet voice.

To help preserve those memories, Greg used to record the Burl Ives songs of the mid-40s on a recording machine that produced home-made wax discs at 78 revolutions per minute. Sometimes it seemed that that machine was totally superfluous. Ives arrived one early Saturday evening and, like the Man Who Came to Dinner (whom he so closely resembled in those days) stayed and stayed and stayed.

He came for a Saturday night party and slept most of the following Sunday in time to take part in a slightly less raucous gathering in the evening. Greg had to report at the studio at 7.30 that morning. When he returned home, Ives was still there – curled up on the carpet looking, says Greg now, like a beached whale.

He left on the Tuesday.

Greg's idea was to use Ives for what he was able to do best – show his bulk, and use his at once soothing and menacing voice to demonstrate that there was no man on earth who was going to deny him his rights, even though Bickford was in fine suitings and he himself wore the same check shirt and soiled trousers every day.

To that end, Greg suggested he have an opportunity for what the French theater calls, in a unique phrase, "*le tirade*."

He wanted Ives to have a speech that was not merely spiced by invective, but one which consisted almost entirely of the kind of salty Western abuse that would be recognized as such by any man who genuinely spent his day rustling cattle and breaking in horses.

Ives committed to memory a page of invective in a manner that allowed his full 350 pounds to sit on the audience without their feeling crushed by it. Apart from a couple of cross-shots in which Bickford in evening dress at a big fashionable party at his ranch is seen to be taking this verbal assault on his dignity, the speech was uncut in the finished movie. It won Ives the Oscar for the best supporting performance of the year.

No one set out to win Academy Awards when the picture was first conceived. One of the early understandings between the two producers was that the first aim was to make a popular commercial movie. But the spirit of happy partnership was not to last.

One of the earliest difficulties in the picture was selecting a suitable writer for the screenplay. Jessamyn West, who had written *Friendly Persuasion* was the first to be brought in, and then discarded. The budget for the picture, which started out at $1,100,000, had by this time escalated through this and other causes to $1,250,000.

Leon Uris, who had just written *Exodus*, was invited to produce a more acceptable script, at a fee of $25,000.

Uris actually wrote two different versions of *The Big Country* story. When he was first brought in, he looked at the material then available and declared disdainfully, "This is bullshit. It's all cliche. Totally unplayable."

He was hired because he was known to be a fast writer, very energetic as well as extremely talented, a man who had shown by his previous work that he could come up with the goods. The hiring had also followed an enthusiastic interview in which he was brimful of ideas. But at the first serious story conference, the combination of Uris and William Wyler was like the rubbing of two sticks together. The sparks flew and it was left to Greg to liaise with the writer.

Uris's work, too, was to be largely discarded although parts of it were used. Burl Ives's tirade – on which Greg worked closely with him – was the one section that was not totally abandoned.

But after weeks of talk, script consultation and actual writing and editing, there was still not enough on paper with which to make a picture, certainly not one of the kind they wanted *The Big Country* to be.

Wyler brought in his brother, Robert. It was Greg's job to work with him now, and with another writer called Robert Wilder. Every morning at six o'clock, Greg would be working on Wilder's script, editing, dictating memos to his secretary and consulting with the writer himself. Sixty-five pages of script were produced, all of which

William Wyler pronounced: "Not great writing but shootable." But Robert Wilder was also to be replaced and so was his successor, the author of the original *Saturday Evening Post* story, Donald Hamilton, who had flown over from Sweden to produce the Big Script for *The Big Country*.

Eventually James Webb and Sy Bartlett were retained to try to make a movie. Bartlett was a partner in Greg's own company and much of what eventually went before the cameras was the work of this team.

Probably a million dollars' worth of extraneous film was cut from the final picture seen in the cinemas, an expensive lesson for an aspiring film producer. It was a lesson that should have been learned earlier on in the production schedule – when Greg and Willy Wyler accepted a script that extended to 170 pages. It was plainly too long.

Into that mistake went the bulk of the movie's profits. Each of the two producers had a 25 per cent stake in the profit share-out, but as it turned out there really were no profits at all. All either of them earned was a nominal $50,000 – their fees as producers – which was not a lot in return for what was effectively a year's work. In the end, both of them got caught up not only in their own pride but also in the desire to create the great classic Western for its own sake, a work of art.

The writing was just one of the problems that Greg has since said – although he did not think in such kindly terms at the time – was part of the "blood, sweat and tears" of producing.

The first row between the two producers concerned the order that Greg had put in for 4,000 head of cattle which he had requisitioned at $10 each per day.

It was a lot of money, $40,000 a day, but Peck considered it essential for a scene in which Bickford demonstrated the full extent of that Big Country. In one huge panoramic shot of 180 degrees, the camera would take in the breathtaking beauty of it all and the wealth it represented. Peck, who had had a bit of experience with Western locations in his time, knew that meant showing a lot of cattle. That was why he picked on a number like 4,000.

Wyler, who considered he had a lot more experience in organizing motion picture budgets, thought it was woefully extravagant. He countermanded the order and changed the 4,000 to 400. The day that the camera team turned up to take this all-important scene, Greg was plainly underwhelmed by all that he surveyed. There, sure enough, were the rolling acres of land that would bring conceivable prosperity to people like the Bickford landowner. But somewhere, in the distance, were what appeared to be 400 ants.

Days before, Greg had ordered his 4,000 head from neighbouring ranches from the sort of people whom he knew so well. He had gone through the tortuous process of arranging for them to be brought to the location overnight, so that they would all be there together – if there were not one giant herd, there would be no point to the operation at all. But then, on the Big Day of the Big Country, only a tenth of them was on hand.

Greg greeted the appearance of the 400 like a schoolmaster faced with a mass truancy demonstration or an industrialist in the midst of an unscheduled strike.

"What happened?" he demanded, looking out at what in other circumstances might have seemed a simple, picturesque pastoral setting, uninterrupted by animals. As it was, it spelt disaster.

One of Wyler's men was on hand for an explanation. "Well, Mr. Wyler heard about it yesterday afternoon and said he wouldn't spend $40,000 for one shot."

"But there's nothing out there," said a now desperate Gregory Peck learning the harsh reality of commerce-versus-art. "Hundreds of thousands of acres with four hundred miserable little cattle. You can't even see them out there. Get Mr. Wyler over."

Mr. Wyler came – to be greeted by a less than sanguine co-producer. "What's happened, Willy?" he asked angrily. "Where's our panorama shot? Where's the vast cattle herd?"

Wyler was a little disturbed by the effects of his peremptory action of the previous afternoon. Nothing could hide the fact that it was a vast, very empty panorama.

"Oh, it'll be enough," he replied. "It'll be enough."

Previously, Greg and Wyler had come to a decision about their respective roles as co-producers. It would be Wyler's responsibility to act as director, and on the set he was boss. He would be responsible for the editing. The office work of casting, preparing the script, the general preparation of the picture would be shared. But it would be Greg's responsibility to hire and rent the horses and saddles, the Western gear and the cattle. Greg, a man who knew wranglers, who understood the way the Western people thought, would be best able to organize such things.

Greg reminded Wyler of the agreed division of labour. "I thought *this* was to be *my* decision?" he asked. "It is my obligation. Those 400 head of cattle just aren't going to show."

Wyler answered with a comment that amounted to "Goddammit – $40,000!" The importance of what he was saying was not lost but as far as Gregory Peck was concerned, the scene was.

In truth there was nothing that *could* be done. You just couldn't whip up another 3,600 head of cattle at a moment's notice. So it was just 400 that were used in a scene that took all day to photograph – by patiently shifting the same 400 cows and steers from one part of the panorama to the next.

Additional friction between Greg and Willy Wyler was rather more intense – and Peck now believes it was a pretty good demonstration of why directors and actors shouldn't try to be producers at the same time. The double act they have to perform by constantly switching hats (and forgetting on occasions which one suits them best) is too difficult for comfort.

Looking back now, Greg says, "It all turned into such an outlandish brouhaha, I can't understand how it happened, especially since Wyler is one of the directors I love and respect the most. Somehow, though, at times like this you lose touch with reality and little matters become magnified out of all proportion."

The row really took off from the moment that has become enshrined in Hollywood Western folklore as The Buckboard Scene – a buckboard being a Western horse-drawn waggon. After seeing the rushes of the scene, in which he and Carroll Baker were in close-up, Greg asked to be able to do it again. He didn't like the way in which he was photographed. Not only did it seem to him to be a very bad close-up shot, but he hated the way he acted in it. "I'm amateurish and wretched and must do that again, Willy," he said.

"We'll see," said Wyler in a tone of voice that seemed to indicate that he had thought about it already and the answer was no.

About five times, Greg pressed for the scene to be reshot and five times Wyler was non-commital. Finally, the unit was about to leave Stockton for new locations on the Mojave desert. The buckboard scene had to be reshot immediately or be lost forever.

"Willy," said Greg on the evening of their departure, "we've got to do that close-up today or it's going to be too late. This is the last chance."

Wyler was now as firm as he had previously been uncommunicative. "I'm not going to do it," he declared. "I'm the director of this picture," implying that he believed his producer colleague had overstepped the bounds of his terms of reference. "I don't need a new scene. I can cut around it. I don't want to take any time to do it and I'm sick and tired of hearing about it."

Greg suddenly felt a cold chill inside him. He walked away to his trailer and thought about the situation in which he was now placed. As he thought, the chill inside him seemed to intensify to freezing point.

A few days earlier, Veronique had left the location at Mojave with Anthony and gone home to Los Angeles, a hundred miles south. The location work was practically finished.

Without saying anything more to Wyler or to anyone else on the set, Greg decided to follow the rest of the family. He moved his personal things out of the trailer into his car, sat behind the wheel and started driving – all the way back home.

"What are you doing here?" asked a pleasantly surprised Veronique when her husband walked though the door. "You weren't due back until tomorrow."

Before he could finish his explanations, the telephone rang. It was George Chasin, who had heard only Wyler's side of the story and was anxious to prove for himself that his client had not left his senses behind on the acres of land scrub at Mojave.

Wyler had meanwhile agreed that any filming lost could be made up later on in the studio. Greg was told that there would be another week of studio shooting to do. He said he wouldn't go back at all – but good sense told him to reconsider.

Everything was all set for a return to work when Wyler – until *The Big Country*, one of Greg's dearest friends – insisted on a condition: Gregory Peck would make a public apology for walking out in front of the whole crew. Greg stubbornly dug in his heels and refused.

Wyler was now faced with the alternative of either allowing Peck back or losing the entire film. The day that Greg re-appeared on the set, there was an impenetrable void between himself and his director-cum-co-producer. He wouldn't speak to Peck and Peck wouldn't speak to him.

The row lasted for long after the picture was completed. The biggest fight of all came when it was all finished, just before an important preview was scheduled. It was a showing that was to take place before some of the most influential members of the press and the Hollywood community. Greg heard that Wyler had decided not to allow the Peck name to be featured in the credits as a co-producer.

All the old anger flared up inside the Peck frame once more. And this time, he was not allowing it to rest at a mere show biz feud. Now he was calling in his lawyers and a battle-by-correspondence began that was to add to the frosty atmosphere between the two men.

Although the precise details of the correspondence have never been published, the feud was the talk of the town. A year later, Greg told Louella Parsons, "It's true that Wyler and I had words but what I had to say I said to him, not behind his back."

But subsequently when they were in the same room together at parties or other social evenings, it was obvious that they were not on speaking terms. They would gravitate to different parts of the room and avoid the possibility of having to say anything to each other.

Their wives tried to make the previously close friends see sense and make up. Neither of them would. By the time several months had gone by, Greg was beginning to feel that the whole thing had been a bit foolish – and, if put to the test, of course it was the director who had the final say as to what scenes should be let alone. Peck now recalls that when the truth of that situation dawned on him he was just waiting for an opportunity to shake hands with his adversary.

It came when Wyler won an Oscar for *Ben Hur*.

It was three years after the Big Row. Greg was backstage at the ceremony waiting to go on himself when a beaming Willy Wyler walked with the Award straight into his path. On an impulse, Peck stuck out his hand and said: "Congratulations, Willy. You really deserve it."

Both men smiled and shook hands. Wyler looked Greg straight in the eyes and said, "Thanks, but I still won't retake that buckboard scene!"

Wyler and he have stayed friends ever since. The buckboard scene was virtually eliminated and the embarrassing moments that Peck said worried him so much were cleverly cut around. He admits that probably only he is aware that for a brief second he thinks he "looks like a cretin".

Fourteen

So Gregory Peck had demonstrated one thing: he could be quite a difficult customer. He wasn't always altogether the smooth, Mr. Nice Guy the columnists had delighted in writing about. Sometimes, reported Veronique, he could lose his cool and demonstrate that he had a strong temper.

But there was little doubt that he had now at last found the complete happiness he had always wanted. "Veronique," he told reporters, "is the woman of my life and I couldn't ask for more. I'm the luckiest man in the world."

Because there still had to be occasional joint parental decisions about their boys, when Greta and Greg met, they did so warmly and pleasantly.

Any disagreements that she and Greg continued to have centred around the boys' schooling. He wanted them to go to school abroad once they had gone through their first few years in the classroom. It was wrong, he thought, for a child to be brought up in Hollywood in the shade of their rich and talented parents, where they could grow soft. They needed to show that they were their own people, able to make their own decisions based on their own experiences. Greta wanted them much nearer at hand, and since she had legal custody of the boys, she won.

Jonathan, Stephen and Carey were in turn all to go to the Harvard School, an establishment that has nothing to do with Harvard University, but one that proved good enough as a training ground for the college life that followed. Jonathan certainly was proving himself to be an athlete of exceptional ability. He was already a runner and would soon become a champion half-miler.

He was the only one of the boys who closely resembled their film star father, the handsome hero of many a woman's dreams, the man of whom, when *The Big Country* had its premiere in London, a titled lady said: "He's the only one for whom I'd leave home."

And Jonathan's relationship with Greg was particularly strong. While still at school, he asked his mother if he could change his home and go to live with Greg and Veronique. It was arranged without any difficulty – just as all the boys were always able to come and stay at Greg's house whenever they wanted to do so. Their initial shyness had worn off completely now and Veronique was accepted as a close friend – which was precisely the relationship she sought.

Meanwhile Anthony and Cecilia were developing into normal kids who just happened to have a famous father – but weren't overly impressed by it.

Greg wasn't all that excited about talking about himself either. He told one reporter in 1959, "It's all rather second-rate to expose one's insides to the public view. I'm not interested by the vogue for actors to tell all. I think it's in poor taste. My performances are the only forms of self-revelation that I go in for."

And because it was self-revelation, he was choosey and, some would say, very difficult about the roles that he did accept. But if he wanted to do a part, he was able to adapt to the circumstances and take the consequences without calling for his lawyers.

The two Gregory Pecks spent a lot of time with each other. Gregory Senior loved telling people his name and delighted in proving it with his credit card at a gas station or supermarket. "You sure you're Gregory Peck?" tradesmen would ask. And if they added, "You don't really look like him," he was happy to answer in his lilting Irish brogue: "Ah, but you see, I haven't been well."

He was four inches shorter than his son but there was a distinct family resemblance. He was also proud of his offspring. "Gregory is just the same sensible lad he was before he became famous," he would tell people. "He's unspoiled, unchanged. A clean and upstanding boy."

There were plans to team Greg and Clark Gable in a movie called *Toward the Unknown*. The only problem was that Greg always had top billing – and so did Gable. Since both men were represented by George Chasin, this seemed like the conventional meeting between the irresistible force and the immovable object. But Greg saw the difficulty for what it was.

"George," he told his agent, "no problem at all. Me take first billing over Clark Gable? Out of the question!"

The idea was never put to the final acid test of signing a contract. The film was eventually made with William Holden and Lloyd Nolan.

A similar situation arose in 1959 over the plan to co-star Greg with Marilyn Monroe in *Let's Make Love*. Once more George Chasin was representing both parties and once more Greg had an agreement that he had to have top billing. But so did Marilyn. That fact was not lost on the Twentieth Century Fox executives trying to set up the deal. Chasin was called into the office of Lew Schreiber. "Well, genius," he said, "you're so smart. You worked out these contracts. What about the billing? How are you going to get round *this* little problem?" It was a question worth asking because not only did Greg like to be top star in his productions, Marilyn wasn't averse to being difficult either. There was, however, one important mitigating feature; Marilyn had been complaining for years that – Laurence Olivier apart – she never had a leading man or a director of international importance.

The "genius" decided that this could be the one way to get round her.

"Marilyn," he said. "You know that clause in your contract – the one we worked out for you?"

Now Miss Monroe knew her contracts from A to Z, but she thought it was worth being as naive as her coy dumb blonde roles always made her out to be. "Explain it to me," she said, while her lawyer listened too.

"You know," said Chasin, hesitantly, "you have first billing and you can only be preceded by a male more important in the industry than you." That was the kind of legal language which could be interpreted safely by no judge. "You know, we've been talking about Gregory Peck . . ."

"My God," she said. "There's absolutely no problem. To think that I could be working with Greg Peck. Of course, he should be billed first."

Marilyn also had approval of director. That was more difficult. For the director chosen for the film was George Cukor, still a man able to spin stories featuring beautiful women as though building a gossamer web. They were light and silky – and fitted their female stars accordingly. Men trying them for size tended to feel somewhat out of place, just as Greg had on his last brief working relationship with the director.

He liked the idea of playing opposite Marilyn. He also liked the Howard Hughes type character who had been written for him – a billionaire mystery tycoon who falls for the Greenwich Village showgirl played by Miss Monroe – although faced with the triple threat of a young actor-singer-comedian, a man to whom she has given her heart. Because he can do none of the things that the entertainer can do, he takes lessons. There were plans to use Bing Crosby as the singing coach, Milton Berle as the comedian and Lee J. Cobb as the actor.

Greg liked the idea so much that he paid for real lessons of his own. For about six weeks, he took instruction in delivering fast funny monologues, studied singing with a professional coach and with the help of a black dancing instructor, learned how to do a 32-bar-tap routine.

He didn't see Marilyn all that much – usually only when they overlapped their bookings in a studio rehearsal room as she or he were finishing their own dance lessons. "How are you coming on with your tap dancing?" she asked and he would tell her that he thought it was ridiculous, but going to be all right.

And it was – until George Cukor happened to throw into a general conversation: "By the way, we're getting some rewrites done."

Greg was not altogether delighted to hear that. He had been happy enough with the original script handed to him and the more he read the lines himself, the more he liked them. "What rewrites?" he asked nervously. "What's being rewritten?"

"Oh," said the director. "We're going to go through the whole thing. Sharpen it up, put more into it."

"Who's going to write it?" Greg asked, betraying his anxiety.

"Arthur Miller," said Cukor. The mention of Marilyn Monroe's husband's name flashed a warning light to Greg. Looking back now, Greg says that at that moment the unuttered comment going through his mind was: "God Almighty! The whole thing's up the spout. Arthur Miller's going to throw the whole thing to Marilyn."

As the pages rolled off Miller's typewriter, Greg felt that his fears were justified. Marilyn's role became more important and his own faded into a subsidiary position – essential but like wallpaper, hardly noticeable. The fun had gone out of it, too. His own character had changed from that of the scheming billionaire who could buy anything with his wealth and who had his own way of wooing women, into a stuffy humbug in a homburg without humour.

Peck protested. It wasn't right for the picture and it certainly wasn't right for him. "Wait till you see the finished script," said Cukor. "Wait. You'll change your mind."

When the whole thing arrived in its binding for Gregory Peck's attention, he liked it even less. He called for an immediate meeting and one was hastily organized between himself, Cukor and Arthur Miller at the director's home.

He and Arthur had known each other for years. Miller had once offered him the lead in the Broadway production of *The Crucible*, but film commitments had got in the way and there was never really any chance of his being able to do it. Greg didn't think *Let's Make Love* was really the answer to the difficulty of getting them to work together.

He was polite but firm. "Arthur," he said. "I'll always have the utmost respect for you and your work and I've always wanted to be in something by you. But to be perfectly honest, I think this frothy, light comedy romance is now about as funny as pushing Grandma down the stairs in a wheelchair."

Miller did not laugh. He did not agree that the screenplay now emasculated Peck's role. "You really think that?" he asked.

Greg answered, "It just isn't funny any more."

Cukor kept repeating: "What shall we do? What shall we do?"

Greg offered the solution. "Well, I think the best thing would be for me to bow out. I won't take the money and I won't hold the studio to the contract. I'll just step aside. I have a lot of respect for you people and you may be right. I don't happen to think so, but that is a matter of opinion."

A few months later, the part was rewritten again – for Yves Montand who "yielded to temptation" with Marilyn, the last link in a chain of events that began with Gregory Peck's frustrated ambition to become a song and dance man.

Like imagining what Greg would have done in *High Noon*, the question of his part in *Let's Make Love* – remembered now as a disappointingly dull penultimate film for Marilyn – is one of those that will never have an answer.

But Greg wouldn't have enjoyed making a picture from the script that was handed to him. "Everything I enjoy most has the qualities of vitality, creativeness and vigour in theater, sports, conversation, even friends," he told columnist Sidney Skolsky about this time.

People wanted to know what films he would make now. There was going to be an epic he revealed, called *The Guns of Navarone*.

Before beginning *Navarone*, there were to be other pictures, including one in which there was a role for which he definitely did have a feel – *Pork Chop Hill*. It was a semi-documentary about the Korean War and was without the usual heroics offered in war pictures. It centered on the true incident when, while armistice talks were being conducted, a weary band of American troops fought and died to take an anthill of a spot called "Pork Chop Hill" – only for the survivors of the squad to be marched down again when the talks were completed.

The picture was made by Greg's own company with Sy Bartlett producing and James Webb as writer, and was based on the book by a retired General and military historian, S. L. A. Marshall.

James Webb had brought it to Greg's attention and he desperately wanted to make it. For the director, he chose Lewis Milestone, who will be forever associated with *All Quiet on the Western Front*. It was a different sort of war picture this time, but Milestone's reputation was only enhanced by *Pork Chop Hill*. *Time* magazine selected it as one of the ten best films of 1959. "The film does not sentimentalize or patronize its heroes," said the magazine.

It also gave a screen start to a number of actors who have since made it big: George Peppard, Harry Guardino, Bobby Blake of the "Baretta" T.V. show and Martin Landau from "Mission Impossible". But it didn't take any money at the box office – there was nothing for the women apart from the grimy Mr. Peck and no love interest whatever.

It did, nevertheless, focus attention on a war that became a trial run for Vietnam and which amounted to America's first ever defeat – even though that was padded over in the form of an armistice. Despite his left-wing tendencies, Greg himself has held that MacArthur was right in wanting to take over North Korea – that the Russians and Chinese were not ready to embroil themselves in a third world war. It was a theme he would return to.

Sensitivity seemed to be the Peck approach to the role of F. Scott

Fitzgerald in *Beloved Infidel* based on the book by the writer's mistress, Sheilah Graham. Sy Bartlett, this time, wrote the screenplay. Deborah Kerr played the Cockney-born columnist. Despite the rather upper-crust feel she gave to the role, it seemed at the time to be an easier bit of casting than making the tall, dark, still young Gregory Peck play the stocky, blond, blue-eyed Fitzgerald. The critics were not amused and blamed him for taking a part to which they said he was not suited. Some accused him of not realizing how different Peck and the real Fitzgerald were. Looking back on it all now, Greg says he would have been happier had he been playing "just a writer" under a different name. "Chances are," he says now, "that 90 per cent of the audience had no idea at all what Fitzgerald did look like."

Even if the critics didn't like it, Greg says he thinks some of his best work went into that movie. To make sure that he really looked like the sozzled husband who, in one scene, ruins his wife's first broadcast, he went into character – swallowed enough vodka to throw off his inhibitions and allow him to see the role of a drunk through a drunk's own eyes. Even so, his old friend Henry King standing behind the camera was just that little bit shocked.

King, of course, denies it. But he says, "He scared Deborah Kerr half to death. You would think he was a drunken demon. When he gets in to do something, he does it – right to the very limit without hamming it up. Exactly what's on his mind."

He also put the fear of God – or perhaps merely a section of God's children – into the men of the Motion Picture Association of America who were still operating their censorship system, and doing it with a vengeance.

In one vital scene the drunken Fitzgerald – who, after being on the waggon, hears he has been fired from his studio job in Hollywood – flies to Chicago with his wife, his pockets stocked heavy with gin bottles and his breath revealing that a number of them have already been emptied.

He is making a nuisance of himself, talking to the other passengers. When he attracts the attention of a pretty stewardess, he asks, "Have you read any of my books? My name is F. Scott Fitzgerald."

"No," she replies. "I never have, Mr. Fitzgerald." To which Mr. Fitzgerald replies, "You silly bitch!" and toddles off to annoy someone else.

The Johnston Office were in a tizzy about this. "You will have to substitute another word for 'bitch'," they demanded. "You'll have to put in some 'post-sync.' and get it fixed."

King and Peck were both outraged. They pointed out that the word "bitch" was perfectly acceptable in society and was just what a drunk like Fitzgerald would use in the circumstances. The office bowed its head to the Peck argument and so turned *Beloved Infidel* into something of an historic picture – the first one that dared use the word "bitch".

Beloved Infidel was the last of the pictures for which Greg was committed to Twentieth Century Fox. He did it only because of his contract with the studio and at times wondered whether he ought to get out before things got too hot for him. In the end he was glad that he didn't. The picture itself failed to come off in the way most people hoped it would, but the scenes in which the boozed Gregory Peck characterizes Fitzgerald without ever caricaturing him, were worth seeing.

Greg's next picture, *On the Beach* was a lot more successful at the box office. Yet it was one which had him back at his typewriter pouring out a series of memos. Making the picture, he says now, was "pretty grim". He objected to having to take Ava Gardner who, since *The Snows of Kilimanjaro* had become one of his best friends, to bed as he gives up hope of finding any other remaining human life after a nuclear holocaust. It was, he now says, a violation of the novel, and "out of character" for the American Navy captain.

Despite his own doubts, *On the Beach*, the film of Neville Shute's best seller, was distinguished in many ways. One of the most important was the fact that it introduced a new dramatic actor named Fred Astaire. It was the picture that showed that the man who was – and is – almost never thought of without a shiny top hat, a pair of patent leather dancing pumps and a gold-topped cane, could also act. Astaire played the scientist taken aboard the submarine on the last voyage round the earth.

The United States has already been depopulated by the Bomb – the year is said to be 1964 – and the nuclear tide is gradually engulfing the entire planet. So far, however, Australia is still unaffected and it is there that he takes his ship and where he meets and loves Ava Gardner.

It is, however, obvious that even the country "Down Under" is in peril. After issuing poison pills to everyone on board, the captain decides to take the sub back to America where the crew can die on their native soil. Ava waits for an agonizing solo death in Australia. Astaire dies as he always would have wished – sitting in the cockpit of his racing car as the exhaust fumes envelop him in the locked garage.

Neville Shute was less than happy with the way Stanley Kramer, the director, interpreted his characters and he boycotted the entire venture – staying away from the set and from any public showing of the movie. Greg felt that the captain of the sub – the Royal Navy lent H.M.S. *Andrew* for the filming – should have stayed loyal to the wife and child whom he hoped, against all the odds, might still be living in America. Instead, Kramer insisted on the consummation of the affair with Ava. "My character goes out of the window when I do the expected thing and go to bed with Ava," he told the director. "The eccentricity of the character, the peculiar twist that makes him interesting and different, goes down the drain."

Peck and Astaire – who hadn't known each other before the picture – became firm friends during the course of the filming, each admiring the professionalism, the devotion to duty, the charm of the other. They have remained close ever since, occasionally spending days at the races in each other's company, sometimes going out to dinner with Veronique and when the mood takes them, playing a game of three-handed rummy.

The part of the junior officer on the sub's crew was played by Anthony Perkins, whom Greg remembers as shy and "with some complexes he has now been able to overcome. He was a very good young performer." He tended to agree with Tony's co-star in *Friendly Persuasion*, Gary Cooper's diagnosis of the actor who made a virtual career out of playing neurotic young men. "He needs to spend a summer on a ranch."

A great deal of the filming was done in Australia – with Veronique at Greg's side and bringing Anthony, Cecilia and Carey along too.

It was Stanley Kramer's idea to make the film into a plea for world peace – by demonstrating what could happen without it. To get that message across, he held simultaneous premieres of the picture in 16 different capital cities. Greg and Veronique represented the film when it opened at Dom Kino, the film workers' union club in Moscow. Some 1,200 top Soviet officials were present together with the American Ambassador, Llewellyn Thompson and other diplomats. Later, in an adjoining banqueting room, there was a huge dinner for the distinguished guests. When Greg made a speech in which he spoke about hopes for peace, he was warmly applauded by the audience. But when he met a few Russians afterwards and asked them what they thought of the picture, one of them told him: "Yes, it's a very serious film, very well done, but I think we would have given it a happy ending had we made it. We would not have allowed the world to blow itself to smithereens."

When the film was premiered in America, the press was almost uniformly excellent. *Cosmopolitan* reported: "Gregory Peck as the commander of a U.S. submarine and Ava Gardner who plays the loose-living playgirl with whom he falls in love give excellent performances." High praise was also given to Fred Astaire and to Anthony Perkins and Donna Anderson.

Reviewing *On the Beach*, the *Hollywood Reporter* awarded the picture's star something of a back-handed compliment: "The actors are so good, it's impossible to choose among them. As the submarine commander, Gregory Peck under Kramer's astute direction, unfolds a powerful two-sided characterization."

Peck hoped for at least as much from his next picture, *The Guns of Navarone*, which he said he saw as a love story with a dash of the Keystone Kops added for good measure.

One day early on in the filming, he explained his theory to the writer-producer Carl Foreman.

On paper in the script, in Alistair MacLean's original novel and to the casual movie goer who eventually saw it in a theater, it was the story of a professional mountain-climber – turned army officer who leads a group of other troops in an assault on a Greek island in 1943. The object of the exercise is to knock out the huge guns that dominate the island. Anthony Quayle is the original leader of the force and when he is wounded, Greg takes over, as the next in line. David Niven, for once in his life, played a mere corporal.

"Here's the real plot of the picture," as Greg told it. "David Niven really loves Tony Quayle and Gregory Peck loves Anthony Quinn. Tony Quayle breaks a leg and is sent off to hospital. Tony Quinn falls in love with Irene Papas and David Niven and Peck catch each other on the rebound and live happily ever after."

"Greg, you clever rascal," said Foreman, "you've caught me out."

Two factors contributed greatly to the success of a film that cost $6 million to make, recouped all the expenses almost immediately it went out on release, and ended up as the biggest money-spinner Greg had had to that time. No one took it over-seriously and everyone got on well together. As Greg says, "Those commandos were performing miracles. Five or six commandos outwitting a whole German regiment, getting right into the middle of them, stealing their uniforms and masquerading as Nazis. Well, to do that, you have to do with the Nazis what Mack Sennett did with the Keystone Cops. There were 550 chances for them to kill us before we even set foot on the island, but we had to do it with total conviction, even though we were aware that it was flirting with parody."

When they weren't trying to be serious, they played chess, told tales and when it got very cold very late at night, they had a drink. Sometimes they were filming up to their belts in ice-cold water. Only a steady supply of brandy could be calculated to warm the body as well as the spirits. By the time filming for the day was over, some of the team would be near to paralytic. "But not Greg," David Niven has recalled. "He matched us drink for drink – but none of us saw him so much as stagger or muff a line. Really quite disgusting to see a man able to handle liquor like that."

The *Navarone* film had been in preparation for a year or more before work began – first with the interior shots at London's Shepperton studios and then, for the outdoor material, on location on the island of Rhodes. And as usual, it was fraught with difficulties.

The director chosen was Alexander Mackendrick – but a week before shooting began, the director fell out with Carl Foreman and Mackendrick was fired. A new man had to be found quickly. A telegram went off to Greg, suggesting Carl Foreman's own choice – J. Lee Thompson, the director who had recently done *Tiger Bay* and *North West Frontier*. His telegram said:

DEAR GREG: SORRY WE'VE BEEN UNABLE TO TALK TO EACH OTHER STOP HOPE YOU SEE NORTH WEST FRONTIER SOONEST AS I WOULD LIKE TO GO WITH

LEE THOMPSON AND HOPE YOU WILL BE AS EN-
THUSIASTIC AS I AM STOP HE IS HOTTEST DIRECTOR
IN ENGLAND AT THIS TIME AND WORD OF MOUTH ON
HIS LATEST PIC I REACH FOR THE STARS KURT JUR-
GENS EXCELLENT STOP ACTUALLY HE WAS ALWAYS
MY FIRST CHOICE NAVARONE BUT WAS NOT AVAIL-
ABLE . . .

Greg agreed to go with Thompson. Relations with Foreman were
always of the best and Greg admired the way he had worked
practically single-handed on the project until then. Greg flew into
Athens from Paris where he was staying with the family and Carl
came in from Rhodes. In the King George Hotel's own projection
room they spent three days looking at the work of various men and
ultimately agreed that Thompson was the one whom they could
both "go along with".

Thompson flew down to Rhodes before he had even had a chance
to go over the script. He read it on the flight. By the time he arrived
on the island, he had planned out what he rightly believed would be
his big opportunity to break into the international field. Three days
after his arrival, shooting began.

After the picture was completed, Greg sat back to enjoy the results
and said that he thought that any capable actor could have played
his part. To some this gave the impression that he wasn't happy with
his performance. It wasn't true. "Because I may well have said that
there were any number of fellows who could have played my role,
candour on my part was mistaken for a negative view."

One of the frequent points of disagreement between Greg and
Veronique is that she often thinks he is being a little too candid.

For Carl Foreman he saved his candour for comments about the
script. He went through it not so much with a toothcomb as with a
toothpick. Line by line of the writer's prose was dissected and when
he thought it needed some amendment, he put his thoughts in
writing in one of his Selznickesque memos: "P. 14. Mallory's speech
near the bottom, in answer to Jensen's line 'Any questions?' Could
Mallory have a stronger line – not liking any part of the idea.
Humorous and more outspoken than we have now – almost profane?

"P. 17. Mallory, after Franklin's speech: 'Thanks Mallory. I'm
most grateful . . .' nods without enthusiasm. Couldn't Mallory have

a colourful line here? He sees that he's trapped. Even Stravos is waiting for him in the hotel. Couldn't he have a humorous, ironic compliment to Jensen and Franklin, whether in this spot or up above in place of his line 'You think of everything, don't you sir?'"

The speeches were suitably toughened up to meet the Peck requirements.

Greg, as usual, took advantage of his time making *Navarone* to spend what leisure there was in the way that he and Veronique most enjoyed. They socialized with friends like the Nivens, attended the theater a great deal in London and went racing. He had an ambition now – to win the Grand National – the British race which is regarded as the world's greatest steeplechase. Nothing in America, in France or anywhere else for that matter can compare with it.

He wasn't ready for the National when he was in Britain for the interior shots of *Navarone* but he was ready to start taking his place among the racing aristocracy. Greg sometimes strikes strangers as a reserved man and he will readily admit that he enjoys relaxing only with people whom he regards as his "own type". Actors certainly fit this bill. They, he finds, are "more giving and funnier, relaxed and better story tellers than people in most other professions". He also welcomes the company of doctors, writers, painters and musicians – and the horsey set.

Once, he bought a horse in England and took it over to California, a promising animal called Tetread, from the Anglo-Irish Blood Stock Agency, run by Frank More O'Ferrall and his brother Rory, two men whose friendship he had first made while filming *Moby Dick*. Neither Tetread nor a horse he later picked up in Australia during *On the Beach* amounted to anything, but Greg's ambitions for the big race were as strong as ever.

They did, however, lie fairly fallow during the 1960 trip for *Navarone* – although living in Ascot meant that the Pecks had plenty of opportunity to watch the cream of race horses in action. And being 45 minutes' drive away from London, at the house they rented at Burleigh Road, Ascot, there were ample opportunities for evenings at the theater, too.

When they did go to the theater they went in a chauffeur-driven car, a fact they later had some cause to regret. One night, as they drove back home to Burleigh Road, down a dark country lane, a delivery van was seen scurrying in the opposite direction. It was past midnight and Greg nudged Veronique as the vehicle, travelling far in excess of its usual lumbering speed, passed them. "What the devil is that van doing making deliveries at this time of night?" he asked. They both shrugged at the thought and went on discussing the play and Greg's work for the next day on the *Navarone* set.

Three days later Veronique searched in vain for some jewellery. It had gone. So, too, on investigation, had two fur coats – one mink, the other sable.

The local police were called and they began sifting through the remaining Peck property for clues. Later, they came across two tell-tale marks near an outside wall. It was clear, they decided, that a ladder had stood at that spot and had been used to gain access to the house. Did Mrs. Peck leave the window open? Yes, she replied, she did. It was a warm summer evening and with no air conditioning, it seemed a sensible thing to do.

After all, the bedroom was on the second floor and there were other people in the house at the time – a butler, a cook, a maid, a secretary, a nanny and their two children. But the children were asleep and the assorted staff were watching television. All of which seemed to indicate that the burglars had had a tip-off.

Neither the raiders nor the goods they stole were ever recovered, but it was soon established how the robbery had been affected. Mike, the Pecks' chauffeur – a seemingly personable man whom it had been difficult not to like – had a prison record. His speciality was driving rich and famous people – and then tipping off a gang about when his employers would be out of the house and where most of the valuable property could be found. On the day of the theft, the tip was about Veronique's jewels and furs – and the useful additional fact that there was a garden ladder behind a hedge a few steps away from the open second floor window.

Mike had been working for the Pecks ever since they first took the house. He had endeared himself particularly to Anthony who liked nothing better than driving to Shepperton with his father every morning and, like the members of the crew, eating during the break a sausage roll and drinking a cup of tea. To Anthony, sausage rolls were the food of the gods. When the delicacy was chewed to its final crumb, he walked reluctantly away with Mike, who would drive him home – usually stopping at a nearby playground on the way.

Mike was his pal – and everyone else's too. He would tell most of the people with whom he came into contact how he had just scored a killing on the greyhound track. He knew all about the dogs and Greg was happy to invest a couple of pounds with him most days.

There was nothing but his record to tie him with the robbery and Greg refused to sack him. Only another couple of weeks of filming were still to go and he liked the man, despite his suspicions. When it was time to wrap up the work on the film, Greg included Mike in a list of recipients who were given mementos of the star's appreciation for their devotion to duty – a Peck tradition. Following *Navarone*, Mike, together with Greg's stand-in, his make-up man and his wardrobe assistant, were handed Cartier gold watches – all inscribed.

The suspicions might have lingered, but as far as Greg was concerned that was the end of the matter – until a few weeks later when there was a phone call to the Peck home in California. It was from a bewildered but bright assistant at Cartiers of Bond Street. A man answering Mike's description had ordered a dozen watches on Mr. Peck's account – he said Greg intended to present these too, to the crew and had asked Mike to get them for him. The answer down the phone was direct and grateful.

In full spate, Mike booked a suite at the Connaught Hotel. Mr. Peck, he said, was returning to do some post-synchronization work. Meanwhile, Mike had taken possession of the suite himself, had ordered champagne and was blissfully ensconced there at his former employer's expense with a young lady. Greg gave him full marks for ingenuity – and detailed evidence to Scotland Yard. Mike went back to the slammer.

Greg and Veronique had by this time bought a villa at Cap Ferrat on the French Riviera. Veronique's father helped them plan it and for years it would be the place where they could relax, dress and eat casually and where they could meet friends. While Greg continued to work at Shepperton, Veronique took the children to the villa.

Just before flying in to join them, he phoned Veronique and casually asked her what presents the children would like from England. Anthony had no doubt: "Sausage rolls," he called out. Greg bundled up half a dozen in a straw boater and saw the sun light up in the little boy's eyes. "If Anthony had his way," said Greg, "they would form his basic diet."

The *New York Times* review of *The Guns of Navarone* described Greg as "the lean-limbed, laconic mountain climber" in a picture which "even though [it] runs to more than two and a half hours, moves swiftly and gets where it's going."

The film was a huge success both critically and financially.

Nobody now had any doubts either about the success of Greg's marriage to Veronique. Proof of that success came with their decision, some five years after the original civil ceremony, to have their marriage blessed by the Roman Catholic Church.

The Archbishop of Los Angeles agreed on the "chancery annulment" after Greg had filed his marriage licence of 1943 with the Archdiocese together with written approval by Greta to their marriage being officially ended.

With the paperwork out of the way, there was nothing to stop the religious ceremony going ahead. This was performed by a friend, the Jesuit Father Jim Deasy, in the one big Catholic church in Santa Barbara. The only witness was Greg's rancher friend, Channing Peake – the man on whose land the first ceremony had been held.

After the joy of seeing the plaudits for *Navarone*, Greg switched to making a film for his own company, *Cape Fear*, and handed the plum role not to himself but to another actor, Robert Mitchum.

It was a calculated move. Greg knew that Mitchum's part as a newly-released sex criminal seeking to avenge himself on the lawyer whose evidence put him behind bars, was much stronger than his own as the man's prey. But he thought it needed the Mitchum type to carry the part and that he would benefit both the movie and Greg's company.

Although Greg still thought he made a good producer – despite all the pitfalls – he always steadfastly resisted any suggestion that he now try his hand at directing. "On the floor there can be only one boss. Otherwise, it's anarchy and everyone is uncertain. You have to look to one fellow. He's the one who says 'print it'. Those are virtually the most important words in picture making. I've never wanted that responsibility."

After *The Big Country* experience, he thought it wiser to bring in Sy Bartlett to act as producer of *Cape Fear*. But he still had the problems thrust in his own lap. Early on in the production, Rod Steiger's agent kept up a barrage of telephone calls asking for his client to be given the role of the ex-con. "What's the matter?" he asked.

"Doesn't Greg want a good actor in the part?" He did – but he saw it more as a Mitchum role than one for Steiger.

All through the production it seemed he had made the right choice. Mitchum was perfect in the part, didn't fluff his lines once. The notices proved the point that Greg knew that they would. Mitchum got all the best reviews.

A couple of times, Mitchum was quoted as saying that he had wiped out Gregory Peck in the finished movie or that he had not been given much opposition from his fellow star.

"I didn't think highly of him for that," Greg now recalls. "I don't dislike him. I've seen him since and we've been friendly. But I had given him that role and really I'd paid him a terrific amount of money. It was perfectly obvious that it was the better role. I had done it rather idealistically to get my company moving. I thought he would understand that, but apparently he thought that he had simply acted me off the screen."

Greg says now that he wouldn't mind the chance of getting his own back. He says he is just "human" enough for that. Not to "wipe out" Mitchum completely, but to have the chance of a 50–50 situation where each man has a role of equal importance. "Bob shouldn't depend on my generosity next time. We would see then, who wipes the other out," he says with a grin.

There was now, however, something marvellous on the way. It was called *To Kill a Mockingbird*.

Fifteen

It was the big peak of Gregory Peck's career to date – a picture for which he not only received an Oscar nomination but the one that actually earned him the coveted gold statuette. The film of which he now says, "I'm not falsely modest about it. I think I was good in that picture."

It is the movie which for years gave him the greatest sense of satisfaction, the film which people have mentioned ever since when they bump into him in a parking lot or in an elevator. "I saw you in *To Kill a Mockingbird*," they say, "and I'll never forget it."

Some movies have the right chemistry to suit both the performers and their audience. *To Kill a Mockingbird* is one. It was, he says, for him like "putting on an old suit of clothes – just comfortable."

He had the feel about it from the moment that it was first mentioned to him. Of course, he was aware of the pitfalls – about never working with dogs, children, motorboats or Charles Laughton – and in this film he was to play a hard role with some youngsters who, just by smiling, charmed the birds out of the trees. But he was convinced he would be able to cope.

He had read Harper Lee's book about an impecunious widower called Atticus Finch, a lawyer who takes on the seemingly hopeless task of defending a black man charged with raping a white woman – and in a small town deep in the Deep South.

The part of Finch was based on Harper Lee's own father and it was more than just a mere story – albeit one that earned a Pulitzer Prize. It was a statement of faith: that there were people in the South who could surmount the prejudices that seemed to pervade all human life there; people who could stand by principles simply because they believed them to be just.

Harper Lee told me she saw Gregory Peck as her Atticus the moment her novel was bought for the screen, but he was not the first to be considered for the role.

It was originally brought to the attention of Universal Studios by Rock Hudson. But it was turned down by Universal – either because they genuinely didn't want to make a picture called *To Kill a Mockingbird* or because it was the polite way of saying they didn't see Rock Hudson as Atticus Finch.

It turned out to be one of those fortuitous combinations of circumstance that led to a result which everyone now takes for granted. Greg had an office on the Universal lot at the same time that the book was being talked about and just then was looking for a suitable vehicle for his independent production company. Bob Mulligan and Alan Pakula who were working as a team of director and producer respectively, wanted him to star in one of their operations. They had read *Mockingbird* too, and now they gave it to Greg to read.

Racial pictures weren't exactly the surest recipe for box office success in the early 1960s and George Chasin tried to talk Greg out of it. "You know," he said, in the quiet soothing tones that indicate a man who understands what he is talking about, "you will lose the entire South." It sounded like the prognosis of a political machine before an election and in a way it was. For Peck the convinced liberal, *Mockingbird* seemed to be the best demonstration of his own philosophy since *Gentlemen's Agreement*. It was also a very warm, telling story.

Finch's middle-class values were essentially Greg's own. His reaction to racial intolerance matched Finch's perfectly, although there were not too many men willing to risk taking on a case that looked set to end in a legal hanging only so long as the lynch mob didn't get to his client first.

He saw himself wearing Atticus Finch's white suit from the moment he started turning the pages of the novel.

Everything about the picture was right – the story of Atticus Finch at home, his reasoned explanations of life as they were living it to his children, their own torment. Emotional touches like the shooting of a mad dog, all helped to turn the movie into a very human document indeed. But it was the court scene – as Greg knew it would be – that made the film.

To Harper Lee, certainly, it was seeing Gregory Peck in front of the witness stand, first talking to the judge, then addressing the jury in the kind of homespun language that they understood that made the "old suit" fit so well.

Greg had worked out the fine points of the story as it unfolded in the courtroom. On the margins of his script he had scribbled: "A battle shapes up. This man is innocent . . . He'll be lynched . . . be clear. Don't sit around like Whistler's mother. Do not look away from the judge. Lawyer – look him in the eye. Atticus is a fighter."

On another page was scrawled: "No medical evidence. The key to my case."

When he asks the father of the alleged rape victim: "Mr. Ewell, did you call a doctor for your daughter?" he had underscored the question: "MEAN IT."

One only had to venture on to the sidelines of the set, taking up a position between a lighting engineer and a sound technician, to see that this was a part Gregory Peck was enjoying hugely. When it came to his delivering the nine-minute close-up speech to the court, it was clear that if he had never before done anything quite to his own satisfaction, now he had found his great moment in pictures.

The day Harper Lee saw him for the first time walk out of his dressing room in his Panama hat and three-piece white linen suit she burst into tears and called, "My God, he's got a little pot belly just like my Daddy!"

"That's no pot belly, Harper," said Greg, "that's great acting."

Of course, Greg had researched the Atticus Finch role as though he were playing a Pope or a President; to make him seem less than real would be to invite derision. Peck knew that Harper Lee greatly loved her still-living father and he didn't want to be guilty of distorting the truth about a very real man.

With Mulligan and Pakula, he made the trek to Alabama and Harper Lee's own town of Monroeville. It was between Mobile and Montgomery, the scene of the civil rights marches, names inscribed forever in the history of the American Black struggle.

There, he met the real Atticus Finch, Harper's father, Amasa Lee, crippled with arthritis but so obviously proud of the success of the daughter who had joined the ranks of that incredible band of Southern writers: William Faulkner, Tennessee Williams, and Truman Capote, to say nothing of the fact that she had walked off with a Pulitzer Prize for telling *his* story.

He had really been a widower who raised his children single handed, a man who at the same time was always ready to defend a black man accused of crimes he did not commit, even though the *Mockingbird* case was fictional.

Monroeville in 1962 didn't look a lot like the town of 1931, so it was decided to use studio sets for the Maycomb County setting. By the time that filming was over, her father was dead, but Harper had the uncanny experience of seeing him each day virtually duplicated on the set.

Nobody was happier with *Mockingbird* than she was. "In that film the man and the part met," she told me. "As far as I'm concerned, that part is Greg's for life. I've had many, many offers to turn it into musicals, into TV or stage plays, but I've always refused. That film was a work of art and there isn't anyone else who could play the part. I was one of the luckiest people in the world."

She showed her appreciation of that luck with a gesture of seemingly incredible generosity.

Her father had a habit of toying with an old pocket watch – a watch that went with him to court for 40 years and which he never failed to handle deliberately and affectionately in the course of every action before the Bench. Harper told Greg about this and schooled him in the art of using the timepiece to its most telling effect.

With the film over and the model for his part dead, Harper gave Greg the very watch her father had used. He decided then that it had to be his talisman – the good luck charm that he now wouldn't want to be without.

He isn't really a superstitious man – although he had conveniently accepted the show business dictum of trying to avoid seeing a peacock on opening night, which isn't really all that difficult. At the same time, he never likes to travel without a small, cheap crucifix which he has carried since the time it was given to him as a ten-year-old at St. John's Military Academy. (Nowadays, Veronique keeps it for him and always has it in her handbag on every visit abroad.)

Greg had the old pocket watch firmly in his possession the night that *Mockingbird* won the Oscar in 1963 – the night that the fate of his fifth nomination for the precious Academy Award statuette was revealed.

His hand was on the watch throughout the evening. Then, when it came time to announce the award for the outstanding performance by an actor that year, he was clutching it tightly. He saw it as a symbol of the whole project – all of it a gift from Harper Lee.

The atmosphere in the Santa Monica Auditorium was tense, but Greg, as he fingered the watch, was trying not to work up either any undue excitement or nerves. As he has said a number of times since, he had lost before and fully expected to lose again that night.

His principal competition was Jack Lemmon for his brilliantly expressive role in *Days of Wine and Roses* and it seemed a lot of Hollywood money was on him. Greg had seen the film himself and he thought Lemmon had been superb. They were sitting about four feet apart from each other as both waited anxiously for the announcement to be made.

The suspense was broken by Sophia Loren. "The winner," she declared, "is Gregory Peck."

As an elated and surprised Greg got up from his seat to take the hurried but still majestic traditional march to the podium – holding the watch in a more relaxed way now – he reached out to Jack to lightly touch his shoulder. Veronique witnessed the gesture and says that she thought it a tremendously moving demonstration of one actor's feelings and admiration for another.

A few years later, when Jack received his own Oscar, for *Save the Tiger*, it was Greg who presented it to him at the ceremony.

It is not easy to describe the attitude of an actor given the accolade that the name "Oscar" symbolizes. It has become a much abused award to some. Marlon Brando and George C. Scott have tried to totally deride its value. Others considering themselves "in the know" on the Hollywood scene, have dismissed it as more of a back-scratching symptom of the film capital's love of saying thanks for past services than a genuine tribute for current achievement.

Greg says that it occurred to him that it was the culmination of many years' work, but a tribute only to his *Mockingbird* role. He was thrilled, happy at the judgement of his peers – and lucky that the right part had come along when it had.

The memories *To Kill a Mockingbird* recur every time it is shown on a television set in any one of fifty-odd countries and every time someone feels called upon to review the career of Gregory Peck.

* * *

Of course, *Mockingbird* was the triumph to crown Greg's career. It came at a time when, though just 48, Greg was already telling some close friends that he thought he had another five years of picture making in him and then he was going to retire.

The news shook a few Martinis in Hollywood, but most people believed he had passed through another watershed – and now was going to celebrate his even more enhanced status in the industry with more and more work.

But he did have other diversions. He was increasingly being asked to sit on committees connected with film and the arts. He was a close friend of President Lyndon B. Johnson and he and Veronique were enjoying the kind of social whirl that the fan magazines just loved.

At one party at the Rainiers' Monte Carlo palace, a woman approached them diffidently: "Mr. and Mrs. Peck," she said reverently, "Miss Greta Garbo is here and would love to meet you."

At that point, they were like any of the other married couples who over the years have been thrilled at the opportunity to meet Gregory Peck. Garbo was a legend, still on the same pedestal that her films and her reputation had placed her, and the Pecks were as awed as anyone else at the opportunity to meet her.

The now mature lady, her cheekbones still as firmly set as ever, giving a clear indication of her previous uncanny beauty, looked up into Greg's face and said, "Oh – we meet at last, so far from home." The beauty, the voice, the accent captivated Greg and, particularly, Veronique, as much as they would have enthralled people who knew nothing of the life of a film star.

People whom Gregory Peck was captivating at this time were the English racing fraternity. The Californian cattle rancher, and movie cowboy felt completely at home with these people whose mode of living hadn't really changed in half a century. They talked horseflesh every day of the year and were never happier than when dressed in tweeds.

If this ever looked like being the year of the Oscar, with any luck, Greg thought it could also be the year of the Grand National. The excitement of the world's most important steeplechase still fascinated him as no flat race in America ever had. Now he had bought a horse with the strange name of Owen's Sedge. He thought it might just allow him the prize of leading a winner into the owner's enclosure.

178

The betting began at 25 to 1. The horse was to start the race as joint favourite.

Greg was proud of his acquisition; it meant he could register his own racing colours – navy blue with white seams and a red and white quartered cap. He had only one worry: the calendar.

The big race was just two days before the Oscar ceremony. The coincidence of the two dates led the Pecks into a travel schedule that would not have been out of place in Jules Verne's *Around the World in Eighty Days*.

Greg was filming *Captain Newman M.D.* all week, but the notion of missing the race was unthinkable. The problem was that because he couldn't get away from the studio before Thursday, he was going to have little more than 24 hours in which to reach Liverpool.

An even bigger consideration was the weather – that notorious English climate which in April could involve anything from fog to snow and possibly both, and was likely to become worse the nearer to Liverpool they got. The forecasts all indicated that the travellers should expect the worst.

The idea of flying from London to the northern city was not practicable, so Greg had arranged for a limousine to meet them at Heathrow and then conduct them up the M1 motorway towards Lancashire. They arrived at the grand, stately Adelphi Hotel at one o'clock in the morning. But that was still time to join the ball, traditionally held on the eve of the National.

Having survived the trans-Atlantic flight from the West Coast (one of the most arduous of journeys) and the limousine trip across country without the benefit of sleep for two nights, the Pecks decided they might as well enjoy their suffering. They quickly changed into evening dress and joined the other owners and their trainers, and danced and quaffed enough champagne to dull the pain.

They collapsed into bed in what could only be described as the late early hours and no more than 120 minutes later were dressed in tweeds and raincoats for the equally traditional walk around the course. They could hardly see in front of their noses in the mist and the rain, but plainly they were enjoying every minute of their discomfort.

"Greg's Grey, the Housewives' Choice," the Press called Owen's Sedge. Greg had to be prepared to organize a winner's party that night if his horse came up to expectations in what was always the most unpredictable race on the English turf. Alternatively, if that did not happen, the Pecks had arranged a speedy exit for themselves so that there was no doubt that they could be at the Oscar ceremony on time.

It was a good thing that the Pecks had made alternative arrangements. Owen's Sedge, with Pat Taafe up, kept on to the end, taking all the fences, but without any exciting show of speed. He finished seventh and Greg and Veronique chartered a private plane to take them to London in time to meet the jet flight to Los Angeles.

The result was a disappointment. Women had rushed to put money on the nag simply because it was owned by their handsome hero. Greg's presence on the Aintree course, looking not the least bit the worse for the wear of the flight, did a great deal to raise the status of racing among Britain's female population.

A year later, Greg had more hopes for Owen's Sedge – even though the horse was now a venerable eleven years old. Other horses had walked into the winner's enclosure at that age before. In preparation for Aintree, the horse was put into a preliminary race at Kempton Park – and died on the course. It was a unique death in the history of racing. Owen's Sedge took a fence and landed in front, spread-eagled with his fore legs out in front and his back legs straight out behind, instead of bending them under him. His whole weight came down on his pelvis, cracking it and in the process, severing a main artery. He managed to get up and stagger on for a bit but then fell down and died in front of the shocked crowd.

Greg was saddened about losing an animal he had grown to love – but not one he ever knew really well. The horse had lived mostly in Ireland and he had rarely seen him at work either there or in England.

The loss, however, did not put him off racing. He had taken quite a stake in the turf industry in recent months, via his friend Frank More O'Ferrall. The previous September, he had bought May First – it was Cecilia's birthday – a yearling, for £3,150 whose sire had been the Queen's Pall Mall, which won the Two Thousand Guineas four years earlier. It was a present for Veronique. In February 1964, he bought another Irish racehorse which he hoped would win the Guineas for him, a two-year-old colt which he named The Pro.

He carried his enthusiasm over the Channel, too. At Deauville, however, his towering presence was not sufficient to get him into the weighing room, the haunt of trainers and the international set who think they know a few things about four-legged creatures.

"My name's Gregory Peck," he said at the entrance. "I am sorry, Monsieur," said the man at the door, "but I am afraid I cannot let you in."

"But I'm an English owner," Greg protested. "Ah, that is different, Monsieur," the attendant replied. "Of course you may enter."

Two years after the Owen's Sedge accident, Greg employed the Queen Mother's trainer, Peter Cazalet, and with his help bought a gelding named Different Class which he raced in the Nationals of 1967 and 1968. It came third in that first race but in 1968 it looked set to do better. The National was the one big race that had eluded Cazalet, and he was determined to do all he could to rectify that situation.

Greg and Veronique had flown in from Hollywood and had again stayed up all night, dancing and knocking back the champagne until it was time to walk the course.

For a while it seemed that this time the race was going well. Different Class was in second place when a hubbub among the crowd of Aintree racegoers showed that something was wrong. Far away down the course, lost in the fog, a pile-up had followed a jump that one horse had not taken as well as it should. Fourteen animals had fallen. Cazalet said as calmly as he could, "I think we're down. Yes, we're down."

Different Class survived but did not win. It did, however, come first in other races. But later it became sick and developed a bad liver, complicated by heart trouble. Eventually it had to be put down. Soon afterwards, Peter Cazalet himself died.

If his trainer had still been with him, Greg would probably have bought another horse or two and kept on trying to win the National – with the man whose dream of winning the grand prize he shared so completely. The race presented a marvellous challenge. No matter what the bookmakers said, the odds were always against *anyone* winning. It is a meeting that some animal lovers have tried to stop. They call it the cruellest race in the world – and it's true that forty-five horses that look as though they are re-enacting the Charge of the Light Brigade could all tumble into a single heap. But there is no sporting event more exciting for an owner who understands his business.

Without Cazalet to guide him, Greg decided that the best bet was to leave racing alone for a time.

Sixteen

The people who now believed that Greg would follow his *Mockingbird* triumph only with pictures of its high standards were to be proved wrong. The title of the film that followed told only part of its story. *How the West was Won* might have been more appropriately called *How Gregory Peck was Won*.

Looking back now all those years later at the cameo role of a gambler he played in that epic, he says quite bluntly, "I wish I hadn't done it. I was charmingly seduced into it by Irene Dunne."

Now that might sound strange to anyone who knows anything about that straight, conservative star of the Hollywood of forty-odd years ago. Seduction, on or off the screen, was distinctly not the bag of the lady who sang "Smoke Gets in Your Eyes" in *Roberta*, who played Queen Victoria in *The Mudlark* and who was the elegant schoolmistress in *Anna and the King of Siam*.

But it was her way of raising money for the Catholic sisters of St. John's Hospital at Santa Monica.

"Irene," Greg recalls, less than happily, "scampered around enlisting everyone into making the film at a nominal salary, and the nuns got ten per cent of the picture's profits."

The arrangement was that all the stars involved – Greg and John Wayne, Debbie Reynolds, Thelma Ritter, James Stewart and Karl Malden included, all took the same $5,000 a week. Greg signed on for one week's work and ended up doing three.

Now he says: "I wasn't particularly pleased with it – it was the best role that they could find for me but Irene had appealed to me as a Catholic and against my better judgement I agreed. I learned a lesson."

Ever since those three weeks, when he saw the Cinerama rushes for the first time, Greg has said that he only wished that he had himself paid to have the new wing of the hospital built. It would have been so much easier than making the film. In fact, he says, he'd have given "a little more besides" only to have been spared the agony of being associated with the project. "I thought the picture was predictable and corny. I didn't like working in Cinerama and artistically I think it fell short, even though it was a box office success." Certainly, it ran for years.

It was the time when the studios, desperately trying to recover audiences from television, thought that the only way to do so was by making bigger movies on wider screens. Hollywood had flirted with 3-D, abandoned it as unwieldy and gone out on a limb extolling the virtues of Cinemascope – which, it was happy to announce, audiences could see "without wearing special glasses". But it still wanted the screen to get bigger. The result was Cinerama – which attempted a wrap-round effect using three cameras shooting three different panels (which producers just had to hope could be joined together without too many people noticing). The result is that today Cinerama movies are shown on colour television – looking as though someone has been busy sewing up three different bits of film.

The joins that the audience did see were not the only problems. At one stage, Greg and Karl Malden were supposedly talking to each other. Greg was in the panel on the right. Malden was in the one on the left and in the middle panel, in-between, was a girl. But although the two men were the ones having the conversation, neither was allowed to look at the other – because in the finished film it would look as though they were talking to the girl. Instead, to chat to Karl Malden, Greg had to look at a tree and say: "I can see you've noticed the Apaches." When there was a close-up to do, something like 800 lb of machinery resembling a high-speed locomotive would interlope between them.

Recently Greg was asked by a well-known figure in the film business to take a cameo role in a picture that would help retarded children. Greg replied, "I'd rather write a cheque for the retarded children. How much do you want?"

The biggest disservice you can do Gregory Peck today is to tell him that *How the West was Won* is on television. "I practically break a leg," he told me, "getting to the T.V. set to shut it off before I come on the screen."

If *How the West was Won* was not the happiest memory of 1963, there was a greater, more personal sadness at the time. Greg's father, Gregory Peck Senior, the "Doc" who had been the bedrock of stability in his lonely childhood and who later had thrilled at his son's success, died. The passing of the elder Peck created a void that for his son was going to be impossible to fill. Gregory Peck senior's early working life had not been easy, but the memory he left was of a good sport who was as grand a source of company in his later years as he had been when he and his son embarked upon their expeditions to Catalina Island.

Happily, there were no remnants at all of the old distance between Greg and his stepmother Harriet and, if anything, they were to develop an even stronger relationship. His half-brother Donald, now an educational film maker, and he were always the best of friends and this bond, too, was to grow.

As far as Greg's work was concerned, he proceeded with the usual determination that every picture had to be regarded as the most important he had done to date – although he had not yet found the elusive second *Mockingbird*.

Captain Newman, M.D. in which Greg played an Air Force psychiatrist, has been described as a forerunner of the *MASH* movie and subsequent T.V. series. Once more it was the comedy about it that Greg particularly enjoys recalling.

He was also fascinated by Tony Curtis, who played his assistant, and who seems to have been perfectly cast ten years earlier as Houdini. Tony is to conjuring tricks what Gregory Peck has been to sex appeal. He had the rest of the cast bemused by his dexterity – and by the way he played the flute and could prepare an artistic-looking collage, seemingly, from nothing.

In recent times, Curtis has lowered his profile as the lovable con-man (the role he had in *Captain Newman* and which was practically duplicated six years later in the Cary Grant film *Operation Petticoat*) and turned to other things. He has knocked the Motion Picture Academy for never having the foresight to give him an Oscar, and more recently still has criticized the publishing industry – for not giving him the money he thought he was entitled to for his first book. Greg took him aside. "Tony," he said. "Stop knocking everything – Hollywood, the Academy. Now you're knocking the publishing world."

He replied, "I promise I'll never do it again."

There could have been a number of natural advantages to *Behold a Pale Horse* – a fascinating story about the Spanish Civil War and its aftermath, coupled with magnificent photography and a demonstration of acting, not only from Greg, but from Anthony Quinn, too. But the big political issues were skirted to the point of being ineffectual.

The result was that the picture was banned in Spain (and for a time threatened to be the cause of all films produced by Columbia Pictures being excluded from the country too). The public never really got to know what it was all about. It wasn't made clear that Greg – playing a man wanted by police in his own country which borders on the Basque sector of southern France – was a refugee from Spain after the Civil War and was marked for execution by General Franco. Franco's name wasn't mentioned.

Even the famous Guardia Civil was called the "federal police" and there were only vague suggestions about the lack of freedom in a country that one assumed to be Spain.

Greg himself now sees this lack of frankness to be the reason the movie never took off. But he admits it could all be hindsight on his part. Nevertheless, as he says, "You can't not take sides about the Spanish Civil War."

The screenplay seemed to straddle the one issue which was at the very nub of the picture. Peck is one of those American liberals of just the right generation to have felt strongly about the war and the Loyalist, anti-Franco cause. It was all going on during his college years and he had even toyed then with the idea of signing up for the Abraham Lincoln division of the International Brigade, which fought alongside the losing Government troops. But he decided to finish his education first. By the time he was ready to go to Spain, that rehearsal for World War Two was over and the main production was already under way in Poland.

After *Behold a Pale Horse*, there were a couple of film projects that never reached an audience. *The Martian Chronicles*, again with Mulligan and Pakula, could have been the *Star Wars* of 1966, but was abandoned when a satisfactory screenplay could not be found.

The Bells of Hell Go Ting-a-Ling-a-Ling got a lot further but was jettisoned after Greg and a whole film company had started work on location in Switzerland. The title came from a World War One song:

> "The bells of hell go ting-a-ling-a-ling
> For you but not for me.
> The angels they sing-a-ling-a-ling
> They hold the goods for me.
> O Death where is thy sting-a-ling-a-ling
> O Grave thy victory?
> The bells of hell go ting-a-ling-a-ling
> For you but not for me."

The picture was about World War One aircraft crews. Costumes were designed, made and fitted. Aircraft of 1917 vintage were adapted and, in some cases, manufactured specially for the film, and over 100 cowbells were included among the props.

Greg and the rest of the company were assembled in Switzerland ready for the off – but it never came. After 25 days of solid rain and three weeks of mist which obscured everything that needed to be photographed, the picture was abandoned.

It was going to be just too expensive to continue waiting for good weather. Even had the sun started to shine at the end of those six weeks, there would have just been no chance of finishing the movie before the mountains were covered in snow. That would have made nonsense of the whole thing. Switching locations – with all the equipment and props involved – wasn't worth the cost either. By the time the decision was made to abandon the whole operation, Greg and the rest of the cast had other jobs to go to.

Everyone was paid and the insurance company was called in to find the cash. Five years later, all the costumes and props – including the 100 cowbells – were duly sold. It was more of a tragedy for the unknown members of the cast – who thereby stayed unknowns – than it was for Gregory Peck.

There were, however, happier outcomes. One of them was called *Mirage*, which may not be one of the great milestones in the history of the cinema, but has a certain style about it which makes it pleasant viewing a decade and a half or so later. Greg is less pleased with it than is its present-day television audience who enjoy it greatly whenever it reappears. He himself says, "I forget what the hell it was all about."

Appropriately enough, perhaps in view of that fact, in *Mirage* Greg spends most of his time on screen suffering from amnesia – not remembering that he is really an important atomic scientist. Leif Erickson played a fascist business tycoon, and there was Walter Matthau as a detective. This was when Matthau had decided to try his hand at what he calls "retirement acting".

Greg had seen him in the theater and thought he could carry a strong, subsidiary role like the one in *Mirage*. He was paid $75,000 for the part. Now Peck says, "I think my main contribution to the film was that I hired Walter and virtually launched him on his screen career."

The film that followed was more in Greg's line and is equally well represented today on the T.V. screen. It began life as *Crisscross* and looked like ending up as *Cipher*. Greg wasn't sure that he liked either name.

In it, he played an American professor of ancient languages at Oxford, called on to translate a message written in hieroglyphics, which both the rulers of an Arab country and a team of plotters are anxious to get hold of. Sophia Loren was retained both to look beautiful and to play the mistress of the chief plotter, Alan Badel. Greg is caught up in the middle of the plot but for much of the time one really isn't sure whose side Sophia is on. This was plainly considered by the director Stanley Donen to be less important than the fact that she was on hand to stun in creations by Dior.

Greg accepted the role of David, the professor, but as usual he had reservations, which he put to Donen in a letter. "To start at the beginning, before I get down to specific scenes and lines, I would like to offer a general comment about David's character.

"I find that he is somewhat inconsistent in that he is sometimes intelligent, sometimes a bit slow. At times, he is active and imaginative and at times he is rather weak, and passive and tends to become, especially towards the end, something of a stooge for Yasmin (Sophia). I would like to see him characterized by more of a spirit of adventurousness and gusto . . .

"The second general point is that I would like to see all of his dialogue gone through and that he be given a consistently urbane style of speech."

Donen went through the screenplay and sent a revised version to Greg – who responded by telegram:

DEAR STANLEY: DELIGHTED WITH NEW PERSONAL-
ITY AND DIALOGUE ON MY CHARACTER THINK
OVER–ALL APPROACH IS VASTLY IMPROVED OUR PLAN
NOW SET TO ARRIVE SUNDAY THE ELEVENTH FOND
REGARDS

But he was also not sure about the title. *Cipher* – the current
proposal – somehow didn't sound quite right for the sort of film on
which he had set his mind. He suggested two alternatives. Stanley
Donen replied warmly to his interest:

VERY PLEASED WITH YOUR REACTION LIKE BOTH
TITLES PARTICULARLY ARABESQUE STOP HAVE REGIS-
TERED IT TO SEE IF AVAILABLE WARMEST REGARDS
DONEN

So *Cipher* became *Arabesque*. The meaning didn't matter very much,
it just sounded right – and was a nice play on the word Arab, which
was so important to the substance of the picture. It became a classic,
single word title in the *Charade* tradition. The film was not really an
arabesque dance any more than *Charade* was anything but a
well-scripted screenplay, also directed by Donen. It was as though the
film makers were searching for a word that really didn't have to come
from a dictionary. In many ways the picture had a lot in common with
the Cary Grant romps – perhaps particularly with his screwball
comedies of the 1930s.

As is often the case, the funniest parts of *Arabesque* were the ones the
public didn't see. One of the most hilarious was when Greg and
Sophia had to get into a shower together, he fully clothed, she
completely naked.

Now Greg is not known as a perfect gentleman around Hollywood
and, apart from the time when she had presented him with his
Oscar, he hardly knew Sophia at all. He decided that the gallant
thing to do was to try to put the beautiful Italian-born lady at her
ease.

The scene came when Greg was hiding from Sophia's lover in her
bedroom. All he could do to save himself was to join her as she
sponged herself in the shower and lost the soap.

"Don't be embarrassed," Greg told her as they got ready to do the
scene. "It's all in the game. Strictly professional."

She fluttered her long eyelashes and looked him straight in the eye – and laughed. "Who's embarrassed?" she giggled as she slipped out of her robe. "What makes you think I would be embarrassed?"

"Absolutely nothing at all," said Greg. Later in the film, the manly Mr. Peck has to try to drag the poor and so feminine Miss Loren away from a murderous threshing machine in an English cornfield. The Arab plotters, having established whose side Sophia is on, are trying to kill both of them as they crawl through five-feet-high corn, desperately trying to avoid the rampaging machine.

The trouble arose because ever since he fell off that horse, Greg's ankle had never allowed him to do more than pace his way through situations in which other men would calmly run. Even with his ankle strapped up as it was, the cornfield race for life was not an easy way for him to earn a living.

He was supposed to be dragging Sophia along. But as he stumbled, she ran – like a thoroughbred at elegant full gallop in the final stretch of the Derby. Every time she nosed her way in front of Greg, Donen had to call: "Cut," and they had to start again.

For Greg, a mere trot could be untold agony, but because of Sophia he was having to go through traumas he had not even imagined when he first approved the script. Finally, he told her: "Sophia, will you PLEASE slow down? Remember – I'm supposed to be rescuing *you*."

She threw back her beautiful head and giggled her musical laugh again. "You'll have to run a great deal faster than that if you want to rescue me!" Plainly, strong measures were now being called for. He pulled his leading lady back while the director tried to get her to slow down. "Make HIM run faster," she demanded.

"I *can't* run faster," he protested desperately.

"Well, TRY," she ordered. In the end, she had to co-operate or there would have been no picture.

But a picture there was, and one that got excellent notices, to say nothing of the box office that suitably reflected them.

Seventeen

His fiftieth birthday was on the horizon – which is a time for thought for any man. For Gregory Peck it wasn't yet the moment to consider retiring, but it was the right time to think about breaking off from the hurdy-gurdy existence of following one movie with another simply because that was his job. Now, before he went on to a studio soundstage again, he wanted to be sure that the script would be just right.

There was another reason: Greg wanted to devote his time to cancer research, the disease which all those years before had killed his grandmother and of which Harriet, his stepmother, was now a victim.

A few years before, he had watched Humphrey Bogart waste away in its last throes. They had always enjoyed their sessions together, frequently with Greg taking the brunt of Bogey's wit. When he discovered that Peck was a Catholic, Bogart turned his face towards him and pointing his finger, rasped: "What is this Immaculate Conception thing? Explain that, will you?"

When Greg last met Bogey, it was just three days before his death. The 85 lb shell of the man who had epitomized the screen tough guy looked dreadful, but he still liked to joke and hear anecdotes.

Greg told a story that he thought would amuse him. It was a long joke, which he tried to cut and edit as it went along. But it was still long. As he manfully worked towards the climax, Bogey butted in. "Greg," he said, "If you don't get to the end of this soon, I won't be around for the punch line."

Greg talked about Bogey when he became Chairman of the American Cancer Society.

"He died gallantly but we would rather have him around living and performing," Greg said in his inaugural speech. "Bogart, Cooper, Charles Laughton, Thomas Mitchell and recently the great Buster Keaton," he declared, "were all victims of cancer." The aim of the society was "by raising funds for cancer research, to be helping to educate the public of the importance of early detection . . . to keep our friends around a little longer. At least some of my friends – and yours – might have been saved."

Other show business personalities who lending their names to good causes are happy – and indeed inwardly content – merely to be listed on the notepaper and to make occasional speeches. Greg embarked on his presidency as though he had just been handed a new screenplay and was bringing in his own company of director and actors to run through it.

He met cancer specialists and asked them for all the information they could provide on the killer illness. He went into cancer wards and spoke to patients. He even donned a green surgical mask and gown and watched tumours and tissues being removed on the operating table.

During his year of office, women's groups were on top of the list of organizations he addressed. The women went along to see Gregory Peck and ended up either signing cheques for cancer research or working for the cause; sometimes both. In the course of Greg's term of office, fifty million dollars were raised.

For the Cancer Society, Greg introduced and narrated a 30-minute colour and sound film in which his co-stars were some of America's top cancer experts. The film was entitled *Investment in Life*.

Greg's 50th birthday in April 1966, was spent on the nearest thing to a flying whistle-stop tour, speaking about cancer once again. He had breakfast with 1200 people in Atlanta, Georgia, lunch with another 600 in New Orleans, and dinner at Houston, Texas, for 1000.

The climax of his year of office was a massive dinner at the Waldorf Astoria in New York.

Greg flew with Veronique to the Philippines when he heard that they wanted to start a society in that country similar to the one in the States. That didn't give him quite the same sense of satisfaction. The islands' *crème-de-la-crème* had been invited and it turned out that they were much more concerned with the social aspects of the function than they were with raising money for cancer research. He made a great plea for them to establish a Philippines Cancer Society, build a special clinic and provide free examinations but he never heard that they did any of those things.

Peck felt no desire to emulate the words of General MacArthur at the same location: "I shall return." "I didn't get too much of a sense of humanitarian concern out there," he says now.

That sense of concern was, however, the impression he had from the doctor who was treating his stepmother. Her pain was so acute that when Greg visited her hospital room the similarity between her fight and the dying days of his grandmother was startling. The climax came when Greg called to see her, together with Donald and his wife. The doctors advised that they should go in one at a time.

Harriet held Greg's hand, and – sure that they were alone – asked him with a pleading look in her eyes: "You've got to get them to let me die. I'm so sick."

From the pinched look on her face, there was no doubt that she was. This was one request she felt she could never have made to her own son.

"I'll try," Greg assured her. A young doctor walked through the door as Greg was leaving and proceeded to connect Harriet to a succession of tubes and bottles.

He was amazed that a woman going through so much torment should be subjected to these additional stresses and indignities.

"What are you doing?" he asked softly. The doctor didn't reply directly. All he said was, "She's going to feel better soon."

It was not a matter Greg wanted to leave. He immediately went to see Harriet's own doctor, a man whose reputation was recognized in every hospital in the country, "You've got to let her die," he said earnestly. "She doesn't want to live. She can't go through any more."

An hour and a half later, the doctor phoned Greg and the rest of the family. "She's gone," he told them.

There were other causes which were less painful for Greg to take under his expansive wings – like getting public money spent on fostering the arts both in California and nationally.

In 1965, he was present at the White House for the signing by President Lyndon B. Johnson of the Arts and Humanities Act. Greg was a charter member of the National Arts Council and one of his first campaigns was to help strengthen the regional theater movement in the United States. With Veronique, Greg went on a scouting expedition, visiting theaters in 26 cities. As a result of this, he wrote a report recommending that federal money should be allocated to 16 of these theaters. Among them were the Long Wharf Theater in Hartford, Connecticut, the A.C.T. then in Pittsburg (it is now permanently located in San Francisco), the Arena Stage in Washington and the Boston Theater Company. It was to be the first time in American history that Government money was used to subsidize the arts.

While Greg was studying the regional theater, John Steinbeck was advising on grants to promising writers; Leonard Bernstein and Isaac Stern were doing the same sort of thing for America's orchestras and Agnes De Mille and Oliver Smith were seeking out the most deserving ballet companies.

Jerome Robbins took a year off his Broadway work to run the Lyric Theater, whose aim was to combine experimental dancing, music and acting under the same roof with a $300,000 grant.

Through Isaac Stern, a German-born craftsman was able to get a $4,000 grant that enabled him to train an apprentice to make special rosin for violinists' bows. The man had learned the art in the country of his birth and without a successor the secret of the rosin would die with him. The committee haggled for an hour over the rosin grant but it was finally approved. As Greg said: "It's very hard to out-talk Isaac Stern! We got pretty heated at those meetings. I remember John Steinbeck at that session growling in tune with the white bulldog that was sitting between his feet.

"'What the hell are we wasting all that money on violin strings for?' he thundered. But it was $4,000 out of just $4 million total for all of the arts in all of the states. Thirteen years later, it's gone up to $200 million."

For three years, Greg was passionately involved in setting up the American Film Institute. Once it was agreed that it should be inaugurated and an initial grant obtained from the Arts Council, Greg personally worked at establishing it.

He and fellow Council members studied ways of, among other things, classifying films and setting up an archive; of promoting grants for non-commercial films to be made by young directors; setting up publications and of developing a cinematheque in connection with the Kennedy Center in Washington, and of cataloging the

American Library of Classic Film, together with the Library of Congress.

All the travelling involved in the work was at Greg's own expense. And that was possibly what tickled L.B.J. most – and began a friendship that lasted until the President's death in retirement in Texas. Johnson was surprised that anyone would want to draw on his own resources. But when he saw Greg's commitment, he decided to back it to the hilt.

L.B.J. was much more sophisticated than his occasional image as a coarse-talking, ill-mannered politician might suggest. He knew, however, how to play the cowboy like a master actor.

It was his professional actor friend Gregory Peck who seemed the obvious choice to narrate *A President's Country*, a 28-minute documentary about Texas – which also turned into something of a biographical work.

The role fitted Greg well. Only a month or so earlier, the public had enjoyed one of his best screen performances – although it was only his voice that any one heard. He narrated *Years of Lightning, Day of Drums* – about the Kennedy "Camelot" years. Greg had done that two years earlier on behalf of the U.S. Information Agency abroad, for no fee at all. Now it was shown at home for the first time. It took Congressional approval to get the film released for American audiences.

Time magazine was cynical about the clamour to see a film that had had its virtues extrolled in "terms usually reserved for such timeless Americana as the Gettysburg Address". Said the magazine: "It is largely for the movie goer who measures the magnitude of an experience by the size of the lump in his throat."

But the words – written by Bruce Herschenson – *were* stirring: "No man could take away the years of lightning with a single day of drums."

It dealt with the Peace Corps, the Civil Rights movement, space projects and J.F.K. saying "Ich bin ein Berliner". Yet, said the magazine: "It is a legend for export, smoothly put together, fiercely partisan and as heedless of history as a love letter written in sand."

Despite that exhibition of cynicism, there's no doubt that Greg felt the film's message deeply. In June 1968 he took Anthony and Cecilia to an 8 a.m. memorial mass for Bobby Kennedy, who a month before had watched Greg at work on location in Arizona. Greg himself later appeared in a concert on behalf of Bobby's Mental Retardation Fund.

He had been working for Bobby, just as he had for his brother Jack and for Johnson and earlier still for Adlai Stevenson. When he thinks about Stevenson, his eyes glint even now. "Ah, he was my idol. He should have been President for eight years instead of Eisenhower. Then, in my opinion, we'd have had a different world today."

The assassination of Martin Luther King also affected Greg deeply. It happened on the day he was to have hosted his first Oscar ceremony as President of the Academy of Motion Picture Arts and Sciences, known to newspaper readers as the Motion Picture Academy and to those in the trade simply as "the Academy". The ceremony was postponed for two days.

Postponement, he said, speaking from the rostrum, was "the only appropriate gesture of respect".

He had never met King but, he said; "What Dr. King would like to have happened is for the whites of this country to grasp the concept that we need the talents, energies and pent-up imaginations of our minority group artists – perhaps even more than they need us. Call it enlightened self-interest, but I feel this country will never be whole until we have achieved total and full equality of opportunity for everyone. Films," said the Academy President, "should celebrate the dignity of man, regardless of race, creed or colour."

That was the evening Greg won his second Oscar – the Jean Hersholt Humanitarian Award. It was given to him as an actor who "lends great dignity and prestige to the movie colony", declared Vernon Scott in the *Los Angeles Herald-Examiner* – a sentiment echoed by most of the country's press at the time.

It was not his only award from his peers – always the most valued ones. The Screen Actors' Award, presented by the Screen Actors' Guild, was given to him "for his outstanding achievement in fostering the finest ideals in the acting profession".

Greg joined with Charlton Heston, Hugh O'Brien and Kirk Douglas – "four gun-slinging movie stars" said one reporter – in urging Americans to have the sale of guns curbed by law. "In the name of humanity, conscience and the common safety of us all," they asked people to contact their senators and congressmen to outlaw mail-order gun sales. Greg told reporters: "The public should send millions of telegrams to demand that kind of legislation to overwhelm the gun lobby – they called out thousands of telegrams that scared Congress off last time. *We* must not be passive."

It was this kind of stand taken on issues of public importance that helped endear Greg to President Johnson.

Every time he walked into the White House, bored and blasé girl typists and secretaries who never turned a hair when the heads of state came to call, crowded around the corridors to watch their hero Gregory Peck being sped on his way to the Oval Office.

The bond between Peck and Johnson was so strong that it swept up Veronique and Lady Bird, too. The couple would enjoy weekends at the Johnsons' Texas ranch as well as intimate parties and gala dinners at the White House.

One evening late in 1968, they were determined to attend a farewell party for the Johnsons given by a group of New York society women at the Plaza Hotel. Greg was seated at the Presidential table, Veronique at another hostessed by Linda Robb, the President's daughter. Sitting next to Veronique was Charles Revson, head of the Revlon cosmetics empire. He took the opportunity to warn his companion that he would not be asking her to dance – a rule that he and his wife had was that they only danced with each other. Veronique was not noticeably shattered by the revelation.

No sooner had Revson finished his sentence than President Johnson appeared at their table – and spoke to Veronique. "Would you care to dance?" he asked. It was, she now says, almost poetic justice.

As they danced, the massive L.B.J. bulk towered over her. But they did manage to talk. "You know, Veronique," he said. "We both have something in common."

"I'm honoured, Mr. President," she replied, "to know that I have something in common with you. What is it?"

"That we both love Gregory," he replied, and then he added; "If I had decided to run for another term, I was going to offer him the post of Ambassador to Ireland."

He then told her of the consolation prize that he was able to offer. He revealed for the first time that he was giving Greg the Medal of Freedom, the highest civilian award in the country.

The ceremony at which the medal was presented was one of the last the President held during his term of office. The medal citation read:

To Gregory Peck – an artist who has brought new dignity to the acting profession. Gregory Peck has enriched the lives of millions. He has given his energies, his talents and his devotion to causes which have improved the lives of people. He is a humanitarian to whom Americans are deeply indebted.
Lyndon B. Johnson
White House
Washington DC
January 20, 1969.

Greg's favorite story about his friend is this: "While visiting L.B.J. at the Texas ranch after his retirement, I said to him one day, 'You know, Mr. President, you will be remembered as the President who put through the Arts and Humanities legislation, the first federal aid to the arts and artists in American history. Wouldn't it be great if the American Shakespeare were to emerge from one of the new federally backed theaters?' L.B.J. considered it, grinned, and always the politician and champion of civil rights, drawled, 'Do you know what would be even greater? If the American Shakespeare turns out to be a black man'."

Inevitably, people talked about Greg now running for elective office. In 1966, together with Gene Kelly and Burt Lancaster, he did a T.V. spot for the Democrats, with Ronald Reagan as their main target. Each said that they would be happy playing a Governor in a movie, but that didn't mean that they thought they would be any good in the real job.

But others thought that Greg might do very well at it indeed. Reagan's predecessor as Governor, Pat Brown, suggested that he might like to aim as far as the White House – although he should start as a senator first. "I'm not recommending him, but perhaps we should go to Gregory Peck," he said at the time.

Greg wouldn't entertain the idea seriously at all. For a time, newspapers thought they detected a spark of interest. "I am far from indifferent to the idea of public service," he said. "Like many men of my age who have enjoyed some success, I am interested in being of service in as many ways as I can in helping solve public problems."

The rest of his statement – that he wasn't going to run for any political office – was conveniently not quoted. But when he accepted the Academy Presidency in June 1967, he declared firmly, "I don't believe in amateur politics. I respect my own profession and that of politics. I can only repeat what I've said on previous occasions when political figures or columnists had thrown my name in the ring – that I'll never run for public office. No one could persuade me to change my mind. I hope to make more films, good ones. That is my profession."

Some people took it as the "protesting-too-much" cry of a man waiting to be railroaded into accepting the acclaim of his public. But he really was not interested in facing an electorate. Yet the following year, it was his name that was being bandied about as a possible Democratic candidate for Mayor of Los Angeles.

Greg remained true to his word and didn't do a thing about running. Recently, he told me, "I like to tell stories, and create characters and entertain. I don't want to manipulate anybody or persuade anybody to my way of thinking or make them behave the way I think they ought to behave. I've never had the slightest inclination for that. As a matter of fact, if anything, I tend to back away from it. I haven't the slightest desire for power."

In fact, in 1967 he was much more interested in his son Steve, who had just been commissioned as a lieutenant in the Marine Corps. On his 21st birthday, Greg sent him a telegram which put his attitude very clearly indeed:

DEAR STEVE: WE ALL SEND CONGRATULATIONS AND A GREAT DEAL OF LOVE AND AFFECTION ON THE OCCASION OF YOUR TWENTY FIRST BIRTHDAY. YOUR FATHER IS BRAGGING AS USUAL THIS TIME ABOUT YOUR SUCCESS IN THE MARINE CORPS PROGRAM

Steve went on to serve with a combat division in Vietnam, a very difficult year indeed for his family.

Looking back at that time now, Greg says, "Despite my later opposition to the war, I was very proud of what he did in Vietnam."

He jokes that there was a "regular air-lift" of goodies from California, but the things Steve most appreciated were the crates of paperback editions of the classics like the works of Dostoevsky, Tolstoy, Shakespeare, Conrad and Balzac that "seemed to relieve the terror and monotony of life in the combat zone".

One of the reasons why Greg was so opposed to the idea of

running for office was that he was inwardly afraid he might be used as a mouthpiece or a front man – in the same way as he occasionally agrees to front a charity function and read a speech written by someone else. He is not over keen on that role, either.

That was why he took his work for the Academy and Film Institute so seriously. If he were to have to do work for them on any kind of regular basis, it was going to be his words that he would recite, based on his own individual research.

Greg was one of the few actors to become President of the Academy and certainly was of the most controversial holders of that office.

He put into operation a massive weeding-out exercise. To protect the integrity of the Academy Awards, agents, P.R. people (except those directly involved in film making) and others on the mere periphery of the business were transferred to an associate non-voting branch.

Greg also worked to discourage the excessive advertising by studios that went on at Award time.

Simultaneously, he initiated a scheme whereby grants were made to the A.F.I., to provide "internships" for young film makers to work side by side with established directors. The idea was to confirm the role of the Academy as above all an educational and cultural organization within the film industry, and not merely the helpful P.R. tool which Oscar-winning studios might have liked it to become.

Greg kept saying, "We are not the studios. The Academy is not synonymous with the industry. The studios may cash in on our awards, but that is not why we are here."

Greg's still unfulfilled dream is that the Award will one day be presented during a "family" banquet, instead of as part of a huge T.V. spectacular. But, he says, realistically, "That's the compromise we've had to make. The Awards evening on TV pays for all our work and keeps us firmly out of studio control. We couldn't begin to do that on the tiny amounts that come in from membership dues."

Greg is also active as a board member of the Motion Picture and Television Relief Fund. Their Country House and Hospital in Woodland Hills provides veteran performers with health care and a comfortable retirement living in a beautiful collection of bungalows in a superb landscape setting.

Another of his interests has been the Inner City Cultural Center. The idea was that a center would be established for the performing arts, the first one located in the heart of a minority community. Partly as a result of his work, there now is a building where dance, theater and other artistic activity for the black community is organized almost daily.

Greg put $100,000 of his own money into Inner City and Veronique organized an early benefit which brought in another $55,000. Months of hard work went into the theater and he gave instructions to the adminstrators to send him all the press cuttings of their work so that he could follow it even when he was away on location.

He gave the fee he received for his first major television program to the Watts Center. This was called The Africa Project, a four hour program which took over the whole C.B.S. network from seven to eleven one evening.

For months, camera teams had been out in Africa filming people, landscapes and wild animals. When the filming was complete, Greg "fronted" the show by doing a commentary on the whole work, sitting mainly in front of a map of Africa.

He hadn't done much television before that – apart from odd appearances on the Sunday evening Ed Sullivan Show, in which he would recite a poem or a speech from a film, mainly as a foretaste of the picture he was about to plug. He has strenuously avoided making T.V. plays. He would rather put his efforts into a movie.

One at the back of his mind for years is a new look at Abraham Lincoln. Lincoln has been a sort of hobby for Greg. He has read almost all the available material on the President and knows his biographical details inside out, yet the actor who has been described as "Lincolnesque" by so many critics has not yet found an opportunity to play him on the screen.

Greg says, "Even more than the chance to play Lincoln as President, I would dearly love to be part of a definitive film on the American Civil War, the most dramatic event in our history. We are what we are today because of the Civil War. It is in our blood, whether we know it or not. It should be an epic film, the American *War and Peace*, complete with full-scale battles. That would be a film to remember – and be remembered by."

*   *   *

Plainly, the late 1960s were not the period of retirement that the film gossip writers were predicting, although Greg and Veronique and their children were now taking full advantage of the Cap Ferrat villa.

As he explained at the time: "I've been a good boy and worked hard for years. Now we have a place where I can relax and walk around shirtless in the village without anyone taking any notice."

He also used his time away from the film studios and location sites to go back to his roots – in Ireland. There, as in France, he was once again the family man, the one who enjoys an easy, lazy joke, rather than the sophisticated film star.

In County Kerry, at a small farm as green as on any Irish travel poster, he visited the Ashe family, cousins of his father and paternal grandmother, and the family with whom Gregory Peck Senior had lived during his childhood. His father's cousin Thomas Ashe was still alive but the farm was run by Ashe's son-in-law, Tom Curran and his wife.

They were no-nonsense people who didn't believe that being a film star necessarily made a man important.

After his initial welcome, Tom Curran looked at his tall cousin and asked: "Would you be after saying hello to Himself?"

Greg looked around. Himself, he took to be the cousin's father-in-law, but no one else was in sight. The problem, however was soon solved. Solemnly, he was escorted up the rickety staircase to a bedroom where, lying on his back like a corpse, was Himself. The old man was wearing a pair of homespun woollen trousers, carpet slippers and, although indoors, a cloth cap pulled down tightly over his head.

"Dad," said Tom, "it's Gregory Peck's come to see you."

The old man turned one suspicious eye in Greg's direction. "The hell you say," he muttered and closed the eye again. The only Gregory Peck he knew of was the one he had played with as a boy in the 1880s. This man was taller than his cousin, and a stranger.

"No, Dad," said the younger man, "it's the fillum star come all the way from Hollywood to see you."

The old man was totally unimpressed. "The hell you say," he repeated. "Go away." Finally, he was informed by his son-in-law that he was being somewhat ungracious. The relationship between his cousin and the younger man he had just met was laboriously explained to him.

Eventually, the old man got up, came downstairs and drank a glass of Irish whiskey which he followed with a cup of tea – all the time drifting in and out of the past. One moment, he knew exactly who it was to whom he was talking; the next, he was being transported 70 years or more to a different world and was convinced that he was talking to his old pal, the original and, as far as he was concerned, the real and only Gregory Peck. He recalled the severed half finger that Greg's father had left on the roadway when the cart's iron wheel ran over it.

From the farm, the Pecks went to Dingle and met more cousins. At the local church, the rector showed Greg the parish records – including the one recording the birth of his grandmother, Catherine Ashe, in 1864.

On the Sunday, Greg went to Mass there. It was one of the eeriest experiences of his life, since everyone there seemed to look either like his father or his grandmother – all dark-haired with the same cleft chin.

Greg had always treasured the family folk tales about being Black Irish, descendants he believed of the Spanish Armada survivors who settled in Southern Ireland. Once, however, Greg discussed this ancestry with Spyros Skouras at Twentieth Century Fox. "That story about the Armada is nonsense," said the mogul. "We (the Greeks) were there 2,000 years ago. That's where the Black Irish come from. Where do you think you got your name of Gregory?"

As he sat in the church with members of his family – many of whom were called Gregory, too – he thought about that.

He also had to remember that he was Gregory Peck, the fillum star. And soon, for the first time in three years, audiences were to get proof of the fact again.

Eighteen

If his main reason now for staying away from the studios was more that he wanted the perfect story than that he needed time for other things, then *The Stalking Moon* turned out to be worth waiting for. Greg had an instinct for a story and this time it was an instinct that paid off.

Several writers described the story about an Army scout who, after rounding up a group of dangerous Apaches, takes a white woman and her half-Indian son to safety in New Mexico as "the first Gothic Western". Greg liked that.

Certainly it had little to do with the traditional cowboys and Indians formula or with Indians being persecuted by the Cavalry. The Indian who stalked Peck and the white woman (Eva Marie Saint) was her husband, who made no bones about being a vicious murderer, anxious to add another scalp to his impressive collection.

The fact that Greg got on so well with the director/producer team of Mulligan and Pakula helped a great deal. Neither of them had made a Western before, but they brought to *The Stalking Moon* a number of the ingredients that had contributed to the success of *Mockingbird*, in particular, a deep sensitivity.

In a way Greg was once more the character he had been in *The Gunfighter*, rough-hewn but wanting to shake off the life of violence he had always lived, yet who finds he has no alternative but to use his fists and his gun again to save the woman.

The critics were enthusiastic. Page Cook said in *Films in Review*, "The role of the retiring Army scout is ideal for Gregory Peck; whose ability to project moral strength plus compassion is one of the most inspiring things today's screen affords."

The film was produced by Greg's own company and released by

National General, the firm that took over Twentieth Century Fox's theater chain when studios were compelled by law to bow out of the cinema circuits. (Although film makers couldn't own theaters, there was no legal impediment to theater chains making movies, with the result that National General went into the movie business and produced 16 features. All except *The Stalking Moon* lost money. Even the Peck film was only to turn in a profit after re-release and when T.V. rights were sold overseas.)

As usual Veronique and the children went on location with the head of the family, this time renting T.V. host Johnny Carson's house in Las Vegas. When they first moved to the gambling city, Greg and Veronique toured the hotels, played the green baize tables a little and tried not to notice the absence of clocks. They saw every show on The Strip – sometimes two a night. But the first thing to know about Vegas is that you can do that sort of thing only for about three or four days at the most, until the pressures to return to normal sanity get too great.

After the first week, they hardly knew who was appearing on which stage, and didn't bother to find out. Their home in the desert was where Greg went after work and where they had quiet dinners together.

This wasn't quite the boring time that the period in making a Western frequently is. Once, in a tiny Colorado town, the Pecks had spent six weeks with only a motel, a market, a gas station and a barber's shop to indicate they were close to what passed for civilization. At least, this time, there was life, a horrendous artificial life that has often been described as a nightmare, in Las Vegas.

It has been an oft repeated story for them – staying at a small motel; Veronique doing the shopping and cooking, whipping up a *boeuf bourguignonne* and a salad that succeeds in being more than just a mass of lettuce and tomatoes, in time for Greg's return. Once the grime of the day's shooting has been washed off, they sit and talk, watch television and go over the lines of the next day's shooting.

MacKenna's Gold was one of those Westerns that is better remembered for the difficult working conditions surrounding it than for the final product. Greg took a part that had already been rejected by Steve McQueen and to which he himself had said "No" as soon as he was shown the script.

Carl Foreman then ran through a virtual casting directory of

Western stars who had all given him the thumbs-down. Greg says he eventually did it out of gratitude for *The Guns of Navarone* and didn't want the creator of that movie to find himself without a leading player. Foreman was also generous in agreeing to script changes.

One of the compensations of the movie was working with Edward G. Robinson – who in a comparatively small role played the blind man who tells of lost gold. Raymond Massey, Eli Wallach, Omar Sharif and Keenan Wynn were in it too.

The trouble was that the product didn't justify the casting. "I'm always put off by the so-called all-star cast," says Greg today. "I can smell a rat. They aim to buy their way into public favour by overpaying stars and featuring important players in small roles." In this case, the rats came to sink the ship.

But not all the off-duty moments were uncomfortable ones. Edward G. Robinson was a man of culture and great intelligence, two factors that endeared him to Greg. "Oh," he says, "he was a darling, funny, warm, actorish, a bit theatrical – relatively guileless, a bit like a grown-up child."

Together, they talked religion, politics and art, the last subject one on which Robinson could talk as though he had wielded a paint-brush for as long as he had been able to walk. He had a collection that was internationally envied and a knowledge that showed he deserved it.

Inevitably, as art collectors do, he would survey the paintings of other people like a trainer contemplating a thoroughbred. In Greg's bar, he spotted a Picasso etching of a satyr climbing through a window, a naked sleeping beauty in the foreground. When Eddie Robinson saw the print, he fell in love with it. "That's Picasso, all right!" he exclaimed gleefully. "That's Picasso, he's got the balls!"

It turned the conversation to the art of Picasso and his contemporaries. Lovingly, Robinson told of visiting the home of Matisse near Nice and seeing on top of a pile of drawings, one of a vase of flowers constructed out of a maximum of 12 lines. It was glowing with life. "You know, Greg," he said. "It's the same with acting. You throw everything that isn't necessary away and just give them what is essential."

Actors love to tell tales about others in their business and Greg is no exception. One of his favourite stories is about the time a State Governor and his family were visiting a Warner Brothers film set and heard Eddie Robinson deliver a complicated three-page speech. He was letter perfect on the first rehearsal.

The Governor was impressed – until Raoul Walsh, who was directing, called out: "All right, fellers. Let's shoot it before he forgets it!" Robinson stormed off the set, muttering, "One-eyed son of a bitch!"

There were four Gregory Peck films released in 1969, and he kept to the success ratio that Gary Cooper had commended. Two succeeded and two failed. *The Chairman* – called in England, where it was made, *The Most Dangerous Man in the World* – came fairly near to *The Stalking Moon* in almost working out the way it had been planned. Greg likes it simply because it appears in his catalogue of "light" films – a fantasy that was never any more likely to be realized than was *The Guns of Navarone*.

And it was *Navarone* director Lee Thompson standing behind the camera once more for this story of a Nobel scientist who takes with him to Peking a secret bugging device hidden in his skull – not realizing that one switch flicked on a computer terminal could turn it into an exploding bomb.

There were some hair-raising moments during filming, too. Lee Thompson wanted to be able to study Greg's facial expression as the actor leaped from the roof of one building to another. That ruled out using a stunt man. It wasn't difficult as stunts go, but had Greg missed a footing – he wore specially adapted rubber-soled shoes – he would have faced a 30-ft drop without the aid of a net.

The scene was due to be shot in the early hours of the morning but he was on call from the previous evening. He had to do a short dialogue scene and then wait in his caravan for make-up, costume and any last-minute negotiations in which he might be involved.

That was when a cousin and his family turned up at the studios, all Irish members of the Ashe clan whom Greg had not met before.

There is only one way to be hospitable to a visiting Irishman – and that is with the help of a drop of the hard stuff.

The cousin came with his wife and two daughters. By the time three o'clock in the morning arrived, the Irishman was under the table and Greg was feeling very happy indeed, convinced he was entirely in control of his senses. Between the two of them, they had killed a bottle and a half of Scotch.

It was when the cousins finally departed that Greg was called to the set to perform his daring leap. He had never felt more ready for anything in his life. Proud of himself at beating an Irishman at his national sport, he was now ready to fly from one building to the other as though equipped with the wings of Superman.

As Greg toddled up the tiles, Lee Thompson decided that the time had come to try to talk his valuable star out of jumping. He said he could move the camera back a bit and use a double.

"No," insisted Greg, "I'll do it myself." Supremely confident, 53-year-old Gregory Peck made the great leap forward. He leapt and succeeded.

"Cut, print," said the relieved director. "That's all for tonight, boys."

Marooned, the last Peck film of the sixties, Greg remembers less affectionately than I do personally. It's a picture that again constantly gets aired on television – one in which Greg plays a space scientist heavily involved in an American astronaut adventure that goes wrong: the men are stranded in space until rescued by a team of Russian spacemen.

Peck feels that the jargon and technicalities got in the way of the entertainment. "I've found that technical types, engineers and people who have to have total control don't make interesting parts. You can't show the inner emotion that the man feels because he has to be supremely efficient." He swears it will be the last picture in which he has little more to do than push buttons and give instructions.

No, Gregory Peck is a man who likes to get involved in every aspect of things once an initial interest is shown. When in 1971 he became Chairman of the Motion Picture and Television Relief Fund, his main concern was to keep the old actors' home going. There was a need for an immediate blood transfusion to the tune of half-a-million dollars – not the sort of figure any one person could be expected to underwrite simply by signing a cheque.

Early one morning, he nudged Veronique from her sleep. "I've just had this idea," he said, excited if still sleepy. "I see the greatest benefit ever produced in this city – or anywhere else in the world. I have a vision of what I want to do – I see a great gala taking place at the Music Center."

The Music Center is, in effect, also the show biz center of the show biz town of Los Angeles – two huge theaters (the Dorothy Chandler Pavilion and the Ahmanson Theater), as well as a smaller third theater. Greg's idea was to have the maximum coverage for his benefit – using both big theaters simultaneously, with talent that was seen to match it.

Greg personally did all of the organizing and lined up a team that represented the cream of show business. No one said no, although Barbra Streisand needed a certain amount of persuasion – personal appearances at big events bring out the shy side of her nature.

In a matter of months, it happened. Jack Benny, James Stewart, Mitzi Gaynor, Pearl Bailey, Jack Lemmon, David Niven, The Fifth Dimension, David Frost, Natalie Wood, Rosalind Russell and Barbra Streisand were on stage. So was Grace Kelly, who flew in from Monte Carlo for the evening in time to be introduced by Cary Grant. And there was the man who was now Greg's very close friend, Frank Sinatra, with the Nelson Riddle and David Rose Orchestras.

It turned out to be an important evening in the Sinatra story. The people who paid about $250 a head heard him sing a repertoire ranging from "Nancy with the Laughing Face" to "My Way" and were told it was going to be the last time they'd ever hear him sing to them live. Sinatra was going into retirement – which, it turned out, lasted about two years. But the fact that people thought it was going to be the last live Sinatra appearance boosted the sales for the black-tie event enormously.

Twenty minutes after the show opened at the Pavilion, the first artistes were repeating their performances before another capacity crowd at the Ahmanson, and so it went on till the early hours of the next morning. After each spectacular turn, the audience were unable to believe it could possibly be followed, let alone topped. Yet the acts kept coming. There had never been a night like it. A night that raised all of $850,000 – an amount that was pronounced unbelievable.

People say that it is difficult to say no to any request from the Greg Pecks. On the other hand, it is difficult for Greg and Veronique to turn down invitations to the dozens of benefit evenings they are requested to attend in Los Angeles. It was at one of these, for the American Film Institute, that Greg had his only face-to-face encounter with President Nixon. It was in 1973, just as the Watergate crisis was reaching boiling point. Greg and Veronique were in a line of celebrities being presented to the President before dinner.

Two or three people were in front of the Pecks. At the stage when the President first allowed his eyes – "those strange eyes of his" – to wander ahead, he focused them on the tall star. It was just a glimmer of recognition, Greg thought. The kind that meant a distant chord was being struck in his brain although he had not yet found the correct point of reference.

When they got to talking, the President pummelled the Peck hand in his familiar way – although Greg said he could see that he was being greeted by a man who was both harried and frightened. "You know," said Nixon, "my parents were both Quakers and my cousin Jessamyn West wrote *Friendly Persuasion* in which you were so good. It's my favorite picture and we show it frequently at the White House."

That was the point when Greg realized why the President's sense of recognition was not as acute as it might have been. Nixon was convinced he was talking to Gary Cooper – who had been dead for twelve years.

The President was waving his arms about excitedly recalling the picture and rattling off other titles which he believed Cooper had made. Greg decided that since Nixon had spent so long on his praise, it would be churlish to put him wise.

"Thank you very much, Mr. President," said Greg. "It was good of you to come."

The party had been hosted by John Wayne. After it Greg went straight up to him: "When you give a cocktail party, Duke," he said, "you certainly give one."

A year or so later, Nixon had no doubt at all who Gregory Peck was: he included him in his so-called "Enemies List" of 200 people who included people like Paul Newman and Jane Fonda and who were being blacklisted by the White House.

News that he was blacklisted came to Greg and Veronique in London as they watched television. They were in a house in Chelsea which they had taken during another working spell in London.

Before that, Greg had no idea even of the list's existence. There had been no letters, no telephoned warnings from anyone. Suddenly, as they watched the B.B.C. news, he and Veronique heard, first that the list existed and secondly, that Greg was on it.

Above: Universal City Studios – with Frank Sinatra, Nancy and Henry Kissinger and Barbara Sinatra
Below: With Bobby Kennedy

Above: With his mother on "Bunny's" 75th birthday party in Monte Carlo
Below: This is Veronique's favourite picture of Greg. She took it herself soon after
the birth of Anthony

UNITED WESTERN NEWSPAPER INC

Above: Greg – the proud father of an ambitious son. Carey's first, unsuccessful bid for Congress, supported by, second left, the President's mother "Miss Lillian" Carter. Also in the picture, writer Garson Kanin and the celebrated actress, Ruth Gordon
Below: Shirley Maclaine, Paul Newman and Bob Hope at a celebrity function with the Pecks

The late Rosalind Russell presenting Greg with his special Oscar –
the Jean Hersholt Humanitarian Award

Above: With Bette Davis on the night of the 1978 Academy Awards Show
Below: Greg and Veronique in the company of Groucho Marx

Above: With the lovely Sophia Loren during the making of *Arabesque*
Below left: For the first time in his career, he played a really evil man –
the "Angel of Death of Auschwitz", Josef Mengele, in *The Boys from Brazil*
Below right: As the Supreme Commander (accepting the Japanese surrender)
in *MacArthur*

Greg and Veronique with Jack Benny's widow, Mary

Above: Three superstars aloft: Greg with friends Cary Grant and Frank Sinatra
Below: With the late Earl Mountbatten of Burma and zany comedy actress Goldie Hawn

Says Veronique now, "It was a real shock. My heart was pounding. It just literally shocked me physically. I was shaking all over, experiencing emotions of outrage and astonishment, shock – everything. I had never thought much of Nixon, but this really was unbelievable."

For the next few days, as they walked through London's Kings Road, young girls would come up to Greg and literally kiss his hand, enthusing not now on *To Kill a Mockingbird* or *Arabesque*, but on how pleased they were that he was listed among America's liberals.

By then, both Greg and Veronique had decided that perhaps it wasn't such a bad thing after all. "I would like to think this one has nothing to do with the President – I don't want to believe that it had," he said at the time.

But, of course, it very soon became apparent that the President had *everything* to do with the list. It also began to bite – and in a way that could only have considerably pleased Nixon. For a time, it seemed that Nixon's mischief was going to affect Hollywood in precisely the same way that McCarthyism had hit it 20 years earlier.

Greg himself lost a valuable contract to produce three big new pictures. Hands had already been shaken on the deal – which to Greg was usually enough, more than once he had made a picture simply after a handshake and then signed the contract when the last reel of film was finally in the can. But in this case, it all suddenly fell apart.

The company's money source was one of the giant corporations which had contributed heavily to Nixon's election campaign.

After Greg had spent eight months searching for properties and having set up his own office and staff, the deal was suddenly called off.

Greg was left high and dry – and out of pocket to the tune of $40,000, to say nothing of three-quarters of a year wasted.

Even so, Peck never used a foreign refuge from which to run down America. "I can't understand the American who goes abroad and stabs his country in the back," he told reporters. "It may well be that in England and France you can walk down a dark street freely with little fear of violence. On the other hand, no country in the world has the same set of complex social problems as the United States."

But he felt strongly about America for positive reasons, and that was why "knocking" the States was not what he had in mind, even when he made pictures that were critical of the country's political system. "I felt that our problems are susceptible to solution with strong leadership," he declared.

That was why he produced a film called *The Trial of the Catonsville Nine* which cost him $200,000. "In the old Hollywood days, we would have spent that on a trailer," he quipped at the time.

The picture was based on the trial of Father Daniel Berrigan, his brother Philip, who was also a priest, and seven others charged with breaking into a draft center at the time of the Vietnam War, and burning Army files with home-made napalm.

Greg put in about a third of the money for the picture himself – the rest came from friends. It was all filmed in eight days, using the same cast and director who had turned the story into a successful stage play in New York and Los Angeles.

Greg hawked the film from studio to studio, hoping for finance towards the cost of prints and advertising. At Paramount, he thought he had struck some of the gold that the studio had picked up from its most recent blockbuster success.

When the lights went up in the preview theater, Greg turned to Robert Evans, the executive in charge of the production. "Will you do it?" he asked him. Evans answered: "These things do have to be said and I'm glad someone had the courage to say them on the screen."

It couldn't be more encouraging, Greg thought.

Frank Yablans, the then President of the company, was there too. He was also full of praise. "This film," he declared firmly, "*must* be distributed, but not with my *Godfather* money."

The picture opened in New York, Boston, Washington and Los Angeles but, Greg says ruefully, it all reminded him of his favourite of all Goldwynisms: "If the public won't go to the theater, you can't stop 'em." Nothing stopped the public from not going to the theaters. The film died.

But although he wasn't satisfied with it artistically, he thinks the picture had to be made. "We were not only killing 50,000 American boys, but no one knows how many Vietnamese women and children, civilians and old people too. We were destroying the countryside and destroying a whole country in order to make it free, according to our concept of freedom. I became convinced that it was, in fact, a civil war in which we should never have been involved. Making the film was my way of trying to influence public opinion to get it all stopped."

That picture wasn't calculated to please Nixon, either, since the President was still pursuing the Vietnam conflict. Others in Hollywood may have talked about the times that Greg entertained visiting Russians. He did that before it was fashionable. In recent years, it has become perfectly acceptable for people to fall over themselves entertaining Soviet ballet dancers, but when Greg was the host to Russian film makers or athletes, it was news.

The athletes were particularly interesting to the Peck family because Jonathan was showing all the signs of being a champion runner and Greg swelled with parental pride at his eldest son's achievements.

He was already Southern California champion in the half mile and was being spoken of as a potential world beater. It was a joy for Greg to be able to take him to athletics meetings and to discuss the field and track results with him.

Greg and Veronique frequently went to see Jonathan compete. They watched him run second and then as it got into the final stretch, cheered as he passed all the opposition to win.

As they hugged and congratulated him, they noticed that Jonathan wasn't as excited as they were. "I shouldn't have won that race," said Jonathan. They couldn't understand what he could possibly mean.

"I let the other guy set the pace," he explained. "And then I passed him at the last minute. That was wrong. I should have set the pace."

Greg doesn't think he ever convinced him, but he tried to explain that that was what racing was all about.

People were wanting to know if Greg intended his children to follow him into show business. His answer was always the same: "I won't pressure them in any way, but the idea of a son stepping into his father's boots is overdone in Hollywood."

Jonathan had chosen to go to Occidental, the liberal arts college in the Los Angeles area, largely because they had outstanding track teams. Stephen went to Northwestern University outside Chicago where he majored in public speaking, theatre and communications. Carey majored in the school of foreign service at Georgetown University.

Anthony and Cecilia were too young for college but when it came to their education, Greg and Veronique had no quarrel at all. When the children were fourteen, both agreed that having enjoyed the early formative years, it was time for them to go away to school.

The children were sent to Switzerland, to attend Aiglon College at Villars, not far from Montreux and Gstaad. They were consulted before a final decision was made and both agreed to start roughing life a bit.

As Greg told me, "Kids get too soft here. They have everything. They're surrounded with affluence. They are apt to lose their ambition, their will to study or to accept the set of rules that they have to live by and become mere appendages of their talented parents. I've seen all too many examples of it."

Aiglon was considered right to help them avoid that fate. It had cold showers and much of the strict discipline of a Gordonstoun. The place did rub off the soft corners of both Peck youngsters – without affecting Cecilia's femininity. There was plenty of ski-ing at the college, but also facilities to learn French, German and all other subjects surrounded by an international bunch of kids.

Of course, they grumbled every now and again – particularly about the food, but on the whole they both enjoyed it greatly.

It was a good investment for the future.

So was the education of Veronique's brother, Cornelius, who was now brilliantly going through medical school in California – with Greg watching his progress with the pride of a father. Veronique's recently widowed mother, whom Greg calls Chouchoune, came to join her children and Greg insisted that she live at their house. She decided, too, that she wanted to drive. Although her English isn't perfect, her son-in-law saw no reason why she shouldn't learn on the Los Angeles roads. It was he who taught her – taught her so well, in fact, that she got a Californian licence.

Greg's love of people meant more to him than the investments he had in a number of financial concerns. He had business managers who reported back on what they were doing with his money. It was not always a satisfactory process but he much preferred concentrating on activities that he enjoyed and found exciting to attending business meetings. He had interests in chains of supermarkets, but didn't want to get involved in the details of the price of washing powders or of jars of instant coffee.

People whose favourite reading is a balance sheet are not the kind whose company he relishes. He would much rather be ensconced over a drink with another actor – or perhaps a comedian, discussing the business of entertaining people. That was why an invitation from Jack Benny to appear on a show with George Burns and himself in late 1969 was like a request to take part in a command performance.

The show was called "Jack Benny's New Look" and the idea was that the three stars would re-enact an old vaudeville act called Goldie, Fields and Glide. Jack had for a long time been trying to think of ways of inviting Greg on the show – but was convinced that a straight actor of his standing would consider it infradig to appear in a T.V. comedy, especially doing a vaudeville act.

Eventually Jack asked Greg to pop down to his office when they were holding a story conference. He went, and when he heard the offer, he was beside himself with excitement. The night that the show was aired, Greg appeared in a 1906-vintage blazer and straw boater and did a soft-shoe shuffle with the two veteran vaudevillians. He also sang "The Shadow of Your Smile", with gestures.

After the show, Greg thanked Jack profusely and said, "Any time you need a song and dance man just think of me."

The two had appeared on radio together in the late 1940s and they were on the same stage at a number of benefits but it was only after the T.V. show that they became firm, close friends.

Originally it was the professional work involved that attracted Greg and Jack to each other. Hour upon hour was spent perfecting the dance, the song and the comedy routine that followed. They proved what Greg had always suspected – that the best ad-libs are the ones that are rehearsed the most.

The songs took even longer – to the point that Jack butted in with a plea, "Greg – stop working at it! The worse you are, the funnier you'll be. Don't sing pretty. Sing funny!" It could have been a rejoinder to Rochester although this time Jack didn't visibly cover his cheek with the palm of his hand. And it was true – Greg rehearsed so much that he got too good. On screen, though, he stood absolutely still, using the hammiest gestures that he could possibly imagine – and allowed a tear to fall down his cheek. It got a roar. Greg always says it was one of the most enjoyable experiences of his professional life.

The personal bond between Jack and Greg extended to their homes. Veronique and Greg also became very close friends of Mary Benny, Jack's wife who had been a household name as Mary Livingstone during the 30s and 40s.

Together, they had quiet dinners at Beverly Hills restaurants like Chasens – where Jack somehow never knew either what to order or how much to tip.

Once the Pecks and the Bennys were at Las Vegas together. It was three o'clock in the morning and Greg said, "Let's do something really silly. Let's go to a topless show." Mary didn't want to go but the pair of super stars with the supremely elegant Veronique descended (not an inappropriate phrase) on a third-rate theater to watch, as Greg puts it, "some rather tired girls bounce up and down".

A few minutes went by when Jack suddenly exclaimed, "What am *I* doing here?" They all laughed and stayed for another hour.

Nothing, however, equalled the time that Jack casually mentioned to Mary that he wanted a big, strong dog around the house. That was all that Greg needed to hear – because just a couple of days before he himself had bought a 90-pound Alsatian.

Greg got a new lead and tied a huge bow on the dog's collar – and sent the live "package" along to Jack's office in the care of a muscular friend who was a physical training expert. The man told the receptionist on his arrival that he had a present for Mr. Benny from Mr. and Mrs. Peck.

He was shown into the office, handed the lead to a startled and annoyed Jack Benny, and departed. With the "gift" was a note – containing a detailed menu for the animal and adding casually that he wasn't yet fully housebroken.

Eventually, Jack followed the man into the back parking lot calling, "Hey, I don't want this dog!" Later, he realized it was all a joke and was to carry the note around with him in his pocket for years afterwards.

Veronique and Greg marked Jack's 80th birthday – they were in London – simply by sending him a telegram. It read:

DEAR JACK. BIG DEAL.

Veronique's first memory of Jack is sitting next to him at a dinner at the home of James and Gloria Stewart 20 odd years ago. Jack wouldn't have recalled it. He didn't know who she was and ignored her for the whole evening. Later, Veronique got to appreciate how good they both felt when the basically shy Jack Benny did speak to them.

Jack gave Greg a money-clip – which, considering the comedian's "mean" reputation, was an honour indeed. It was complete with a caricature of himself and an inscription that read: "To Greg with love from Jack". When it vanished in a burglary after Jack's death, Mary replaced it, and it remains one of Greg's treasured possessions. Greg says simply, "I like to think of Jack every day, and I do."

Soon after they had first got to know each other well, Jack tried to persuade Veronique to appear on T.V. with him. She declined. But he wouldn't leave it there. Every time they met socially, he would kid her and say: "One of these days I'll find the right thing for you!"

Finally, she weakened. There *was* something about Jack Benny that inspired great trust and when he said he had an idea for a sketch that would suit her perfectly, Veronique could only accept. Yes, she said, she and Greg *would* appear together with Jack. The basis of his sketch was that the Pecks invite Jack to their house to dinner the following Saturday. Greg protests that they can't suggest to a big star like Benny that he should come to them at only two days' notice.

Veronique decides to ring just the same. But she can't find the number. Greg says, "Try the yellow pages – under 'Entertainer'."

Finally, they get through. Veronique asks if Jack could come to dinner – and when. He replies: "Six thirty . . . seven . . . seven thirty . . . if I don't shower, I could be there in half an hour!"

She stammers that it's her birthday that day and Greg was taking her to a restaurant. "I'll be there," says Jack.

At the restaurant, he asks his friend, "Say, Greg, did you tell them it's Veronique's birthday? If you did they'll bring you a free cake!"

And so the sketch went on, one Benny-type laugh every line. But the show itself never happened. It was due to go out in December 1974 – but that was when Jack was struck with cancer. Up to the last minute, however, he protested that he intended to make the show. He even arranged a publicity photographic session with them, but was too ill to attend and Veronique and Greg posed, instead, in front of a blow up of the famous Bouchet sketch of Benny. A violin and bow crossed on a music stand was placed in the left hand corner, where the live Jack would have posed with them. On December 26, 1974, he died. A few days later, Greg was one of the pall bearers at his funeral.

Veronique had accepted the invitation to appear on the show after merely hearing Jack go through the outline. There was no question of signed contracts or script approval. It took another four years for Veronique to bring herself to read the actual script of the sketch. "It was the perfect thing," she says now. "I couldn't ever imagine appearing on television with anyone but Jack."

And to that, Greg adds, "We were an odd couple, but somehow I could make Jack laugh. We had a very nice friendship."

Greg was less happy with his next movie, *I Walk the Line*. The script had Greg as a Southern sheriff swimming underwater through the flooded rooms of his childhood home which had been taken over by the Tennessee Valley Water Authority. Director John Frankenheimer suggested that Greg do it nude. He would, he said, photograph him from above so that only his backside was in view.

Greg didn't take kindly to that at all. "I'll wear a diving suit," he said. "I make my living with my brains, not my behind," and that was considered to be the end of the matter. It looked effective enough in the rushes. The film's editor, however, didn't think so. All the swimming scenes were lost, and so, he says, was the effect on the sheriff's mental processes. "It reduced my character to a clichéd middle-aged man with a lust for a young girl," he maintains.

As for *Shoot Out*, the picture that followed: "I shouldn't have made it at all. A trivial Western. A mistake."

The trouble was that Greg had not yet got out of the habit of working regularly. After four films released in 1969, and *I Walk the Line* in 1970, there just had to be one to follow or he would have felt uncomfortably unemployed. He became nervous that, if there wasn't a new one every six months, he might never be asked to make a film again. *Shoot Out* was a potboiler that should never have been allowed on to the stove.

It was *Shoot Out* that persuaded Gregory Peck to take stock of his film work and not to make others like it. The respected *Los Angeles Times'* entertainments editor, Charles Champlin, wrote after seeing the film that the movie "serves mostly as a glum reminder of the inadequate use the movies have lately made of one of their principal personalities, Gregory Peck. Peck strides through this low-budget Universal Western like a giant through corn stubble, outclassing his material and most of his support, acting out the charade with craft and intensity and that riveting command of the screen which defines a star."

Three years went by before another Gregory Peck film was

released – a different cup of tea altogether although perhaps the terminology is not totally appropriate. *Billy Two Hats* was immediately dubbed the first Matzo Ball Western. After the spaghetti Westerns made in Italy, this one was filmed in Israel, because Norman Jewison, the director, was able to set up an economic deal to film in the Negev Desert, which could easily pass for Arizona or New Mexico.

It was different in other ways, too. For the first time since *Moby Dick*, Greg wore a full growth of beard. And for the first time in his life, he had a Scottish accent, as broad as a stretch of heather.

His memories of *Billy Two Hats* – in which he played an outlaw hunted by a sheriff – are happy. The only thing he didn't like was being shot in the leg a quarter of the way through the picture and having to be dragged through the remaining hour by Desi Arnez Junior.

But the linguistic opportunities compensated for that. For weeks, he studied Gaelic diction with a Scottish actor.

Thus equipped as a Scotsman, he was ready for Israel. For nine to ten weeks, he and Veronique toured the country, visited the holy places and the kibbutzim, spoke to Jews and Arabs and admired the way trees grew where once had been only sand and swamp. They enjoyed every minute of it.

Compared with the earlier two pictures, Greg was able to describe *Billy Two Hats* as – at best – an "honourable effort", but finds reason to quote his old friend Bill Goetz, who once said: "If it looks like a duck and walks like a duck and quacks like a duck, it is a duck."

Nineteen

Greg took Veronique and their children to the South of France and made up his mind to try to forget the film business. His acting days, he decided, were finished.

After all, the career of a super star can be notoriously short and he had had a very long time indeed at the top. But now he had made up his mind that it was over. None of his recent pictures had really set the Atlantic Ocean on fire and there wasn't exactly a clamour any more to have him starring in important new films.

So the Pecks went to Cap Ferrat intending to stay for five months, during which time the head of the household would do nothing but swim, ride a bicycle, read and socialize with the many friends who, like him, had homes in the area.

For two months that was fine. He read a great deal, wore down the tires of his bicycle, swam for hours and enjoyed a succession of dinner parties with people like the Rainiers, the Nivens and the Rex Harrisons and had quiet evenings at home. Yet, as the calendar dates were ticked off, he grew more and more restless.

It wasn't the financial aspect that concerned him. His career in Hollywood had been profitable and for the most part he had used that money well. There was not the slightest doubt that he and his family could live out their days in comfort, even luxury – and still have something left over for future generations, too.

What did worry him was the thought that at fifty-eight years of age, he still had sufficient energy to enjoy life *and* keep on working. He decided, therefore, that a man who had spent more than half his life in the motion picture industry couldn't just throw it all off as though he had clocked in at a car factory every day and was now itching to relax.

There was, however, a seemingly irreversible decision to make – and he made it. He wasn't going to do any more acting. The scripts that now tumbled on to the doormat at the Cap Ferrat house were more of the same, Westerns that for economic reasons would all be shot in Yugoslavia.

After the experiences of *Shoot Out* and *I Walk the Line* – to say nothing of *Billy Two Hats* – he wasn't going to make any more like them. Now, he was going to be a producer again.

It was a move that, as usual, he talked over carefully with Veronique. He never embarked on any project without consulting her first. She, too, thought the idea of Greg becoming a producer without taking on an additional acting responsibility was a sensible step at this stage in his career.

And there was just the right project to work on. Walter Matthau, now firmly established as a crusty character and a major star, had agreed in principle to play the lead in a comedy Western. Elaine May, who had starred with him in *New Leaf*, was willing to write the screenplay and the property itself had about it all the hallmarks of a brilliant success. It was going to be called *Billy Boy*. Milos Forman was ready to direct it. There was sufficient financial backing for the project, too.

But then Matthau's agents came through with a salary demand which the backers said was unacceptable. Fearing the worst – that all the costs would escalate beyond all proportion – the backers backed out. The movie idea that Greg believes could have been as great a success as Forman's later major Hollywood debut, *One Flew Over the Cuckoo's Nest*, flew away.

The Dove, on the other hand, seemed a much more tameable bird. Greg read the story that had for months been enchanting readers of the *National Geographic Magazine* – the tale of a 16-year-old boy who had sailed alone round the world in a twenty-three-foot sloop – and fell in love with it. To him, it seemed to contain all the magic of a teenager single-handedly conquering Everest.

There was no question but that only unknowns should play the boy and the girl friends who figured in the shore scenes, but Greg wanted the insurance of an experienced director whom he believed would be just right for the film. He settled on Charles Jarrott; with the Swedish cameraman, Sven Nykvist photographing what turned out to be a magnificent travelogue. Unfortunately, and for the second successive time, Greg fell foul of an agent – this time Jarrott's.

The agent inserted a clause into his client's contract imposing a deadline for starting the film. The result was that *The Dove* began shooting in Fiji while its producer was 10,000 miles away in London – and without a script.

That a completed film is ever satisfactory and actually played before a live ticket-buying audience is one of those miracles that film-goers rarely appreciate.

At one point on *The Dove*, Greg – working from offices at Elstree Studios – had to phone dialogue which had just been written (by a fourth writer retained to work on the picture) to a secretary in Darwin, Australia, who then handed it to Jarrott for the following day's filming. At the same time, Greg was having to look at the rushes which were flown in to London every day from Australia or Fiji, and having seen them, immediately phone the director with instructions about changes he considered had to be made.

It was not the easiest way in which a man who had contemplated retirement could introduce himself to what was virtually a new career.

Part of the time, too, he was having to travel to locations – in Australia or Mozambique or somewhere else on this round-the-world voyage.

Yet all the time, someone had to be at E.M.I.'s Elstree Studios to watch the budget, which had now escalated from the original estimated £1,300,000 to £2,200,000. That someone had to be Greg, the producer, who now had to find the additional money from an American source.

Finally, Paramount came through, but until they did, Greg had to find the money himself. It was in Mauritius that the company actually ran out of cash.

Paramount's money came in just the nick of time. *The Dove* failed at the American box offices but was a tremendous success in Australia, New Zealand and Japan – where it earned enough to take it out of the red.

The picture might have done better had it followed the example of other films of the period and put the emphasis more on the sexual awakening of the teenagers. Instead, although the boy and girl were seen once to be under a blanket together, talking – which a generation earlier would have outraged the Johnston Office – there was no grappling under the blanket. The audience were given sufficient credit for understanding that the couple were having an affair without the creaking of springs to emphasize it.

Now, Greg was going to have a few months off again and he and Veronique would do what they had always enjoyed – relax at Cap Ferrat. Life seemed very good indeed. He could have no inkling that it wouldn't be long before he would rush back to America, enmeshed in the greatest tragedy of his life.

Twenty

It was a much more content Gregory Peck who left for Cap Ferrat in the early summer of 1975. He was able to exercise his gifts as an amateur gardener, growing, he was sure, the best courgettes and green peppers on the Riviera. As he did so, he could plan what he was going to do next on the work front. But these moments of quiet enjoyment were to be short.

It was while he was staying in the French villa that he received the telephone call he knows he can never forget – a direct and hopeless call that stunned him and sent his mind reeling: his 32-year-old eldest son Jonathan was dead. A gun had been found nearby and all the evidence pointed to his having taken his own life.

A father can never take the death of a child without the deepest pain. Greg, who had always regarded his relationship with all his children as the closest possible, was hit like a fighter winded by a punch below the belt. He was grief-stricken, unable to fathom out how or why the dreadful thing had happened.

He knew there had been stresses in Jonathan's life. His workload as a television reporter had recently been unbearably heavy, and Greg himself had tried to ease it slightly. He had been through an unhappy love affair – Greg knew that, too. He had not been well – although no one had any idea just how ill he was. There had been moments of deep depression recently, although none of it seemed to go back very far. There had never been any reason to believe that his three boys had done anything but survive, perfectly, the break-up of his first marriage – and that was all of 22 years before.

Greg and Greta still bore no bitterness to each other, still talked fairly frequently on the telephone and saw each other from time to time. Veronique, for her part, had always got along very well with her husband's sons by continually making sure that she was never regarded as either a stepmother or a mother substitute – but simply as an additional member of their own family who loved their father, and who cared about them, too.

Jonathan's problems didn't occur until he had grown up and found a very independent life for himself. He had gone to Africa with the Peace Corps, before returning to California as a C.B.S. news writer, a job he did well, following his success both as a student and as an athlete. But he had problems he did not talk about.

He was "bugged" by looking like Greg and more so about being constantly reminded by friends and outsiders how closely he resembled him. It was a problem Greg would have understood. It was something he had foreseen as a possibility and why he hadn't named any of his boys Gregory Peck Junior.

Jonathan was also undoubtedly concerned with his health. Doctors had told him he had an enlarged heart, high blood pressure and arteriosclerosis. But only the autopsy proved just how very far advanced the hardening had gone, far beyond most medical men's judgements of what a 32-year-old's arteries should be like.

Greg had noticed that Jonathan's eyes were often red and that he blinked a lot. He was worried that he got very tired while playing tennis and that he was plainly losing vitality. Jonathan was depressed a great deal.

When Greg left for his round-the-world expedition for *The Dove*, he gave Jonathan some money to spend on counselling sessions with a psychiatrist. He didn't know that his son thought they were a waste of money, that he didn't think they were doing him any good, and that he soon stopped attending.

No one either knew at that time about his being turned down by a young divorcee with two children. He had asked the girl to move into his Santa Barbara house with him, but she refused. She had recently been through the torment of a divorce and didn't want to get involved in another intense relationship.

It bore down heavily on him. So, too, did the experience of knowing that another girlfriend, a brilliant Phi Beta Kappa student at Berkeley, who worked in the college library, had committed suicide. For weeks a deep depression had lain over him about that.

It seemed, though, that he had got over it all on a fishing trip which he took with Greg up to the Sierras.

Greg did know, though, that his latest job was getting Jonathan down. He was working in Santa Barbara as the correspondent there for a T.V. station in Santa Maria, a township about 100 miles north of the city. It was a farming community whose signal, by some freak of radio beams, was picked up in the much larger resort of Santa Barbara.

Santa Maria was a small town with a small station that made small-time demands on its staff, much in the way that a tiny local newspaper might 50 years ago have expected its reporters to collect advertising space, set the type and arrange for the bundles to be distributed to wholesalers. Jonathan was required to turn in three reports a day, which meant deciding which stories were worth covering, as well as working the camera, doing the interviews and providing the voice-over commentaries, too.

As any local reporter might, he had first to line up the stories – build up contacts with police, the town's clergymen, the hospital and the university and at the same time keep his finger on the pulse of the Santa Barbara social and artistic set. Then when he had found his three stories – a mind-blowing job on a slow news day in the area – he had to set up his camera and tripod and report and film. And be sure the three stories were on the Santa Maria bus at 1 p.m. every day.

When the news was slow and when there were not three stories already lined up the night before, he would often have sleepless nights before taking up a dawn vigil at the police station and hanging around at the Mayor's office at the start of the day's business, trying to land a story. Needless to say, evening council meetings and other functions had to be covered, too.

When Greg saw the impossible predicament his son faced, he offered what he considered a reasonable solution: "Just tell them there isn't any news."

"No," said Jonathan. "I can't do that. They expect three stories a day."

Greg thought there had to be a solution. "Can't you tell them you need some help, that they must find you a leg man? That they should get someone to write for you, scrounge for you, or just work the camera?"

"No," Jonathan, who knew how the chips were stacked, replied. "They won't. They're a small station on a budget."

So small, so tight a budget that they didn't even have enough film to issue him without severely rationing it. That worried him enormously, too. How could he afford to use so much valuable film on what might turn out to be a dud story? The station wouldn't like it and might cut off his further supplies. His father sent him a dozen cans of film.

He had told Jonathan more than once to give the station two days' notice and walk out. But now it was too late.

Greg flew back to California immediately he received the call about his son's death. On the journey, the bitter, unbearable flight home, he tried to think about the causes that led to the tragedy. Now he says, "Whatever the other causes were, whatever the mistakes his mother and I may have made, whatever influences he was subjected to that made it apparently impossible for him to withstand that particular set of pressures at that particular time I don't know. But my regret that I'll live with for the rest of my life was that I was in France instead of here. I felt certain that had I been in Los Angeles he would have called me, because he often dropped in and talked things over with me. If only he could have picked up the phone and said: 'Things are just bearing down so much on me tonight, that I can't stand it,' I would have said, 'Stay where you are, I'll be there. Come on, we'll go off to Tahiti or somewhere.'"

Instead of going to Tahiti, Greg was now on the flight home from Nice – with Veronique staying behind to make the necessary arrangements for closing up the Cap Ferrat house.

Being able to deal with a tragedy is one thing. Surviving it is quite another. That Greg was able to do both was due to the man's inherent common sense – and, in no small measure, to the support of the people around him.

It was because he had never allowed himself to sail off on the dizzy cloud of super-stardom that sometimes overtakes people who have become public idols that he overcame the trauma into which he was thrust in the mid-summer of 1975. At the times that counted, it was his family that had to come first.

As soon as he arrived in California he went straight to Greta. Once more after 21 years apart, he was sharing with her an intensely personal moment, knowing that, despite all their differences, each understood exactly how the other felt.

But when Veronique flew in for the funeral with Anthony and Cecilia, it was mainly to her that he was able to turn for comfort.

"The fact that he survived this was a great expression of his love for us, for me, for Anthony and Cecilia," Veronique told me. "I believe he surmounted something which was insurmountable because of us. So it must have been all of us together, feeling for the other and somehow doing the right thing instinctively – because we *had* to survive this."

The need that she felt and which she transmitted to a husband who for a time was torn to shreds by his grief was simply to hang on, a realization that everything else just could not be abandoned because of it. That in itself generated a hidden strength, an energy to keep going.

To this day he wonders about the things that led up to his son's death. "Who knows how good a father any man is?" he mused to me on one occasion. "What we did right and what we did wrong? All I know is that I was always conscious of the need to be close to my children and to spend as much time as I could with them. I think I did the best I could, considering the amount of work I was doing. I don't think they suffered from any neglect or certainly from any indifference from their parents."

It has been suggested that parents in the public eye have a special responsibility to be sure that their children are not let down. "Don't all parents have that responsibility?" he asked. "We bring them into the world. We *have* to stand by them until they can take off on their own and even after they do that I think we will always have to be prepared to help and to be there so that they can turn to someone if they're in need. That's a life-long responsibility, surely."

But he also recognized his responsibility to Veronique and the others. He needed to get back to a semblance of normality and the only way to do this was by getting back to work.

Twenty-one

Although he had said firmly that his mind was made up that his acting days were over, Greg had to face the fact that he had been getting bored as a producer. There were other ideas in the melting pot for film productions, but there was no guarantee that, despite his own hard efforts, they would ever reach a camera.

It was, of course, an old producers' story: there were always more unproduced ideas than there were finished pictures. But the endless round of figures and budgets was wearying him. He had been through it all before with those business meetings and now, just as he had with the boards of major corporations, he had had enough of his producer's office. When he contemplated the thought that it would take at least a year to get a new picture produced – plus the time it took to decide whether or not it worked or was even remotely gratifying – he said that it was all too large a slice out of the life of a 60-year-old even to consider seriously.

But now he was handed a script that got all the old Peck juices working again. As with so many other scripts that became important films, this one came to him via George Chasin, who after being off the Peck scene for nearly ten years, was once more his agent.

Chasin had been asked to read a script called *The Anti-Christ Story*. It had resurfaced after lying on a shelf at Warner Brothers for close to eighteen months. Warners decided to abandon it because they thought it might conflict with the sequel they were planning for *The Exorcist*.

Fresh from signing up his new client, George Chasin was at that point able to introduce the name Gregory Peck. Twentieth Century Fox came up with a suitable offer: a quarter of a million dollars, plus ten per cent of the gross. The picture was now to be called *The Omen*.

The rest, as they say, is history. *The Omen* was a smash hit. But it needed a lot of work. The script was terrible at that stage, says Chasin. Another difficulty was getting Greg to accept Richard Donner as director.

The question of Donner's directing was a more difficult problem to sort out than the need to rework the script. Greg knew that the picture would be seen, if at all, as his "comeback" attempt. That being so, he needed to feel that he was working with a top director whom he could trust. And Donner was a completely unknown factor to him.

"Who is he?" he asked.

All George could reply was, "Well, I've met him socially although I don't know him professionally. He's done one or two T.V. specials."

"Nothing for the theaters?" Greg probed.

"I'll have to look him up in the directory," his agent replied – which gives one some idea of Donner's standing in the industry, and Greg's reluctance to go along with the project as it now stood. If this was going to be his comeback, he wanted to take out every possible favourable option going for him.

Chasin soon discovered that Donner had made a couple of "B" pictures but was anxious that nobody remembered them too well. It was agreed that Greg should see the T.V. specials, but he was worried then about liking the picture and not the man.

In the end, he decided to accept an invitation from Donner to meet him. Later, from his house, Greg called George and said, "Don't bother with the specials. I like Dick. We've gone over the story and the changes that will have to be made and we see eye-to-eye all the way."

That was when *The Omen* took off and when Greg made up his mind to make what turned out to be the most financially successful film of his career.

He agreed to play the American Ambassador to London who discovers, too late, that his son was conceived by the Devil. The boy kills his own mother, played by the beautiful-as-ever Lee Remick, and causes the deaths of other people too. Finally, the Ambassador decides to kill the boy himself – except that events work out differently and it is he who is killed.

Greg decided early on that his first ever horror-thriller had to be regarded as "paperback entertainment". That being so, he saw it had to be made believable and, of course, played as though it were the most important picture he had ever made in his life.

Nobody debated the literary merits of the picture. What they did know was that it was colourful, exciting, full of both suspense and showmanship.

The picture not only meant that Greg would be working in England again, which he still loved, but with Donner and Bernhardt whom he now felt he had cause to respect. Most important of all, he was getting back to work, doing what he enjoyed most. He was the proverbial old firehorse, hearing once again the clanging of the bell.

If Greg had not had the opportunity of being American Ambassador to Dublin in real life, he was going to make the most of being the pretend Ambassador to the Court of St. James's. All he had to do now was to make the Ambassador seem believable – which he was to do brilliantly. There was not much chance of getting swamped by the Ambassador's horrific situation or of taking him home to Veronique in the evenings as he sometimes did with his more engrossing roles. He really couldn't take the blood letting seriously when he actually saw it being sloshed from bottles.

As Greg maintains, "We actors are salesmen. We sell every story with conviction and persuasion. I know some people think that aspect of it is disappointing, but that's exactly what we are paid to do."

After what had happened earlier that year, working was an enjoyable experience in the fall and winter of 1975. So also was the company of Lee Remick – "a wonderful partner" – and of David Warner, Leo McKern and Patrick Troughton, all of whom he respects and admires as skilful English character actors.

Greg's work on the picture finally wound up on December 24th, in time for him to take the 2.30 Pan American flight to Los Angeles and join Veronique and the family for Christmas Eve dinner at home.

Everything about the picture pointed to its being a huge success, so he flew home feeling pleased with himself. Even before it was completed, it was clear that once again he was a very bankable star. However, he was not rushing into any new projects.

An idea Greg had had for a long time was to play General Douglas MacArthur, the American folk hero who was loved by the more right-wing elements and hated by the Progressives (among whom Greg normally counted himself). Without knowing too much about him, Greg believed he was a great American and a brilliant administrator who was largely responsible for putting Japan on its feet after World War Two. But he saw the General as a vainglorious and complicated man, a 19th century style patriot who, fortunately for the world, failed to win the Presidency. He was, however, a great character for a film.

In his comparatively fallow period, Greg had tried to interest Universal in the idea, but they turned him down. To them, Greg was no longer associated with success, and if they were going to make the picture, they wanted the best box office name they could get.

They thought of George C. Scott, but his role as Patton now eliminated any chance of his being considered as a contemporary MacArthur. Charlton Heston was mentioned but no deal was arranged. Henry Fonda was considered until he played MacArthur on television and so removed his name from the list of candidates; it wasn't considered right for him to play the part twice, particularly since a big-screen picture would have to take a different stance. They even considered Laurence Olivier who, by coincidence, was to play the General in a T.V. spectacular three years later. Anyone, it seems, but Gregory Peck.

The studios once more were clamouring for Greg's services. *The Omen* had achieved the almost unbelievable feat of taking $100 million at the box office.

At 62, a time when he had probably needed reassurance more than ever before, he was again on top of the heap. As Darryl Zanuck used to say to him when he took out his little blue book, "Success breeds success."

A few weeks after first mentioning the new Peck film, a Universal executive button-holed Chasin: "I've been hearing a great deal about *The Omen*. Do you think you could arrange a deal for *MacArthur* with Greg?" The deal *was* arranged.

Greg would make the picture in a package of three for the studio. That decided, he began, as always, the mind-boggling job of researching his new character. He waded through the veritable library of MacArthur books – the ones that praised him as a glorious patriot, and the ones that cheered the fact that the demagogue never reached the White House.

As he dug and as he read, the screen MacArthur began changing his mind about the original, real-life General. Instead of the man called by some of his detractors "Dugout Doug", he found one who never shirked the firing line, a victim of hearsay whose faults, on analysis, seemed to be trivial. "He was not unique among war leaders in having a love of grandeur and a sense of publicity," he says now. "I found that he was in no sense a dangerous megalomaniac nor did he have a consuming ambition to be President. That's a canard. He was never even close to it."

When Greg walked into the studio for the first story conference he knew how Douglas MacArthur felt after the invasion of the Philippines, how he reacted under fire – "fearless when there were bullets flying" – how he felt when he smoked his corncob pipe and put on his battered, braided cap. With the distinctive MacArthur haircut, parting on the left, instead of the usual one on the right, even the bald patch at the back, he became MacArthur, even though he is quite five inches taller than the General was.

The resemblance to the real MacArthur, in fact, was uncanny. With the addition of the famous sunglasses, the experience of seeing Greg among a crowd of soldiers, with the scene framed as a hundred original newspaper photographs had been, was almost eerie.

Yet he had given up seeking a close resemblance soon after the first make-up tests. They had put him through the usual experiments: rubber nose number one, rubber nose number two, rubber nose number three, rubber jowls, cheek padding. Finally, Greg himself decided that this was not what he was after.

"Forget it, fellers," he said. "I can't do it. I feel unnatural and I won't be made into a ham. I don't want to impersonate him. I want to get inside the man's head."

He talked about the role to Laurence Olivier before filming began. "How's your breath control?" the actor peer asked, poking his finger into Greg's solar plexus – he knew a little about the MacArthur phraseology. "In his speech, you have to have the breath to carry through to the end of the phrase."

But, as he hoped, it was thinking like MacArthur that carried Greg through. An actor of his standing takes his make-believe so seriously that sometimes it can be difficult not to take its schizoid effects out of the studio with him.

He enjoyed the research immensely and surprised himself by the

gradual change in his own feelings from dislike for the megalomaniac general to intense admiration. "I came to understand him – to
love him really," he told me. He was a very, very great man, in my
opinion. I'm sure that in history, when it's all weighed up, the
plusses will far outweigh the minuses."

And that was why he wanted so badly for the film to work.

It was while making *MacArthur* that Greg and Veronique talked
seriously about moving from their house in South Cliffwood Avenue.
At an age when other couples are contemplating leaving their big
homes for smaller, more compact apartments, Gregory Peck, at 62,
and Veronique felt that they should make no concessions to the
calendar. Greg didn't feel old, and since old age is a state of mind, he
was determined to live the way that he felt. Veronique, 20 years
younger, didn't see that their attitudes to life were any different.
Instead of contracting their lives, they wanted to expand.

Now they wanted to live in a house with more open space, more
recreational opportunities to enjoy their free time. It was while Greg
was having a short break on set that an anxious Veronique got
through to him on the telephone.

"I've found a house for us," she said. "The only thing is there's an
offer for it pending and we'd have to make our minds up today."

That was a pity, but there seemed nothing to be done about it.
Greg knew he wasn't going to be able to leave the studio until after
nightfall that day and there was no point in seeing a house in the
dark. But this one was important, she stressed. "All right," he said.
"I'll get them to drive me down during the lunch break."

The people of Los Angeles are used to strange sights, but there
was many a flutter in the breasts of the older citizens when a shiny
staff car purred its way along Sunset Boulevard, through Whittier
Drive and up along the Holmby Hills as General Douglas MacArthur, in a battered braided cap, sunglasses, and military tunic, sat
in the back. When he stepped out of the car, he carried his five-star
general's swagger stick as he kissed Veronique.

Together, they walked through the house on North Carolwood
Drive, from one spacious room to another, through the wooded
landscaped acres, up to the swimming pool, down to the tennis
court.

"Right," he said, pointing his stick as MacArthur had done on the
beaches of the Philippines. "Buy it."

There was, Veronique pointed out, the small matter of that other offer. "Offer $50,000 more," he suggested. Decisive. That was the thing about MacArthur which always frightened Truman.

One of the most memorable lines occurs on the landing craft as it inches its way towards the shores of the Philippines for the famous "I have returned" invasion. With him on the craft is the Filipino President. As the ramp is lowered, the General politely offers to let the President go first. Just as it really happened on the day, Greg hears the President comment, "I hope that the waters are not too deep. My people will find out that I cannot swim!"

To which MacArthur replies, "I wouldn't worry about that, Mr. President. My people will find out that I can't walk on water." At that point, General Gregory Peck steps off into more than five feet of water, loses his balance, and only his cap is seen floating into shore. That classic moment of disappearance is preserved for posterity on film and has been seen with a collection of other "out-takes" on the Johnny Carson Show. Greg came up spluttering and laughing and waded ashore, as he puts it, "like a wet labrador".

He disappeared into his trailer for 15 minutes, found a clean uniform prepared for just such an emergency, and this time waded ashore in water that was no more than knee deep. Once there, and in simulated rain – to recreate the drama of the real occasion – he gave a beachside press conference.

Greg had wanted the director to paint a broad canvas to take the picture to all the locations on which MacArthur worked and fought. Instead of the battles in the Pacific Islands, there were mock-up shots in California. Instead of remaking the massive ticker-tape parade on Broadway, the studio opted to use archive pictures on which Greg, in the MacArthur-style raincoat and cap, was superimposed. But since the original newsreels were in black and white, the curious notion was devised of making it look as though the parade was being seen on television, complete with all the screen lines!

Instead of using the House of Representatives for MacArthur's moving address to the joint Houses of Congress, Universal took advantage of the fact that at the old Republic studio there was a set modelled on the Senate. So they used that instead and hoped no one would notice.

Greg doesn't criticize Joe Sargent for this. But the historical drama was lost on the conglomerate mentality of the studio. Instead of this becoming what Greg had hoped for – a twentieth-century American equivalent of a Shakespeare chronicle play – it had the look of a movie made for T.V.

He was not altogether denied his thrilling moments making the picture. He did get to address 4,000 cadets at West Point and to feel something of the magic that MacArthur himself must have felt as he made the famous "Duty-honour-country" speech. "My hackles rose at that," he recalls. "It was quite an inspiring moment to stand there and deliver his words in the same spot that he had done it and to get that reaction from the boys – the same cheering and stamping ovation that they gave him."

Once more, he covered his script with comments and directions to himself. One speech, he noted, is "anti-climactic". Another "doesn't say anything".

Across another speech, he scrawled the one expressive word: "Bullshit."

These were notes he wrote to himself. To the executive producer, Frank McCarthy, early on in the progress of the picture, he wrote a letter in which he said he had no choice but to break a promise.

"Dear Frank, I have tried to keep my word and not bombard you with memos. This has taken a great deal of self-control, since I am a graduate of the David O. Selznick school of memo writing."

He was basing his feeling that things weren't going right, he said, on what he had read in two books – one by MacArthur's aide Courtney Whitney, the other by Clark Lee. He had found in those books aspects of MacArthur's behaviour which needed to be brought out in the movie.

One example he quotes was the decision of the Joint Chiefs of Staff not to strive for total victory in Korea – which MacArthur saw as a violation of all his own training and experience. Says Greg, "According to Whitney, he had never seen MacArthur in a moment of greater sorrow or distress. To me, this seems like the beginning of MacArthur's downfall ... he was never able to swallow that directive. It was a dramatic turning point. All of the heroism that precedes this event, the impressions of his early career almost uninterrupted by any failure, the retaking of the Pacific Islands ... all of this success sets him up for the tragic downfall. It is the opposites that make the drama."

And again: "May I suggest that we let MacArthur state his

position with full passion and conviction? But it must not be a one-sided affair. Let the Joint Chiefs, Truman and Bradley, state their views as well."

And: "How about Burgess and Maclean who, according to Whitney, kept the Red Chinese fully informed on the secret plans and policies of the Allies on the conduct of the Korean war? Are we not going to offend anyone in this picture?"

There was a sting in the last comment that reflected Greg's fear of being set up to make a soft as well as a cheap film – not at all the project that he had in mind. He recalled his disappointment over *Behold a Pale Horse* and the efforts made not to offend General Franco with that film.

"I think if we are not going to make anybody mad – including the Pentagon, the British or the Japanese – then there is going to be a softness at the core of the picture. It is going to lack edge and force in building up to the dramatic conflict that brought MacArthur down."

He wanted to hear MacArthur say in a speech "God Bless America" – which was admittedly corny and which he himself always disliked, but he said, "It is so typical of MacArthur . . . that it was almost inevitable that he said it." He pressed for the inclusion of lines like, "By God, it was destiny that sent me here." Said Greg, "It seems overblown and Shakespearean to a lot of his critics, but that's the way his mind worked. If he doesn't say things like that, it won't be MacArthur."

The producers Richard B. Zanuck (Darryl's son) and David Brown were impressed with his work. They replied, "Based on what we have seen so far, we are confident that your performance as MacArthur will be one of the most memorable and distinguished performances of your career.

"Our aim and that of the studio is to make this a *great* motion picture. Should you ever find that this is for some reason significantly less than what you and we expected and hoped it would be, you will find us *totally* supportive."

The memos, nevertheless, continued – at first with more script suggestions.

"MacArthur's speech beginning: 'Starve Hansa Bay' etc: it has two inconsistencies or confusions. What has the jungle to do with it? And what has 'Attack! Attack! Attack!' to do with a strategy of bypassing strong points and leaving them to wither and die on the vine? This is one of my favourite scenes, but I believe I can make it much more effective and predatory by staying with the theme of starvation, thus: 'Starve Hansa Bay! Starvation! That is my ally! Splendid! Splendid! Splendid!'"

The following month, he was criticizing the emphasis put on certain parts of the Korean conflict which – from his own studies – he thought were totally misplaced.

"Scene 215 is grossly unfair to MacArthur, is not as strong a scene dramatically as it should be. Historically speaking, it distorts by omission. I believe that while MacArthur was wrong in attempting to make U.S. foreign policy decisions and rightly was dismissed for it, this screenplay is wrong in pinning the Chinese intervention on him. It does not present a balanced account of what really happened. Militarily, he was right. The Chinese, having entered Korea, were engaged to the limit of their capabilities."

It was not something he could leave behind at the studio or at his home office. He discussed the point with Henry Kissinger at a special Washington dinner held in honour of the then retiring Secretary of State. For fifteen minutes, they talked of MacArthur.

In a letter to the director, he put forward Kissinger's point of view:

"1. China, at the time, was not ready for a major war. They did not have the industrial capacity for it.

"2. The Soviets would not have intervened. They were not vitally concerned with North Korea.

"3. Intelligence on both sides was poor. The Chinese attacked because they were afraid MacArthur intended to invade Manchuria. He went too far to the North. If he had stopped at the 'Narrow Neck', the Pyongyang Line, the Chinese would not have come in and we would have remained in control of three-quarters of the peninsula.

"4. Within the past three years, high Chinese officials have intimated to Henry that they made a mistake in entering the Korean conflict. It cost them more than they gained, and North Korea is a continuing drain on them.

"5. Truman and the Joint Chiefs were wrong in assuming that we were on the brink of an all-out war with China and the Soviets."

As Greg now comments, "The truth seems to be that everybody

screwed up." That was also fast becoming his view of the people behind *MacArthur* the film.

Meetings were called to discuss his dissatisfaction. He wanted to be able to use the full Congressional speech made by MacArthur as they had filmed it.

"How can we lose by trying the full version . . . on an audience? The worst that can happen is that they will shuffle or cough a little. The best is that they will be aroused to the point of applauding. The present cutting insures that they will not. Where is the theatricality in that? It is what actually happened on that day; it is the truth. It does not change the fact that Truman prevailed and a constitutional crisis was forestalled by MacArthur's dismissal."

The producers realized that their star was unhappy. In a telegram they wrote:

DEAR GREG: YOUR FEELINGS REGARDING MACAR-
THUR AS EXPRESSED YESTERDAY ON THE PHONE ARE
TREMENDOUSLY APPRECIATED BY US. YOUR DEDICA-
TION AND CREATIVE CONTRIBUTION TO THIS FILM
HAVE BEEN OF ENORMOUS BENEFIT TO US ALL. WE
WILL ALWAYS BE DEEPLY GRATEFUL. DICK AND
DAVID.

The film was "locked up" and ready for previewing but still Greg had reservations. In May 1977, he wrote to director and producer: "It may be lacking in dramatic red meat, as it is now cut. It may draw unfavourable comparisons to *Patton*. The critics and public may say that it lacks the blood and thunder of *Patton*. I think they may well say it is too balanced, too tame and fence-straddling on the Truman-MacArthur controversy."

The picture gave the impression that Truman was a hundred per cent right, he said. "I think this is editorializing, righteous and simplistic. I am afraid we're going to get tame reviews and a tame response from the public unless we throw aside the fear that the audience will like MacArthur too much.

"I cannot help but point to *Rocky* as recent evidence that audiences like to identify emotionally with the main character. By defusing MacArthur, we may be being too clever by half, too proper and 'balanced'. We may be cheating the audience of the chance to cheer, takes sides and argue. This picture cannot be lacking in passion. If that is going to be the verdict of the critics and the public, God forbid, then it will fail."

Until the end, Joe Sargent and the producers were saying that they believed they had a winner. "I truly regret that you have reservations about the points you mention in your memorandum," said McCarthy, "but I must tell you that the reaction on the part of people who have either seen or worked on *MacArthur* has been unanimously highly enthusiastic. A Universal executive friend of mine told me yesterday that there was a rumble through the Black Tower [the Universal Building] based on the opinions of other executives who have seen the movie that this is the best film ever produced by Universal."

But it was not to be the last word. Telegrams still went back and forth. When it was all over, he wrote Zanuck yet another letter: "It may run successfully at the Music Hall for the summer tourists and no doubt with this short version they will get in an extra showing per day, but I cannot express to you how painful this compromise is to me. Had I known that you would allow this to be done to the two big speeches and the Derevyanko scene [in which Greg tells the Russian representative in Tokyo that he will not allow the Soviets any control over occupied Japan; it was subsequently restored at his insistence]. I would never have undertaken to play the part.

"I thought we had a chance at some degree of greatness, a powerful emotional historical drama, a *cause célèbre* in film. In the name of quote balance unquote we are giving them instead a kind of military tear jerker. It is a terrible disappointment for me because I will never again have such a part. I don't think I failed to deliver, but the picture as directed deliberately diminishes the character in colour, dimension and audience impact. Only the audience matters. I have not lost objectivity and I cannot stop fighting in the only way left open to me as long as there is a chance to serve up to the audience a richer, more emotionally involving picture."

It was as though he himself were now MacArthur, the studio was his Truman and strips of film represented the Yalu River. The difference was that it was a battle he was still not going to admit was lost.

In another note he said: "The picture is too tame. The conflict should rage. And MacArthur must have all his facets shown – emotionalism, tenderness, some degree of humour, religiosity, toughness with the Russians – as well as the vanity, the self-assuredness, the obsession with anti-Communism. What is wrong with the picture is that the editing is just that. Choices have been made to editorialize by slanting, omitting and switching emphasis."

And so it ended. On the whole, the critics did enjoy Greg's work immensely but disliked the film.

The *New York Daily News* said, "Unlike the snappy, smartly-dressed *Patton*, *MacArthur* is so stiff-necked and generally undistinguished that it leaves one wishing that Hollywood would have allowed this old soldier to fade away quietly."

Charles Champlin stood by his earlier comments to Universal. "Inevitably," he wrote in his paper, "the riveting interest stems from the masterful performance by Gregory Peck. At moments, notably when the dark glasses work as a partial disguise, the physical resemblance is astonishing. The role is possibly the most difficult and demanding that Peck has ever undertaken and provides his most impressive performance since the gentle lawyer in *To Kill a Mockingbird*. His stature, his resonant voice, his innate dignity make him a logical choice for the part and, as you think about it, virtually the only choice."

Newsweek was more reserved, but came to Greg's aid abundantly: "This prosaic, limited, naggingly honest film finally achieves a strangely touching quality – thanks mainly to Gregory Peck whose voice and bearing evoke exactly the 'transcendant sincerity and essential rectitude' that historian Trumbell Higgins found in one of the most enigmatic heroes in American history."

There was a succession of phone calls from people like Jack Lemmon and James Stewart congratulating him on his performance. A famous director rang and said: "The picture is not worthy of your performance."

It wasn't a catastrophe, but *MacArthur* must be written down in the Peck diary as a "lost opportunity".

Greg now says, "It was made by the wrong studio. They are not used to making pictures with any real content. They ran scared. Made it on the cheap. The executives at Universal are creatures of the M.C.A. Conglomerate. I suppose they enjoy scanning stock reports, counting grosses. They grind out mindless drivel for T.V. They must watch the stuff in their home projection rooms. They all seem to have Henry Moore's in the garden. I don't understand them."

Twenty-two

After portraying a national hero Greg was now, at 62, to be cast in *The Boys from Brazil* to play the first real villain of his career. He had depicted bad people before – but usually men who were misunderstood and who wanted to make up for their past, as in *The Gunfighter*. The character of Josef Mengele, known as "The Angel of Death of Auschwitz" was, however, unredeemingly, perniciously evil.

As the man who, in the Ira Levin story, had perfected a means of "cloning" 94 boys in the identical image of Adolf Hitler, audiences saw a totally changed Gregory Peck. His hair was dyed blue-black. His familiar front quiff and widow's peak were gone, his eyebrows partly reshaped, and a moustache added that would have had Spyros Skouras rummaging through his contract file.

The name of Simon Wiesenthal, the Nazi hunter, had been changed to Lieberman because it was difficult to feature a living person in such a way-out story, no matter how skilfully it was made to look real. The Nazi hunter himself said he didn't like the idea of being made into a "Jewish James Bond".

Mengele was a different matter. "I think we'd welcome him showing up and trying to sue us for libel," said Greg. Mengele, of course, has been on the run since 1945.

The director, Franklin Schaffner, as all good directors should, had definite ideas about the way the film should shape up. He saw it as essentially a battle between two aging men, the Nazi and the Nazi hunter. But he couldn't work out who should make up this partnership of hate. He had always thought about casting Lieberman first, and came adrift when he tried to align his opponent. He thought none of the top actors who wanted to be tried for the part were right for it. Greg's name was talked about.

Certainly, he was wrong for Lieberman. For one thing, his physique wasn't at all right. Lieberman had to look old and frail. For another, despite the success of *Gentleman's Agreement*, Schaffner couldn't see Greg being accepted as a Jew. Mengele was a different matter.

Once that casting was settled, it was easier to decide on the right Lieberman. The choice fell immediately on Laurence Olivier – who only recently had himself had a Mengele-type role as the Nazi dentist in *Marathon Man*.

To some people, it was difficult to accept the notion of Gregory Peck as a villain quite as unpleasant as Mengele. So Greg went about the job of making himself feel like Mengele. To help his characterization, he carried pictures of Mengele around with him in his pocket all the time, like a medium who needed some personal link with the man whose body he was taking over. And he took the character home, too. But the Mengele-at-home had to be different from the one on the set. The Nazi role was played to the outlandish hilt – for laughs.

In the house, he demanded his dinner and his drinks in loud, shrill barks in a gutteral accent to the accompaniment of heel clicks. He would dissect his meat with the surgical sadism of a man who had been indicted in his absence for the crime of murdering by medical experiment. Veronique and Cecilia played along, cowering at his approach and at the sound of his Teutonic tirades.

It is always important for Peck to try to have the best relations with the other people working on a film, not just the stars and the director, but the technicians and the secretary too.

Greg told me he found Olivier "beautiful – a darling. He was gallant, funny, easy to be with. Not at all intimidating to the others." For his part, Lord Olivier told me how much he admired Greg's professionalism and his style before the cameras. The same mutual good relations extended to everyone else, to James Mason, as Mengele's principal lieutenant, to Lilli Palmer, as Lieberman's sister. When the film was all wrapped up, Greg sent about fifty of the technicians bottles of 20-year-old Scotch malt whisky or of Napoleon brandy. "It's one of the good old–fashioned Hollywood customs," he says.

He also had cause to thank the librarians who helped him with his research – once more going into every book that could possibly give him an inkling of the character he was to become. The best source book, he believed, was Simon Wiesenthal's own *The Murderers Among Us*.

As with MacArthur, he felt he was not so much playing a man but taking on a cause. "It's a reminder to people who may have forgotten and who prefer not to remember the horror of the Holocaust," he said.

Women who met him at this time didn't like Greg as Mengele. Even Veronique, who is used to being married to a man who invariably becomes the character he plays, said, "It's a shock every day that I wake up and look at Greg. All the women who have seen him are terribly upset at his appearance. But it's a great challenge for him. He enjoys doing it so I don't mind much because he's so happy with the part."

Time magazine talked about "the fascination of watching Gregory Peck, Mr. Integrity himself, playing Mengele. He sports a nasty little moustache and a stiff posture and seems to be enjoying his change of face and pace."

The strangest effect of the role was simply that people didn't recognize him. "One of the great benefits of being a film star," he laughs now, "is that you can always be sure of getting the best tables at restaurants. But in Lisbon and Vienna, we were twice turned away. And that hadn't happened for 35 years."

Once, travelling in an elevator in Lisbon, he was aware of an American woman sizing up his moustache and his dyed black hair. They got out on the same floor, close enough to each other, in fact, to hear the woman say to her husband, "Did you see that weird creep in the elevator?"

But, said Greg: "Mengele was a human rattlesnake. If people are shocked by my part in the movie, I'll be glad."

Shocked they were – and grateful.

Twenty-three

Gregory Peck, at the age of 63, was a star who looked forward to a future that in its way has remained as promising and as undefined as that of any youngster on the threshold of a brilliant new career. He had offers of more work – but until signing the contract for his 1980 film with Roger Moore and David Niven about the breaking of a Nazi spy ring in the Indian Ocean, *The Sea Wolves*, none was tempting enough to accept. After completing *The Boys from Brazil*, he told me disarmingly, "Who can tell – I may be retired already and not know."

Gregory Peck's appearance belies the calendar. He is often willing to say self-deprecating things about himself. True, when the black dye he had worn for the Mengele role was washed off and the widow's peak restored, there was a streak of white in his hair that had never been there before – but it didn't make him any more look his age than he felt it.

A visitor in the morning to Holmby Hills might well find the owner of one of the large houses there shuffling around its tennis court in an elderly red shirt and a pair of running shorts.

Or perhaps at a party given by his next-door neighbour, Rod Stewart – attempting with his still very attractive, wide-eyed wife the latest in disco dancing, although confessing that he preferred the fox-trot.

"Anything goes, Da," said Cecilia when she took over from her mother in guiding Greg between the flashing coloured lights. He was happy enough that it should. If he and Veronique bought the house with the long drive and the electrically-operated gates because they felt there was still much more to do, they have lived up to their philosophy. Of course, nobody believes Greg is now approaching his mid-60s any more than they would have accepted the idea that he could grow that moustache and be savaged to death by a pack of Doberman pinschers in *The Boys from Brazil*. Neither has he given them cause to believe it.

He has always made very clear where his priorities lie – always with his family. When in 1978, Carey decided to embark on a serious political campaign and run for Congress, Greg gave the idea the same all-out support he has always allowed people working on his movies.

Carey's politics were a further demonstration of the differences between his children and himself. For years courted to run as an official Democratic candidate, Greg always contented himself with offering his support to people like the Kennedys and Adlai Stevenson – and with having an infinite faith in democracy. It was not too long ago that he lost his temper at a golf club when he heard a member say something he considered offensive about a minority racial group. "Take your drink and get lost," he demanded. "I won't sit down with a man like you – understand?"

That kind of private stand was plainly not enough for Carey. He was running on a platform aimed at securing a better deal for old people, a more reasonable distribution of taxes and fairer education opportunities – while Greg went on the appeals circuit, wowing matrons at lunchtime meetings, talking to firemen and having fund-raising parties at home at which he would buttonhole names like Walter Matthau and George Burns for contributions – something of a backscratching operation; a few months later Greg appeared momentarily on a T.V. special for Burns, a 17-year-premature production called "George Burns's 100th Birthday".

"I don't understand why Carey wants his political career," Greg told me in an off-guarded moment – and then he added, "But I suppose I do in a way. It's a very tough job and a tough life, but an exciting challenge." Greg did try to talk his son out of it. But Carey was adamant.

"I want a measure of power of my own," he told his father, "so that I can bring some change and make some difference. You've got to win an elective office to make changes and improve things."

Greg decided that was well put. "It was then that I understood what every father has to understand sooner or later – that his son is entirely his own man and that if he isn't, he's in trouble. My son is a different breed of cat. I've never wanted power." Which is, of course, one of the reasons why he never had any ambition to direct movies.

Carey didn't win his election, although he had blasted through the primary campaign and finished up in the main election a hair's breadth away from the winning post. Close enough, though, for disappointment – for his father as well as for himself. But there were compensations. Carey had recently married and he also now had a good job in the housing industry.

For Greg, the memory of the tragedy of Jonathan is still a bitter one. He has no desire to forget either his eldest son or Jonathan's achievements. But he has always been intelligent enough to know that it is more productive to dwell on the pleasures that his other children continue to give him – like Steve, who is now making a successful career for himself as a documentary producer, director and writer.

His two youngest children, Anthony and Cecilia, are a constant source of joy, too. Both of them worked with him during their college breaks on *The Boys from Brazil* – Anthony happily calling out "Quiet please" as an assistant director and Cecilia acting as assistant unit photographer – for which she got a credit at the end of the picture. Cecilia has done some acting and stage managing at school. Now, a senior at Princeton University, she seems headed for a writing career.

Her pictorial work has already appeared in *Vogue* and in a British national magazine and both her parents speak of her with the kind of pride that is uniquely reserved for an intelligent, attractive daughter.

Anthony is at the Juilliard Institute in New York studing acting and has no doubt whatsoever that he wants to follow in his father's footsteps, although Greg hopes he will content himself with being his own kind of actor. "If he were to adopt any of my characteristics and attitudes, without branching off on his own in directions that I never undertook, I'd be worried," says Greg. But he delights in the fact that Anthony moves "like a rocket", is "superb" in comedy and that he played a blind Vietnam veteran in a college play for which he "got notices better than any I've ever had".

Now that he himself has escaped from the treadmill of following one picture immediately with another, he has found time to enjoy a quality of life that he always knew was there but which at one time merely served as a gap between movies.

He enjoys gardening at home, which he stresses is his only manual ability. There are two gardeners employed full-time but he's always at his happiest helping them, either tearing away old bushes or tending indoor plants, preparing the soil and planting seedlings. He delights in growing his own vegetables and seeing his own chrysanthemums, foxgloves, columbine and zinnias bloom.

On the set, he is always helped by the people Veronique calls his nannies – his own wardrobe and make-up men. Just as important is the fellow who keeps Greg in trim when he is not working. Three days every week, Greg is tended by a Japanese American called Kim Lee who for an hour and a half puts him through a series of exercises which would have merited a place in the Spanish Inquisition. He says they help him to limber up and keep his weight down.

He has now left the executive control of organizations like the American Film Institute and the Academy to others, but he works enthusiastically for them when called upon to do so.

Veronique, with whom he still discusses every project that comes his way, has done a great deal to shape him into the man that he is.

"He is a man of strengths and weaknesses," she told me. "He is certainly mercurial – a complex person, not of one colour. If I had to paint Greg, I would need a whole range of colours to do a portrait because there is great variation. If you say strength, you have to say weakness, too, because otherwise there would be no balance. A sensitive artist like him has to have both. He can do unexpected things – not a predictable person at all, I am glad to say. In spite of his 'good works' and his awards and honors, he is still in private life what he has always been, a bohemian who does pretty much as he pleases, doesn't conform and refuses to be labeled. He is fiercely supportive of children, old people and underdogs of every description. He is scornful of people he calls 'users'. He has no time for them, and in his world, prefers the company of 'the people down in the trenches, the artists and technicians who do the real work'. He is sentimental; in fact, I once caught him watching T.V. with tears rolling down his cheeks. He was watching Lassie playing nursemaid to a sick eagle."

While he was filming *The Boys from Brazil* at Lancaster, Pennsylvania, Greg, together with Lord Olivier and Franklin Schaffner, was awarded an honorary degree at Franklin and Marshall College. He took advantage of the opportunity to give a few hints to budding actors and actresses on the campus.

"Do not neglect the fundamentals," he told them. "Train your voices. Have a decent respect for breath control. Stretch your vocal range and stamina as far as it will go. Learn to move with precision and purpose. Fence, dance, exercise, do gymnastics. YOU are the only instruments you will ever have with which to express your talents and imaginations."

History will judge that he used the instrument called Gregory Peck exceedingly well. Unlike many actors, he says he enjoys watching his old work on television, somehow the less important films benefit by being shown on the small screen, complete with cuts.

Occasionally, these days, he will go to the Academy to see a new picture by someone else. He isn't thrilled with a lot of them. The actor who fought to be allowed to say "silly bitch" in *Beloved Infidel* marvels at what can be got away with today. "It's the only way they talk on screen. Of course, it's a crutch, a downgrading of language, using the same four or five words over and over again so casually that it means nothing. It's a corruption. They're in a bad way because our language is a magnificent thing."

Early on in our chats, he told me:

"I enjoy practising my craft as well as I possibly can. It's a little like being a cabinet-maker or a person who is skilled at putting things together. I enjoy the work for its own sake. I suppose I could have played it safe, and gone on repeating one of several characterizations. The idealist of *The Keys of the Kingdom*, or the hard-bitten loner of *The Gunfighter*, or the breezy reporter of *Roman Holiday*, or the martinet (with a heart of gold) of *Twelve O'Clock High*. Played with variations, any one of these surefire characters might have lasted out a career. I think they call that giving the public what they want. But somehow I liked the risk of pushing out into deep water more than being typed. When I start working on a new part, I don't bring along much baggage from previous roles. I start from scratch each time, and before shooting begins on a new picture, I am semi-terrified. I have a fear that I will not be able to stand in front of the camera again and produce anything like believable human behavior. It wears off, but the first days of every film are very trying for me."

Certainly, he thinks he is lucky at being able to do well what he enjoys doing most – and to have found a public for it. He doesn't believe he has any mysterious brilliance. Other people will be more generous to his talents than he is prepared to be himself, although occasionally he will agree to say that he sees no reason to be "unduly modest" about certain movies that have both delighted critics and had the right sort of reception at the box office.

If he did make mistakes, and he makes no secret of this, the over-riding truth is that every time he went in front of a camera, he treated the film he was making as the most important he had ever tackled – whether it was a deeply-felt moral story like *To Kill a Mockingbird* or a Western like *The Gunfighter*.

Looking back now on one of his most successful pictures – *Roman Holiday* – a film that has to stand out as one of his favourites, Peck says, "If now and then through luck and circumstance, we get into a film that someone might call a work of film art, so much the better; that's an extra bonus. If now and then we get into one that has something to say on a social issue or that gives people food for thought on something of importance in their lives or in terms of social problems, that, too, is a bonus. But really, the name of the game is to entertain – never to bore – and to do it well, with expertise and precision and professionalism and with whatever degree of personality or attractiveness or charm you are able to bring to it. Then people want to go and see it, enjoy it and be glad they went. That's what it's all about. . . ."

"It's not too late for new adventures," he now says. "If the Civil War epic materializes, that would be fine. Meanwhile, I'm a gardener who goes off now and then for a few months to make a movie somewhere. I adore my wife. We have good friends. I haven't a grumble." And if some future President of the U.S. were to offer him a job as Ambassador to Ireland? "I just might try it. Catherine Ashe from Dingle Bay might like that."